Geoff King is Professor of Film and TV Studies at Brunel University and his books include *Indie 2.0: Change and Continuity in Contemporary American Indie Film*, *American Independent Cinema*, *Indiewood, USA: Where Hollywood Meets Independent Cinema* and *New Hollywood Cinema: An Introduction* and *Spectacular Narratives: Hollywood in the Age of the Blockbuster*, all published by I.B. Tauris.

'With *Quality Hollywood*, Geoff King provides yet another astute assessment of contemporary cinema and contemporary culture. In incisive case studies of films like *Inception* and *The Social Network*, King demonstrates how issues of authorship, style and storytelling still matter – and how quality filmmaking has somehow persisted – in the current age of formulaic blockbusters and dumbed-down billion-dollar franchises.'

Tom Schatz, Mary Gibbs Jones Centennial Chair of
the Department of Radio-Television-Film at
The University of Texas at Austin

GEOFF KING

QUALITY HOLLYWOOD

MARKERS OF DISTINCTION IN CONTEMPORARY STUDIO FILM

I.B. TAURIS
LONDON · NEW YORK

Published in 2016 by
I.B.Tauris & Co. Ltd
London • New York
www.ibtauris.com

International Library of the Moving Image 28

ISBN: 978 1 78453 044 0 HB
        978 1 78453 045 7 PB
eISBN: 978 0 85772 885 2

A full CIP record for this book is available from the British Library
A full CIP record is available from the Library of Congress

Library of Congress Catalog Card Number: available

Typeset by Out of House
Printed and bound by T.J. International, Padstow, Cornwall

Contents

Acknowledgements

Thanks to Janet Staiger and Tom Schatz in particular for commenting on a draft of the manuscript and making a number of useful suggestions for improvement. I am grateful also to Mark Jancovich, Michael Newman and Piotr Cieplak for providing additional feedback on all or part of the manuscript.

Figures

Introduction

Quality and Hollywood: history and motivations

The terms 'quality' and 'Hollywood' are often treated as if mutually exclusive rather than belonging together. Hollywood, especially the corporate-owned system prevalent today and in recent decades, tends to be associated with a commercial bottom line in which the sole emphasis is on blockbuster-scale franchised products designed to appeal to the widest possible global audience. So dominant is the contemporary form of the blockbuster that Hollywood is often treated as if entirely coterminous with this realm. This is not, and has never been, the case. The studios also embrace a wider range of production, even if commercial motivations are (of course) usually strongly to the fore, and even if the blockbuster/franchise remains very much, or increasingly, the dominant core of the business. This includes 'mainstream' (i.e. large audience) oriented films of less than blockbuster scale, including familiar/conventional genre and star vehicles. Contrary to the impression often created by many commentators, both journalistic and academic, Hollywood has also maintained a persistent if sometimes embattled strand of what is usually taken to be at least *relatively* more challenging, ambitious or culturally aspirant filmmaking, the kind of cinema to which the term 'quality' has been applied.[1]

If Hollywood at its most commercially oriented is often assumed to rely on lowest-common-denominator factors such as incessant action, spectacle, star appeal, simplistic narrative and broad varieties of comedy, the notion of the quality film brings rather different associations. Such works might be characterised, in some cases, as dark, gloomy and sombre; subtle and nuanced; relatively complex; serious, sometimes perhaps morally ambiguous. These are not the kinds of terms generally associated with Hollywood production but qualities more usually expected in films from beyond the realm of the main operations of the studios, including the art and independent film sectors or the 'speciality' divisions employed by some of the majors for the production and/or distribution of relatively less mainstream work. A number of studio films have exhibited such characteristics, however, along with others such as a proclaimed 'worthiness' that aspires to a similar cultural status, and been received as distinctive from the mainstream/commercial norm, both in the recent/contemporary period and in the longer history of Hollywood. How this might be understood, particularly in the context of the early decades of the twenty-first century, a period in which Hollywood has often been assumed to have reached something like an artistic nadir, in its overwhelming focus on large-scale corporate franchise properties, is the subject of this book.

A supposed turn towards what was widely interpreted to be a strain of higher quality production in Hollywood was noted by a number of prominent sources in the American press towards the end of 2010, one of several such conjunctures. *Inception*, in particular, was cited as an example of 'quality' or 'classy' filmmaking at the high-profile level of expensive blockbuster production itself. Other titles from the same year, including *The Social Network*, were viewed in a similar manner, having enjoyed critical and commercial success. A number of explanations were offered for this apparent phenomenon. A feature in *The New York Times* speculated that the prevalence of social networking might be undermining the marketing of weaker films, the result being that Hollywood was being held to a higher standard than had been the case in the past.[2] A note of scepticism was also sounded, but the writer concluded that 'the message that the year sent about quality and originality is real enough that the studios are tweaking their operating strategies' to take such factors into account – although no specific evidence was provided to substantiate such a claim. Another explanation offered by the same feature was that widespread talk about 'originality' and 'quality' in studio films at the time was an outcome of the closing over the previous two years of some of the speciality divisions. These had been the principal source of the kinds of prestige films upon which the studios had come to rely for success at the Academy Awards, creating a gap they needed to fill for themselves (not to mention their ability to exploit a particular market niche). A move to quality was also seen, somewhat more questionably, as a response to general uncertainty about the state of the marketplace.

A writer in the *Los Angeles Times*, another prominent source, concluded in the form of a question. Is *Inception* 'really a sign of the changing times or just an exception to Hollywood's business as usual?'[3] This is, in broad terms, much the same as the initial question addressed in this book (the debatable merits of the explanations mooted above will be considered further below). If *Inception* is seen as offering qualities not typical of the summer blockbuster – in particular, its relative complexity of narrative structure – how might its existence in this shape be explained? Should it be viewed as part of a specific, local tendency at the time of its release? Can it be located in the broader history of notions of higher-than-usual quality, of one kind or another, in Hollywood? Or should it be seen as an anomaly from which few broad conclusions might be drawn? Either way, what might such a film – and other examples examined in detail in this book such as *The Social Network* (2010), *The Assassination of Jesse James by the Coward Robert Ford* (2007), *Mystic River* (2003), *Blood Diamond* (2006) and *A.I. Artificial Intelligence* (2001) – tell us about the space available within the blockbuster-dominated contemporary studio system for productions that can be categorised in this way, however prevalent or otherwise they might be in any particular period?

It is necessary at this point to consider what exactly is meant by the term *quality* as used here in reference to such films. The term is clearly a loaded one (as is the concept of the *mainstream* to which it is often opposed). In general usage, it implies something that is considered to be superior to the norm, in this case the norms of Hollywood studio production. It is hard to avoid the strongly evaluative connotations of

the term, but its meaning in the usage intended here is not restricted
to that dimension. A good account of this distinction is made by
Robert Thompson in his study of the 'quality television' of the 1980s
and 1990s, forerunner of a wave of small screen material that has
been accorded such status in the following decades. Quality television
became the label given to a type of programming recognised by critics that was judged to be 'better, more sophisticated, and more artistic
than the usual network fare'.[4]

In the same way, quality film, in Hollywood, is that judged to be,
or that seeks to position itself as, 'better, more sophisticated, and more
artistic' than the usual studio fare. (But, I would add, generally in a
manner that is not quite the same as the positioning in similar terms
of films from the independent or art-film sectors, a question of relative degrees of departure from mainstream norms to which we return
below.) In neither case is this as simple as it might first appear, however. As the terms of this formulation suggest, this is not an evaluative
judgement simply of how *well* something is done. It also suggests
the doing of particular *kinds* of things that have 'higher' associations
within the broader cultural arena. Quality, in this sense, does not suggest something particularly well-made or accomplished – although
that might be a contributory factor in many cases – but something
with a particular location within an established *hierarchical* system of
cultural evaluation and taste patterns, an issue explored in more detail
in this Introduction and in Chapter 1. Skill of accomplishment might
be considered to be a necessary but it is not a sufficient factor for
the attribution of this kind of quality label (the exact relationship
between these notions of quality is one to which we will also return).

In television, as Thompson suggests, quality has come to refer to
something akin to a generic style rather than an aesthetic judgement,
as is suggested by the tendency of some writers to give it a capital
'Q'. The term tends to connote a particular kind of programming
(although not really a genre, as usually understood) rather than an
evaluative rating as such, although the relationship between the two
remains slippery.[5] Much the same is the case in film, both generally
and in the particular context of Hollywood, although notions of quality of this kind have received more attention in recent years in the
sphere of television, particularly but not exclusively American, than

in that of commercially mainstream cinema. In television, quality has been viewed as an expanding category since the 1990s, a major factor in the attention it has received, alongside other less positively coded growth areas such as 'reality' programming. Its relative prevalence here is explained by a number of institutional/economic factors specific to the medium. The position of its equivalent within Hollywood has tended to be seen as either endangered or subject only to occasional, periodic upsurges, which is one reason why the term (or the notion more broadly, whatever it might be termed) has gained less currency in this context.

Particular types of Hollywood filmmaking have been associated with notions of quality of the kind considered in this book, although not always by the term itself. A category more often used within traditional studio discourse is the 'prestige' film, one that has some overlaps with but is far from exactly coterminous with quality, as is suggested further below. A number of specific historical manifestations of this heritage are sketched here, to provide a broader context within which to locate the more recent case studies from the twenty-first century that form the central focus of the book. This is followed in Chapter 1 by a more detailed initial general outline of some of the specific textual features with which ascriptions of quality are associated, many of which are rooted in the manner in which they mark some degree of distinction from the characteristics associated with dominant mainstream norms.

It is worth emphasising at this point that the distinctions involved here are relative rather than absolute. What is generally involved in the Hollywood quality film is a *degree* of difference that is combined with plenty of more familiar mainstream-conventional ingredients. This tendency can thus be situated within a wider spectrum of American film that differently balances more and less mainstream/commercial qualities with markers of distinction, from the American indie/independent sector to the realm known as Indiewood, constituted in particular by the output of the studio speciality divisions. (If American quality TV has been associated most often with material from cable providers, freed from some of the constraints faced by the main networks, its position is in some ways akin to that of the non-studio or Indiewood sectors; the quality Hollywood film might, then, occupy a position broadly similar to that of the quality network series, although there are a number of institutional/industrial factors that complicate any direct parallel.) This book represents, in this sense, a continuation of my previous work on Hollywood, Indiewood and the indie sector.

In one chapter of *Indiewood, USA: Where Hollywood Meets Independent Cinema*, I examine two features produced from within the main divisions of the studios, rather than their speciality wings: *American Beauty* and *Three Kings* (both 1999). This book is, in effect, a development from that chapter. In the context of a study focused primarily on the output of the speciality divisions, I used the term Indiewood (or 'Indiewood inside the studios') to embrace such productions, on the basis of some points of similarity with the products of the divisions and a blurring of lines in some instances either side of the studio/speciality divide. But 'quality Hollywood' seems a more useful designation for the broader examination of the particular textual features and production contexts of such work and its place within the longer history of studio production. The term also highlights some significant points of similarity to the texts and contexts of quality television, along with some important differences, a reference point often cited in contemporary discourses about quality (or its perceived absence) in Hollywood.

If one point of influence on the films examined below comes from an indie sector that had, by the end of the 1990s, grown to a point at which the lines between it and Hollywood were in some cases blurred, these mostly remain solidly Hollywood-type films in other respects, elaborated in each case in the chapters that follow (although the balance varies from one to another). A key aim of this project is to spell out exactly how the balance between more and less mainstream qualities works, and the basis on which this might appeal both within the industry and to viewers. This includes an effort to specify in some detail the terms in which the often slippery concept of the mainstream is defined and functions rhetorically, as a negative point of reference; and some of the wider historical contexts, dating back to the eighteenth and nineteenth centuries and beyond, within which such discourses can be located. Much of this deeper background context could also be applied to our understanding of the basis on which films from the independent or Indiewood sectors (or the products of quality television) are distinguished from – and often valorised in comparison with – the norms of the Hollywood (or network) main-stream. One strand in my work in this area that has expanded over time – from *American Independent Cinema*, to *Indiewood, USA* and the current volume – has involved an attempt further to pursue the roots of this process (while also examining the specific dynamics at work in particular sectors) as it operates across the spectrum of contemporary American film.

A brief history of quality

Notions of some kind of higher quality of film production, involving the marking of hierarchical distinctions, have probably existed as long as the medium itself. Such ideas were certainly put into play in overt form before the end of the first decade of the twentieth century and have represented a persistent, if minority, presence in the subsequent history of Hollywood and the discourses through which it has been understood. An outline is offered here of some moments in this his-tory, which might help to shed light on the more contemporary phe-nomenon – although a number of differences can also be identified in the terms in which quality is defined and the importance such a concept might have had in one period or another. At stake in some instances is the status not just of individual films and their producers but that of the institution of cinema itself, from early attempts to establish the respectability of the medium to challenges made dur-ing the 'culture wars' of the 1990s and subsequent attacks on what Hollywood is taken to represent in the wider social context.

An early example of a turn to films identified as possessing an elevated sense of quality is found in some of the productions of the Vitagraph Company of America, the largest operation of the pre-studio era. Film was often viewed as of low cultural status in the period of the institutionalisation of the cheap nickelodeon storefront theatre from approximately 1905 to 1912. As William Uricchio and Roberta Pearson argue, it became a focus of wider concerns about the role of popular culture at a time of great social upheaval.[6] This was a period of large-scale urbanisation, mass immigration and labour unrest, the result of which was to pose a number of challenges to the social/cultural status quo. The production of works bearing markers of culturally sanctioned quality offered a source of respectability and protection from threats of censorship or closure. Increased revenues were also available from the courting of a more educated audience of higher social class, increasingly so as films moved in some cases to higher-toned specialised venues.

The production of a strand of quality films by Vitagraph can be understood as an outcome of a combination of these broader industrial and socio-cultural factors and others more proximate to the company at the time. The latter included the disposition of co-founder James Stuart Blackton (a figure lacking in cultural capital – an issue to which we return below – who might have been seeking to increase his own status) and the studio's strategy of trying to differentiate its output from that of its rivals.[7] The quality films constituted a relatively small proportion of Vitagraph's slate but, Uricchio and Pearson suggest, they were foregrounded strongly in the company's publicity – as has often been the case with quality films in subsequent periods – and used to a greater extent than by its rivals as a way to distinguish its output from others. Uricchio and Pearson divide the Vitagraph quality films into three main categories that remained prominent in many later instances of this kind of production: those based on literary, historical and biblical sources. In each case, what was offered was a combination of that which could be seen as educational and respectable with materials that were already sufficiently familiar to be accessible to a wide range of viewers. Other formats developed elsewhere included a type of 'uplifting' moralistic melodrama, associated particularly with the work of D. W. Griffith at Biograph. As Eileen Bowser suggests, audiences of this period 'got perhaps more than they wanted of classical dramas and of sentimental melodramas preaching sermons at them'.[8]

The development in the 1910s of the feature-length film, and of more upscale theatres that attracted higher-paying and more middle-class audiences, led to 'a renewed call for respectable film fare and uplift', Bowser suggests – suitable material being found 'in part through a reversion to the classics of theatre and literature'.[9] Such properties also provided material sufficiently pre-tested to justify the higher production costs that were often entailed. For Neal Gabler, a powerful drive came from the personal motivations of the men who created the entities that became the major studios, a group of first or second generation Jewish immigrants for whom a film business shifted in this direction offered access to a realm of respectability and prestige that they were denied in other fields.[10] A strong desire of this kind, an aspiration to graduate from a working-class to a more middle-class audience and to gain an increased personal sense of refinement in the process, is associated with some of the most influential shapers of the studio system. These include Adolph Zukor and Jesse Lasky (founders of Paramount Pictures), Marcus Loew and Louis B. Mayer (two of the forces behind the creation of MGM) and Carl Laemmle (founder of Universal). That all the major studios invested in notions of quality – to some extent for broadly similar reasons – appears to be widely accepted in studies of Hollywood in the period from the 1920s onwards. As Thomas Schatz suggests in *The Genius of the System: Hollywood Filmmaking in the Studio Era,* 'any studio needed its occasional prestige picture to reinforce its artistic credibility', although little attempt is made in this case to explain the underlying reasons for such a commitment.[11]

The emphasis on moral uplift that forms a central part of the motivation for some quality productions, offered in the face of what was seen as a threat posed by 'disruptive' forces from the lower classes and more popular forms of entertainment, can be situated as part of a broader historical phenomenon that dates back particularly to the period of the Industrial Revolution in Europe, starting from the late 1700s. The eighteenth century was a period that, as Raymond Williams argues in his classic study *Culture and Society,* saw the shaping in their contemporary form of a number of concepts key to the underlying discourses of quality examined in this book. This includes the institutionalisation of the use of the term 'art' to suggest a particular type of 'imaginative' or 'creative' skill (rather than its previous usage to denote any kind of human skill), and 'artist' for a special kind of person to be distinguished from the artisan or craftsman.[12] Central to the evolution of such terms, for Williams, was the development of a particular notion of 'culture' in the sense of 'cultivation', as in the spirit of moral uplift suggested above, a process that for many thinkers of the period (perhaps most famously in, but far from limited to, the work of Matthew Arnold) offered a response to the threats perceived to be posed by the development of industrial society, the rise of democracy and the conditions faced by the working classes.

Further historical context for the development of these discursive oppositions between art and popular culture is provided by Leo Lowenthal.[13] Popular forms of art have probably existed in some form since the beginnings of social stratification, Lowenthal suggests, but did not give rise to 'intellectual or moral controversies' of the kind discussed above until the development of social forces that undermined the feudal structures of leading European states such as Britain and France. In the feudal period, no sustained point of cultural contact existed between the elite and the masses, and no middle class existed 'to complicate the picture or to bridge the gap'.[14] Controversy began to rage in earnest – 'in terms that have stayed with us' – from the middle of the nineteenth century, when the creation of the beginnings of a middle class led artists 'to worry about the demands of an increasingly broader, more "popular" audience'.[15] A variety of responses resulted, ranging from the more optimistic – who believed that the standard of popular culture could be raised – to negative pronouncements, the inheritors of which can be found in pessimistic judgements of contemporary products such as popular film and television.

An emphasis on notions of the elevated quality or prestige of certain productions can be seen in the release strategies of the newly created Hollywood studios in the 1920s. A useful case study is offered by Robert Allen and Douglas Gomery, focused on the production by Fox of F.W. Murnau's *Sunrise* (1927) (see Figure I.1).[16] As Allen and Gomery suggest, the appearance of the film, often viewed as something of an anomaly, can readily be understood as a product of both general and more specific industry concern about issues of quality/prestige at the time. *Sunrise* is located here within the industry category of 'highly artistic pictures', the economic performance of which was less important than their public relations value. 'There is evidence,' Allen and Gomery suggest, 'that the studios financed some films in order to enhance their prestige, and, by doing so, create an image of themselves as not only businesses but as producers of popular art.'[17] A limited number of such films was intended both to appeal

Figure I.1. Selling artistic prestige: poster for *Sunrise* © Twentieth Century Fox Film Corporation

to a minority 'high-brow' audience, especially in major cities such as New York, and to 'elevate the "tone" of the entire studio release schedule'.[18]

As in the preceding era, the value of prestige of this kind can be situated within ongoing attacks on the moral status of the industry – including a series of scandals relating to leading stars and directors – along with threats of censorship and investigation by the Federal Trade Commission into potential breaches of anti-monopoly laws.[19] If this forms part of a general explanation for the presence of certain kinds of quality films, more specific factors can be found in the situation of individual studios – in this case that of Fox. The production of *Sunrise* is located by Allen and Gomery as part of a 'carefully orchestrated plan' by William Fox to elevate the prestige of his previously middle-ranking studio. Murnau had the necessary artistic credentials and was, as a result, given almost entirely free reign over the production. Releases such as *Sunrise* could contribute to the prestige of the studios, but they could also backfire in cases in which executive interference was deemed to have damaged the pursuit of art, confirming a rhetorical sense of fundamental opposition between the two. Some critics complained about the 'happy ending' of the film, which Richard Koszarski suggests resulted in 'an unjust attack on the Fox hierarchy, and the elevation of Murnau to the status of a martyr in Hollywood's long battle between commerce and art'.[20] A similar debate surrounded the release of Erich von Stroheim's *Greed* (1924) – an adaptation of the novel *McTeague* by Frank Norris – the nine-hour original of which was cut against the wishes of the director to two-and-a-half hours, the uncut version becoming for some critics 'an icon of authenticity, a "holy grail" whose loss could be blamed on crass studio executives'.[21]

A wave of productions based on literary and/or historical sources or events similar in cultural status to those drawn upon in the earlier period appeared in the wake of a subsequent round of attacks on Hollywood morality in the 1930s. In this case the trend, started in late 1933, coincided with the enforcement of the Production Code as a form of self-regulation by the Motion Picture Producers and Distributors of America (MPPDA). The head of the MPPDA, Will Hays, had tried to persuade producers to move in this direction, as part of a broader campaign of seeking to impose certain moral standards on the industry. The motivation for this policy was largely self-serving for the industry, as before, in an effort to prevent censorship by others, and also in this case to refocus critical attention away from threats to the increasing development of oligopolistic strategies by the studios in this period.[22]

Examples from this cycle include literary adaptations such as *A Midsummer Night's Dream*, *David Copperfield* and *Anna Karenina* (all 1935) and biopics such as *The Life of Emile Zola* (1937). These would fit quite clearly into the notion of quality examined in this book, although for Tino Balio they are part of a broader category of prestige production (similar to that employed by Schatz), the bounds of which are somewhat wider.[23] As Balio puts it:

> The prestige picture is not a genre; rather, the term designates pro-
> duction values and promotion treatment. A prestige picture is typic-
> ally a big-budget special based on a presold property, often as not a
> 'classic', and tailored for top stars.[24]

Prestige, in this usage as a category employed within the trade, embraces all the most important 'A-list', high-cost studio features, including big-star, action-adventure films such as *The Adventures of Robin Hood* (1938) and a multi-star melodrama such as *Grand Hotel* (1932) – the equivalents of which today might be less likely to be considered within the quality bracket as primarily defined in this book. From the studio perspective, the notion of prestige might often be expected to include how much is at stake in a particular pro-duction – in terms of budget, profile and spending on promotions – either as well as, or instead of, prestige in the sense of aspirations to a higher cultural status or 'worthiness' of the kind implied by examples such as the literary adaptation. What might qualify for the latter var-iety of prestige might also be changeable over time. Particular types or genres are sometimes subject to historical shifts of position within the broader film hierarchy (see, for example, the account of the chan-ging status of the thriller offered by Robert Kapsis in his study of the reputation of Alfred Hitchcock)[25].

A number of strategies were used in the 1930s to target a more upmarket, middle-class audience for such films, and to generate asso-ciations with higher culture and education, including large-scale direct-mail marketing to teachers.[26] As far as the films themselves were concerned, it is debatable how far they offered much in the way of substantial departure from the Hollywood norms of the time. A key figure behind some of the higher-profile qualities of the period was David O. Selznick – either during his tenure at MGM or as head of his own company working as a supplier of films for studio release – producer of literary adaptations including *David Copperfield*, *Anna Karenina* and *A Tale of Two Cities* (1935). For Thomas Leitch, the imperative was entirely economic rather than aesthetic, such films offering 'the mixture as before, with the added seasoning of a brand-name property that can provide largely conventional period melodramas with a literary-historical imprimatur'.[27] Whatever conclusion is reached about the nature of the films themselves, the pursuit of such a strategy indicates a real investment at some level in the promotion of notions of distinction of this variety.

Literary or theatrical properties continued to provide sources of quality production in the postwar period, although in this case they joined what became known as the 'social problem picture' in providing in many cases a darker and more socially critical vein of studio production than was typical of earlier quality traditions (the social problem film itself, considered in more detail in Chapter 5, can also be traced back to the silent era and the Depression of the 1930s). Thomas Schatz identifies the emergence of 'a distinctive form of prestige-level "male melodrama"', the most successful example of which was *The Best Years of Our Lives* (1946).[28] Markers of quality here included an emphasis on a certain variety of social realism and confrontation with a number of social problems that were thrown into renewed light after the war years. Notable examples included two treatments of anti-Semitism, *Gentleman's Agreement* (1947) and *Crossfire* (1947), films that might appear somewhat tame today but, as Schatz suggests, were considered daring and progressive at the time. The studios largely withdrew from such production by 1950, in the face of the growing campaign against alleged communist influence in Hollywood, although dark and pessimistic visions continued to be produced in some upmarket theatrical adaptations, including *Death of a Salesman* and *A Streetcar Named Desire* (both 1951).

The variety of quality marked by the social problem film of this period can be seen as part of an historical reconfiguration of notions of prestige that has significance for the contemporary manifestations that are the main subject of this book. Chris Cagle argues that such films represent a distinctly different mode of prestige film from that which had gone before. The earlier variety, he suggests, was an industrially defined production category, while the latter gained its acclaim from both within and outside the industry, on the basis of its claims to serious status or social critique. As he puts it:

The industrial mode looked outward, conspicuously, towards higher cultural forms to lend Hollywood narratives the aura of respectability. The socially-defined mode looked inward, internalizing an aesthetic and form of perception that itself was meant to be culturally more elevated.[29]

This analytic distinction, Cagle adds, 'is also a historical one', the Hollywood prestige film having over time transformed its 'overwhelming reliance' on the former to an increasing emphasis on the latter. The second part of Cagle's distinction in particular – a shift from an emphasis on overtly external sources of quality to those rooted in particular approaches to film itself – is borne out to a significant extent by the analysis in the chapters that follow, although the difference might not be as clear-cut as his formulation suggests. The kinds of aesthetics internalised by the films are often themselves, as I argue below, implicitly drawn from or likely to resonate with those of other cultural products considered to have high standing in prevailing hierarchies, even in cases in which such associations are less overtly marked or highlighted.

The more critical vein running through some quality films of the postwar period can be attributed to a combination of broader socio-historical context – including an awareness of persisting American injustices at the end of a war supposedly fought to create a more equal and enlightened world – and factors more specific to the Hollywood of the time. This was an era in which the studios faced a number of challenges, including the culmination in 1948 of the legal action that forced them to sell their cinema chains and a dramatic loss of audiences from 1946 onwards. Although the studios still sought to appeal to a large or 'mass' audience, particularly with various forms of high-cost blockbuster productions, their response included moves to cater for somewhat smaller niche markets, including the expanding youth audience and those who might be responsive to more frank or critical material of more 'serious' or 'adult' nature. As Cagle suggests, the social problem film, with its emphasis on low-key realism, provided a cheaper source of prestige in troubled times than the kind of literary-oriented quality film that relied on lavish production values, a factor that contributed to its spread from one studio to another.[30] The typically Hollywood approach, Robert Ray suggests, was to try to combine different bases of appeal to the viewer. If the studios tried, to some extent, to satisfy an audience attracted to overseas imports such as the works of Italian Neorealism – shown in a growing art-house sector in the postwar decades – they sought to do so 'without losing the majority of filmgoers who clearly wanted more of what the industry had always produced – entertainment films predicated on the assumption that hard choices could be avoided'.[31] The result was the kind of mix typical of the social problem picture, films that in most cases had happy endings that belied the real status of the problems around which they were based.

The darker and more questioning dimensions of some of the postwar films cited above seemed to come to a fuller fruition in the period during the 1960s and 1970s that has been marked variously by the labels 'the New Hollywood' or the 'Hollywood Renaissance'. The products of this tendency have since been valorised in many accounts of Hollywood history, often serving as a benchmark for notions of this variety of quality in the spheres of both studio output and television. The Renaissance can, again, be seen as the outcome of a combination of socio-historical background and further stages in Hollywood's response to its postwar loss of audience and structural changes. The advent of the ratings system in 1968, after years of challenge to, and eventual reform and removal of, the Production Code, institutionalised the process of targeting films to more specific audience constituencies. Such changes have also been situated by Shyon Baumann as part of a broad process through which legitimation was achieved for the notion of Hollywood production being capable in itself of claiming the status of 'art', rather than only being able to borrow such standing in a second-hand form from other properties or cultural associations.

Baumann attributes this process to three main factors operative both within and beyond Hollywood, coming to a head particularly during the 1960s. First was the creation of an 'opportunity space' by broader social phenomena such as the consequences of world wars and demographic, educational and technological changes within American society.[32] These included a shrinking of the film audience and an overall increase in its level of education. The growth of television contributed further to the position of film – potentially, at least – in the cultural hierarchy. When television took the place of film as 'the default entertainment medium and the primary source of amusement, film was eligible for redefinition and also compared favourably to television as an art form'.[33] A series of developments within or alongside Hollywood contributed to the process by giving it some of the kinds of features associated with existing art worlds, in the sense in which these have been defined sociologically by Howard Becker.

An art world, for Becker, is constituted not just by a body of work but also its accompaniment by a range of institutional and discursive practices through which claims to the status of art are made, legitimated or contested – processes central to the notions of quality explored throughout this book.[34] Significant changes of this kind included 'the institutionalization of resources dedicated to film as art', such as the development of a network of film festivals and the creation of Film Studies as an academic discipline. These were accompanied by changes in production practices that gave potentially greater prominence to the film director, encouraging an 'auteur'-centred mode of reception, drawn primarily from overseas forms of art cinema and its critical celebration – in which the work in some cases could be seen as the distinctive product of the individual creator – along with other developments mentioned above including the growth of art-house theatres and a relaxation of censorship.[35] The idea of the creative individual author/auteur, working either within or at the margins of the studio system and being seen as able to transcend it to some extent, has remained an important source of notions of quality, bringing with it key associations with broad notions of the 'artistic' and the kinds of industrial products to which it is conventionally opposed.

A final factor considered by Baumann is the growth of an appropriate discursive context, the 1960s being a period in which

> film reviewers began to employ a discourse of film as art that was characterized by a vocabulary and a set of critical devices that provided a way to talk about film as a sophisticated and powerful form of artistic communication.[36]

The outcome of all these developments, some of which had ante-cedents prior to the period that is the main focus of Becker, was 'upwards status mobility' for film as a whole, a retrospective canon-isation of 'old' Hollywood and a differentiation of various strains of production of the kind that is central to this book, including the marking of distinctions between 'serious Hollywood' and the more mainstream-oriented domain of the popular blockbuster.[37]

A number of tensions can be observed among the types of films that might have qualified for 'quality', 'prestige' or 'art' status across the period covered in this overview so far, including those identified by Cagle. Perhaps the most notable difference lies between the notion of cultural 'uplift' at work in some of the earliest examples, along with many subsequent works that occupy the same kind of cultural sphere as the classic/historical literary adaptation, and the darker and more questioning tenor of some of the films of the immediate postwar years and those associated with the Hollywood Renaissance. The latter tend in many cases to oblige the viewer to share considerably less 'uplifting' experiences as far as their diegetic worlds are concerned – see *Taxi Driver* (1976) for a striking example – even while this process in itself is marked as material designed for the more discerning or educated viewer. For some more recent critics, as we will see below, a sharp div-ision is made between these two different strains. What some would consider to be classic instances of the Hollywood art film of the 1960s and 1970s have been taken by conservative commentators to represent a nadir of quality of the 'respectable' kind sought on various occasions by both external moral guardians and some influential parts of the industry.

It is also notable that it was against a notion of a capitalised 'Tradition of Quality' that François Truffaut made his polemical intervention in favour of an auteurist directors' cinema in the pages of *Cahiers du Cinéma* in 1953.[38] In this account, and for those who took up its position, the traditional literary adaptation – what Truffaut terms a scenarists' cin-ema – is a byword for all that is dull and second-hand in comparison with the more directly cinematic creativity of auteurs of the kind later associated with the French *nouvelle vague* or the Hollywood Renaissance. A developing cinephilia among a younger generation in the 1960s and 1970s – an advocation of the merits of the cinematic in its own right, as part of the broader process outlined by Baumann – entailed a rejection of any sense of requiring to look elsewhere (particularly to the overtly literary) as a source of prestige.[39] The latter seems still to play a broader role in the kinds of quality ascriptions examined in this book, however, even if not always directly signalled as such.

There is, clearly, a political dimension to all such interventions and the texts to which they relate, 'respectable' versions of quality tending to be broadly conservative in their adoption of a certain range of largely ameliorative or elitist middle-class perspectives while a more radical potential can exist (although it may be far from guaranteed and may also be elitist in its most likely audience constituency) in more ambiguous, questioning or negatively framed varieties. Ascriptions of quality to some productions also tend to have political implications in the negative valuation of other works against which they are defined, either implicitly or explicitly: for some Hollywood films to be labelled as of higher quality, others viewed as representing the norm have to be denigrated in terms that tend to be ideologically loaded, including a general distinction-marking elitism and a common tendency for the 'popular' negative object to be characterised in patriarchically feminised gender terms.[40]

If the decade up to the latter part of the 1970s is often viewed as a period in which Hollywood was more than usually open to at least some influences from the varieties of quality associated with international art cinema – a picture that is easily exaggerated, given that such films were never the norm even at this time – the following decades are ones in which the studios are generally seen to have offered much less space to such work. An overall return to profitability, and the development of a new generation of franchise blockbuster production/strategy in the era in which the studios became parts of large media conglomerates, undercut the perception that Hollywood was a viable place 'for filmmakers to make meaningful films', as Baumann puts it.[41] The period from the 1980s onwards was one in which marketing and market research became more important in Hollywood than had been the case in the past, part of a broader tendency that resulted from the intensification of the activities of the major cultural industries of the time.[42] The increased role of marketing executives at early stages in the *conception* of projects, David Hesmondhalgh suggests, threatened to reduce the relative autonomy possessed by symbolic creators such as filmmakers and others, an autonomy that generally distinguishes cultural from most other forms of production.[43] A reduction of space for less obviously commercial-mainstream filmmaking in the studio sphere in this period (although not its entire disappearance, contrary to the rhetorical manner in which this might sometimes be implied) was one of a number of factors that appeared to have contributed to the growth of the more artistically oriented parts of the independent sector in particular forms during the 1980s and into the 1990s.[44]

The boundaries between the two sectors become blurred in some instances, however, as the studios sought to share the revenues generated by the most successful independent films of this period. By the mid 2000s, all had created their own semi-autonomous 'speciality' divisions to distribute and/or produce independent or 'indie' films, as they often became known from the 1990s, or titles that mixed indie and more commercial/mainstream qualities. The speciality divisions were hotbeds for the production or release of films that bought heavily into long-standing quality templates of the traditional kind, including numerous classic and other literary adaptations released by leading players such as Miramax – under the control of Disney from 1993 to 2010 – and Universal's Focus Features. Distinctions between different perceptions of quality have also been made within the indie or Indiewood sectors, along lines similarly hierarchical to those explored within Hollywood in this book. Generally most likely to be valorised here is what Yannis Tzioumakis terms 'the low-budget, low-key quality film', often viewed as being authentically independent and juxtaposed with what are seen as more compromised products from the speciality divisions or more commercial-exploitation-oriented varieties of indie film.[45]

Another designation used in some cases in academic work (more so than in any broader discourses) is the term 'smart', particularly in the light of an influential essay by Jeffrey Sconce, a term he uses to suggest a particular sensibility in some work from the indie and Indiewood sectors, marked primarily by a tone of ironic detachment associated with the 'Generation X' sector of the audience in the 1990s.[46] The same term might be applied, but somewhat more loosely, to the kind of studio quality film examined in this book, to suggest productions broadly positioned as 'smarter' (sharper, some degree more intellectually challenging) than the studio norm. It is worth noting, however, that where a distancing of the viewer from central characters is found – particularly in *The Social Network* and *The Assassination of Jesse James* – this tends not to involve the particular *ironic* form of distance identified by Sconce in his examples. Films located closer to the mainstream, either in the studio main or speciality divisions, also tend to combine any of the detachment suggested by Sconce – a clear marker of distinction – with more mainstream-conventional appeals to emotional allegiance, as I have suggested in the case of Indiewood-oriented examples such as *Little Miss Sunshine* (2006) and *Juno* (2007).[47]

If the 1980s was a decade in which Hollywood ceded ground in the art world of film to the independent sector, it was also a period in which the industry came under renewed attack on moral grounds – particularly for the levels of sex and violence in some films – including controversies around titles such as *Cruising* and *Dressed to Kill* (both 1980). Such criticism was 'unusually intense' during the 1980s, suggests Stephen Prince, resulting in a substantial erosion of Hollywood's general cultural standing.[48] Conflict of this variety continued into the 1990s, particularly when such issues became part of the discourse of 'culture wars' surrounding the presidential election campaign of 1992. A prominent intervention in this period was conservative film critic Michael Medved's book *Hollywood vs. America*, which accused Hollywood of being 'an alien force that assaults our most cherished values and corrupts our children'.[49] Medved accused the studios of going out of their way to challenge 'conventional notions of decency' through a litany that includes: attacks on marriage and religion; revelling in graphic brutality and a celebration of vulgar behaviour; the advocation of contempt for all authority; and the promotion of a dark and cynical view of American history and the major institutions of the nation.[50]

Somewhat ironically, it is the very aspiration of filmmakers and studio executives to be recognised as producers of higher-status 'art' – rather than just 'entertainment' – that Medved blames for such tendencies. The arts establishment, Medved argues, 'encourages all-out assaults on our sense of comfort and coherence, while turning a suspicious eye on any efforts that respect convention, including representational painting, rhyming poetry, melodic music – or life-affirming movies'.[51] Such a characterisation seems closer to capturing a sense of how art might often be understood in the contemporary context than Medved's book is in offering anything like a balanced account of the nature of the output of Hollywood in general. It is striking, however, that it is a pursuit of one variety of quality that he identifies as the source of the problem, counterposed to something akin to the traditional notion of moral uplift witnessed in some of the earlier movements examined above, further underlining the tensions that exist within different conceptions of what constitutes quality from one perspective or another.

Medved's intervention appeared to strike a nerve, the book gaining widespread coverage, claiming 'bestseller' status and remaining in print at this time of writing. How representative his views were, or might still be, of more broadly prevailing social opinion is hard to judge, but it is far from clear that the kind of polarised moral split usually associated with the 'culture wars' of this period is grounded in more widely spread reality. Key issues within these debates include attitudes towards abortion, homosexuality, feminism, multiculturalism and the contents of popular culture including Hollywood films – attitudes that survey data has suggested are far more ambivalent and internally incoherent than tends to be assumed in media debate.[52] But it is often in the very nature of such debates for differences to be exaggerated and subjected to hyperbole of the kind found in the writing of Medved and those who have followed in his footsteps. So, what of the background context to quality productions of more recent years? To what extent can this be understood as a continuation of the same kind of process, in both what might be at stake in the production of such work and the kinds of textual sources and qualities involved? And what can we conclude to be the motivations for quality production?

Motivations for quality production: economics, prestige and cultural capital

It is clear from the above outline that a history of quality production of one variety or another has existed within the Hollywood studio system, one that continues today. In some cases the presence of such work can be viewed more or less directly as part of a response to attacks on, or threats to, the status of the industry. This seems most clearly to have been the case in the early period, when the standing of film/cinema as an in any way legitimate medium/institution was at stake. Issues of quality have subsequently often been tied up more or less directly with questions of regulation and censorship, but not in such a way as to relate to the very existence of Hollywood itself as a firmly consolidated and recognised, if sometimes heavily criticised, part of the popular-cultural universe. Attacks of the kind mounted by Medved continued into the twenty-first century, regular sources of such material including the conservative *Washington Times* news-paper.[53] Hollywood is also subject to frequent attack from the other side of the political spectrum, variously, for providing what are often viewed as reactionary texts that appeal to 'lowest common denominator' tastes and that unduly dominate the global market, an argument the intellectual roots of which include the postwar attack on the culture industries made by Theodor Adorno and Max Horkheimer.[54]

The primary motivation for the production of quality films is usu-ally economic at some level, even if this might in some cases be indir-ectly so, as in cases in which such films might have been made to add 'tone' to a broader release slate in an attempt to avoid externally imposed regulation that the studios would see as interference with their ability to pursue profits in ways of their own choosing. Prestige of the kind that carries higher cultural associations might often be valued, but usually as a way to achieve economic success, whether that is by attracting a higher-paying audience than previously in the 1910s, seeking to reach more educated audience sectors in the 1950s and 1960s, or through the achievement of Academy Awards and other status prizes or nominations that generate publicity that can trans-late readily into box office revenues. It is for this reason that in most cases markers of quality and distinction have been combined with more familiar Hollywood dimensions, designed to remain attractive to something more than a small niche audience. The economic basis of quality production remains distinctly less clear-cut than that of its equivalent in recent/contemporary American television, however – the latter being rooted in factors such as the appeal to advertisers of atypical programming that reaches particular upmarket, high-spending niche audiences or the role of such material in the formation of brand identity in subscription-based cable.

The quality Hollywood film occupies a position, therefore, somewhere in between two poles identified by Pierre Bourdieu in his study of the dynamic relations that exist between different fields of cultural production.[55] At an institutional level, it is situated clearly within the arena of large-sale market-oriented production, governed by what Bourdieu terms the 'heteronomous principle', according to which creative works are subject to the prevailing rules of the market, just like any other commodity. The opposite of this, in Bourdieu's account, is the 'autonomous principle', in which all that counts is artistic prestige in its own right, applicable in areas that lie entirely outside the market. Hollywood quality clearly leans much more strongly towards the former than the latter, although with more investment in certain kinds of prestige than is usually associated with the products of the studios (this is another framework in which we can locate, at least approximately, the relatively different positions of Hollywood at its most mainstream-oriented, the studio quality film, the products of the speciality divisions, and work from the unattached indie or art-film sectors). Various tensions can result from the pull of these different imperatives, depending on the context of any particular case.

Medved argues that Hollywood's pursuit of artistic recognition and respect has been to the detriment of its commercial success, a central part of his case being that the industry has become out of touch with the preferences of the public. The 'Hollywood community', as he terms it, 'wants respect even more than it wants riches; above all, its members crave acceptance and recognition as serious artists.'[56] That such a desire should actively override the profit motive to the extent that Medved suggests seems unlikely, especially for studio executives, even if such a case might potentially be made to some extent in relation to the ambitions of certain individual filmmakers. The notion of art being pursued in Hollywood directly at the expense of commercial success might have gained some traction during the exceptional circumstances of the Hollywood Renaissance period, many exemplars of which performed poorly (although in most cases on modest budgets), but this is far from typical of the balance between the two imperatives.

Notions of quality or artistry, of whatever variety, usually require expectations of at least reasonable financial performance if they are to be supported within studio operations. Even within the Hollywood Renaissance, the considerable room for manoeuvre given to some directors (for example, Robert Altman) was largely premised on the revenues earned by previous films (in the case of Altman, the success of *M.A.S.H.* [1970] that kept him in credit with the studios for a decade afterwards). To stray more than a short distance from commercial norms usually requires counterbalancing factors such as the presence at the heart of such projects of a filmmaker with an exemplary box office track record. A classic case is the space Steven Spielberg had to pursue less commercial-seeming features such as *Schindler's List* (1993) and *Amistad* (1997), although even in examples such as these markers of quality and seriousness are combined with more familiar narrative and other dynamics (for more on Spielberg, see Chapter 6). Without evidence to the contrary, it is probably best to start from the working hypothesis that, in order to be pursued in any substantial manner, projects in which quality or any other alternative emphasis is to the fore also require other grounds on which to offer expectations of commercial viability or longer-term payback.

Quality or prestige can be converted quite directly into commercial success, the most obvious example being the role performed by major prizes – and particularly, for Hollywood, the Academy Awards. Prizes of this kind, as James English argues, can be viewed as the most effective instruments for the conversion of one kind of capital (economic, political, social, cultural) into another. In one direction, symbolic or cultural capital can be 'cashed in' (English's example is the new Nobel laureate's out-of-print titles suddenly appearing in attractive new editions); while, in the other, economic fortunes can culturally be 'laundered' ('Nobel's profits from the manufacture of deadly explosives converted into a mantle of supreme literary achievement').[57] The latter appears particularly appropriate to the history of the Hollywood quality film, in which expenditure on potentially less profitable but more 'artistic' productions has in various periods been seen as bringing a potential pay-off at the level of elevating the broader status of the industry as a whole or that of individual companies. The most immediate explanation for the presence of at least a minimal number of quality releases in contemporary studio schedules – and of the attention some of them gain – is, with little doubt, their role in the competition for the status of Academy Awards, along with other relatively high-profile awards and festival appearances that contribute further to the economy of prestige.

English suggests that cultural prizes in general have tended in recent decades to offer larger economic boosts to winners than was the case in the past. They have, in this sense, he argues, become more implicated in commerce and more powerful as marketing instruments. This is not because of a decrease in their autonomy from commercial performance itself, however. English suggests that a comparison of the bestseller lists in fields such as literature, film and popular music with the lists of winners of awards such as Pulitzers, Oscars and Grammys reveals 'a general pattern of divergence, with less alignment between the two lists now than there was fifty years ago, especially in literature'.[58] It is the specific form of symbolic or cultural capital produced and circulated by prizes that has become more valuable in economic terms, he suggests, 'while sheer commercial value has become less liable of conversion into, or even convergence with, this kind of prestige'.[59] The historical context of such change is associated by English with a growing importance of cultural capital and of the symbolic and cultural economy more broadly in the period since the early 1970s.[60]

For English, then, prestige itself, in its own terms, has an economic value, the context of which can be understood via further elaboration of the concept of cultural capital and what it might offer to the consumer/viewer. Cultural capital is the term used by Bourdieu – and subsequently widely adopted – to signify the particular kinds of resources required for the pleasurable consumption and appreciation of one type of cultural product or another, including (but far from limited to) the products of the arts. Different kinds of products – including different kinds of films – require different resources of cultural capital in order to be appreciated, this form of capital being acquired through a combination of formal education and more general upbringing, and thus unequally distributed along class or other social lines in much the same manner as economic capital. The 'higher' arts – for example art or avant-garde film – generally require quite specialised knowledge in order fully to be appreciated, while the most popular-commercial forms are designed to be accessible to as broad a constituency as possible.

A key dimension of this phenomenon for Bourdieu is the process of *distinction* that results. The pleasure of consuming work of this kind (and a much wider range of cultural products) is based to a large extent on the sense created of being different from – and, specifically, 'superior' to – those not equipped with such resources. A spectrum of points of distinction might then be identified across the range from products considered to be most culturally elevated to those positioned at the lowest end of the scale. Relative degrees of distinction of this kind are seen in Bourdieu's account, and that of others who have adopted this approach, as being especially pertinent to particular sections of the middle classes, as ways of marking fine degrees of difference within and between different sectors that might be less clearly differentiated from one another in economic terms. It is to a large extent in this kind of territory, for example, that Claire Monk locates taste preferences for what became known from the 1980s as the 'heritage' film, a now-familiar part of the broader quality landscape to which we return in Chapter 3, in a survey of audiences for such productions in Britain.[61]

Monk notes, however, a number of important differences in the grounds on which such films are appreciated by her respondents. She also suggests that taste investments of this kind, which are likely to apply to the quality field more generally, can be understood as demonstrating *in*security and/or aspirations about class locations of individuals as much as any reflection of achieved position or security – a conclusion that fits with the broader understanding of such processes offered by Bourdieu. A growth in middle-class sectors of the population as a result of various social and economic changes in America, Europe and other 'Western' societies is often seen as underlying an increased significance of the kind of cultural prestige identified by English and others (including Cagle), a factor I discuss at greater length in *Indiewood, USA*. An increasing segmentation on class lines is also viewed by Lawrence Levine as a major factor in a longer historical process through which the hierarchical positions of various forms of cultural production have shifted over time, including what he terms the 'sacralisation' of formerly more popular works of Shakespeare, among other artistic forms, during the nineteenth century.[62]

The Hollywood quality film might be understood, in these terms, as offering a particular kind of mixture of elements associated with higher and more commercial-popular culture, the particular invest- ments in which on the parts of viewers can be complex and varied, and, as Monk suggests, cannot simply be read-off unproblematically from textual features alone. If the avant-garde or experimental lies at one end of the scale, and films aimed at the largest possible audience are at the other, a number of different positions can be identified in between. These would include the particular kinds of mixtures found in the indie and Indiewood sectors, as suggested above and which I have examined in more detail elsewhere, each of which can be char- acterised in large part through the extent to which they draw on the conventions and traditions of more or less distinctive or commer- cially mainstream components from sources including the art film, mainstream Hollywood and various forms of exploitation cinema.[63] Quality films made by the studios themselves might be expected in some ways to lean a degree closer to the mainstream than, for example, the output of their speciality divisions, although the exact balance is likely to be subject to some variation. Films that offer com- binations of qualities of these kinds are likely to appeal primarily to specific audience demographics, particularly among certain sectors of the middle class, an issue I explore at greater length in some broadly similar territory in *Indiewood, USA*.

In one of the few academic works to have acknowledged the existence of the quality film as a significant presence in contempor- ary Hollywood, David Andrews locates each of these sectors (along with the avant-garde and films of the Hollywood Renaissance) within an enlarged and inclusive concept of art cinema. The kinds of films on which *Quality Hollywood* focuses are termed 'mainstream art cinema'.[64] I am not convinced that this is a helpful terminology, tending effectively to collapse real, if relative, differences between the output usually associated with indie, art and quality Hollywood film. My aim, here and in previous work, has been to pin down the varying balance of textual qualities and extra-textual strategies usu- ally associated with each, across a spectrum of possibilities – even if the differences remain far from absolute. In its established usage, art cinema seems to connote a mixture that can be reasonably clearly distinguished from that usually found in the studio quality film. Some quality films lean more closely towards the art-cinema end of the spectrum – as is the case with *The Assassination of Jesse James by the Coward Robert Ford* examined in Chapter 4 – as might some, but far from all, examples of indie film. Many similarities can be traced, as Andrews suggests, in the discursive and institutional processes through which notions of distinction are articulated in all of these realms, including a central and usually mystifying focus on the role of the individual 'auteur' filmmaker. What is missing from this account, however, is any consideration in detail of the particular balance or range of *textual* qualities that usually serves as a marker of one or another specific position within the broader spectrum.

Jim Collins suggests that adjustments in taste hierarchies in the United States in the 1990s and 2000s contributed to a further undermining of some traditional dichotomies, particularly in a popularisation of the literary as a concept and a shift in the power to arbitrate on such values from academia to more mainstream-oriented sources such as book superstores, Amazon recommendations and media-celebrity endorsements.[65] The conception of the literary that resulted includes a blurring of lines between books and popular film adaptations, particularly those associated with Miramax. Central to this process, for Collins, is an 'increasingly easier access to what were formerly considered elite pleasures, which are carefully cultivated to retain the vestiges of exclusivity, even as they become increasingly ubiquitous'.[66] Something of this cultural dynamic might also be identified in instances of the studio quality film, alongside products from the speciality divisions, although this is a realm in which the making of an appeal on the basis of an *overt* literariness (as in the direct literary adaptation) seems to feature to a lesser extent.

A market value of some kind can certainly be put on notions of quality or prestige – in film as in other social or cultural products – as part of a broader process through which the consumption of goods can be understood to involve mechanisms through which various senses of self- and group identity are constructed and asserted in non-material as well as material terms.[67] Elements of quality, mixed with others associated with greater popular appeal, are ingredients that can appeal to parts of the audience on particular grounds, potentially expanding the audience for individual features. They can, of course, also risk alienating other, potentially larger constituencies, but have often formed one part of the overall strategy employed by the studios (if usually a minority component) across a slate of films, for reasons of both commerce and prestige.

Industrial strategies likely to result in critical recognition in terms of artistic-prestige value might contradict those most likely to bring large-scale box office success, however. A quantitative study by Morris Holbrook and Michela Addis suggests that what they term 'marketing clout' (an aggregate calculated through measures including size of production budget and the intensity of theatrical distribution on the opening weekend) correlates negatively with measures of critical and popular evaluation in artistic terms, while correlating positively with the size of box office returns.[68] Enormous marketing clout signifies something other than artistic or hierarchically located notions of quality, as might be expected given its dominant association with the most mainstream varieties of blockbuster production. The industry 'must choose between competing positioning strategies', Holbrook and Addis conclude, highlighting a dilemma confronting films of the kind examined in this book that seek to achieve the best of both worlds – the release strategies of which vary from blockbuster-size (*Inception* and *A.I.*) to solidly mainstream (*The Social Network* and *Blood Diamond*) and indie-scale (*The Assassination of Jesse James* and *Mystic River*).[69] A strong correlation is suggested in each of these examples between the balance of qualities in the text and the scale of release, although this is not entirely fixed, some space being available for choices to be made about exactly what strategy to pursue in any particular case.

As products that combine more and less popular or 'artistic' dimensions, films that might be grouped under the quality label are also potentially subject to criticism from both directions: as either 'pretentious' – in relation to notions of the mainstream – or compromised by certain popular ingredients from the opposite direction. If, for some, such work might offer the best of both worlds, for others it risks being attacked for failing to supply the virtues of either the genuinely

popular or the authentically artistic. The classic expression of the latter view is Dwight Macdonald's notion of 'Midcult'. For Macdonald,
Midcult has the same essential qualities as mass culture – 'the formula,
the built-in reaction, the lack of any standard except popularity –
but it decently covers them with a cultural figleaf'.[70] In Masscult, as
he terms it, 'the trick is plain – to please the crowd in any way. But
Midcult has it both ways: it pretends to protect the standards of High
Culture while in fact it waters them down and vulgarizes them'.[71]
Among the examples he cites is 'the Museum of Modern Art's film
department paying tribute to Samuel Goldwyn because his movies are alleged to be (slightly) better than those of other Hollywood
producers'.[72]

Macdonald's is clearly an attempt to defend existing hierarchical
boundaries, one that can be situated within the longer historical tradition outlined above. It is the ambiguity of Midcult, he suggests, that
makes it 'alarming'.[73] From his perspective, the danger is a threatened corruption of 'High Culture' but what appears really to be at
stake here is an undermining of a clear sense of ideological distinction between the popular and the artistic, and of all the broader social
distinctions that follow. A term that has passed into wider usage to
describe a similar cultural realm is 'middlebrow', another label that
tends to be given negative connotations and for much the same reason: for what Janice Radway terms 'its failure to maintain the fences
cordoning off culture from commerce, the sacred from the profane,
and the low from the high'.[74] Processes of distinction-marking can be
enacted at various levels around products such as the studio quality
film, then, which might be the object of either positive investment or
disdain, depending on the perspectives of those involved. If we might
not wish to make any great radical claims for films of this kind on the
basis of their difference from mainstream and often broadly conservative norms (the bounds of their difference tending to be constrained
and its basis far from necessarily progressive in political terms), their
presence and the reactions they sometimes provoke has potential to
open up to question the existence and function of the type of cultural
hierarchy defended by figures such as Macdonald.

If aspects of quality might appeal to certain viewers, on the basis
of their ability to mobilise particular resources of cultural capital, the

same is broadly true of its appeal to the studios themselves, as we have seen, in their efforts at various times and to various degrees to associate themselves with something other than just the lowest common economic denominator. A similar argument can be made in relation to the role of some individual executives, as suggested by Gabler in relation to figures such as Zukor, Lasky, Loew, Laemmle and Mayer; by Uricchio and Pearson in the case of Vitagraph's James Stuart Blackton; and as might be said of some aspects of the personal motivation of a figure such as Harvey Weinstein at Miramax and subsequently The Weinstein Company in the indie/Indiewood territory. The importance of this dimension can be difficult to pin down exactly or to demonstrate in concrete terms, but it appears likely to be part of the explanation for the production of work that aspires to this kind of cultural prestige. This might most clearly have been the case for some of the earlier studio heads, whose intensely hands-on control of production could give them more scope than was subsequently available to impose their own personal imprint on the entire company output. Zukor and Lasky, for example, are described by one contemporary as being 'dedicated men who would produce pictures that they thought should be done, even though they weren't going to be profitable'.[75] How far, then, might individual executives – particularly those below the level of traditional studio heads – have the freedom or scope to pursue such projects for their own ends, including, potentially, the furtherance of their own prestige? If the existence of the quality film can sometimes be explained, at least in part, at the level of broader strategies, an important role is also played by more local and specific factors relating to those involved in any particular project, from the filmmakers themselves to the corporate-era 'suits' who have the power to give or withhold the all-important green light.

Individual freedom, constraint and motivation

It is worth stating from the start that it is unlikely that studio executives of recent years would pursue prestige/quality products that increased their own stores of cultural capital directly at the expense of *any* likelihood of commercial viability, either immediately or in the shape of some kind of future return. The latter might include the development or maintenance of relationships with key talent, by giving them greater than usual freedom in some instances in the hope of securing their future services in more profitable work. The nature of studio business within the context of the operations of larger media corporations is such as to create greater constraint than the conditions enjoyed by some of the earlier studio chiefs of production in the 'golden age' of the 1920s and 1930s. In most cases, it seems likely that quality will be expected to pay its way, as would generally also be the case in earlier periods, even if not at the potential level of profitability enjoyed by some productions that are more clearly designed to appeal to the largest possible audience. To accept a much lower likely commercial threshold remains a significant departure, however, in an industry often assumed to have little interest in anything other than the commercial bottom line, although such a characterisation of Hollywood has always risked over-simplification.

Certain filmmakers themselves can carve out considerable freedom, as suggested above and as will be examined in more detail in the case studies that follow in the rest of this book. Support from sympathetic executives is also an important dimension of the process through which particular films manage to survive the often lengthy and difficult Hollywood development process, particularly in cases in which the director or another individual participant does not have an overwhelming degree of clout. If this is the norm, such a requirement is likely to be even stronger for any project that is less obviously commercial or is seen as involving higher than usual levels of risk. An example I have examined elsewhere is the role played by Bill Gerber and Lorenzo di Bonaventura in the production of David O. Russell's *Three Kings* in the context of a period at Warner Bros. when creative rather than marketing executives were credited with being given more than usual leadership of the green-lighting process.[76]

The nature of the contemporary Hollywood development and production process is such as to allow some leeway of this kind, if usually limited and subject to particular aspects of individual studio structure and practice at any time. The extent to which space for such individual freedom or creativity exists in industrial-scale cultural production systems, including but not limited to Hollywood, has been the subject of considerable study by sociologists focused on the functioning of organisations. As Paul DiMaggio and Paul Hirsch argue: 'Cultural production systems are characterized by a constant and pervasive tension between innovation and control' – managers and gatekeepers tending to develop their own formulas to control the boundaries of novelty.[77] In the case of television, Robert Pekurny suggests that cultural industries of this kind cannot fully be rationalised in their production operations, despite the efforts of management to achieve such an effect through the use of mechanisms such as reliance on audiences figures, the track records of producers and established formulas.[78]

A similar range of 'coping mechanisms', as Pekurny terms them, are employed by Hollywood in an attempt to introduce a degree of rationalisation into the processes of development and production, including such devices as advanced concept testing and other forms of market research, along with reliance on established track records, pre-sold properties and formulas (the latter categories including generic templates and multi-film franchises). The very existence of such practices constitutes one of the grounds for the association of studio output with the opposite of what passes for quality, precisely because of what are perceived to be their 'mechanical' and contrived basis. Here, too, any idea of complete rationalisation remains illusory, a fact regularly acknowledged by Hollywood insiders (most famously, the screenwriter William Goldman's assertion that 'nobody knows anything', as far as predicting what will be successful is concerned)[79]. Such figures are likely to mystify the development/production process and paint it as more intuitive than might really be the case, however, in order to maintain their own sense of individual creative agency. Whatever the exact balance might be in reality, and it is likely to change to some degree over time and from one local context to another, some margin remains available to sufficiently powerful players in the right circumstances, either to go beyond the usual constraints provided by the likes of track records and formulas or, as in the cases from television considered by Pekurny, more often to find space within these for varying degrees of departure that might be marked as more creative or challenging than the industrial norm. The latter is certainly the case in some of the examples analysed in depth in the remainder of this book.

The degree of space likely to be available for innovations within cultural production systems can be related to both the broader state of

particular industries and more local developments. Studies of industrial innovation cited by Joseph Turow, in an examination of earlier
less-conventional programming in commercial television, suggest that
innovations that involve substantial departures from the norm are less
likely to be developed by firms that experience relatively stable organ-
isational and environmental conditions. They are more likely to be
found in conditions of 'tension-inducing' change or threat.[80] Such a
framework might help to explain the relatively large departures from
commercial norms found in some examples of films associated with the
Hollywood Renaissance period (a time of considerable crisis within
the industry) and, perhaps, the relatively limited degrees of departure
generally found in the other quality traditions considered above and in
the following chapters. This might not be an exact correlation, however. Stability and success in Hollywood can also be precisely what
create space for innovation – even if the scope of this remains limited –
such as that enjoyed by a select group of the most powerful individual
filmmakers. Stability has also been a key factor in the creation of space
for less conventional releases by the studio speciality divisions, a notable example being Sony Pictures Classics, the longest-standing of the
contemporary subsidiaries with the most stable management team, the
most autonomy from its parent, and the strongest leaning towards the
less commercial art-film sector of any of the divisions.

If space for the pursuit of some degree of quality-related innovation can exist for executives as well as for more obviously creative
figures such as the filmmakers themselves, John Thornton Caldwell,
in a more recent study of the attitudes of film and television personnel from various points in the production process, identifies a number
of practices through which executives have sought to gain some of
the cachet associated with the creative dimension of the business.[81]
These range from what he terms 'credit commandeering' – the pro-
liferation of 'producer' credits on some films, including the names of
many individuals seldom or never seen on set during the actual process of production – to lapses into 'creative-speak' by executives when
they discuss business among themselves. The implication is that they
are encouraged to position themselves as 'artistic' as well as business
figures.[82] As Caldwell puts it: 'Some executives, with enough clout,
actually take over creative functions within film/television companies.

Others simply cultivate artistic talk and thinking as part of their personal brands and leadership styles in the trade sphere.'[83] In various ways, he adds, 'the "suits" in film/television continue to find ways to emulate the "creatives" in Los Angeles's entertainment work worlds'.[84]

Such practices are followed in pursuit of personal business objectives and career advancement, much of which might have little to do with any specific investment in support for the kinds of quality production on which this book is focused. They create a context in which this might be at least a part of the picture, however, in the kinds of qualities that might be deemed fitting to the creation of the variety of 'personal brand' to which Caldwell refers. The usurping of aspects of the creative function involves, in Caldwell's terms, a hijacking of 'visionary intuition' for executives, giving 'buzz' to production companies and showcasing 'executive charisma'[85] – all of which might suggest some potential investment in the pursuit of projects that mark themselves out at least to some extent from those associated with the most direct targeting of the largest commercial bottom line. The most immediately important dimension might relate to rational matters of career development in a sector in which individual job tenure is often short. But creative prestige of this kind can also have currency at a broader social or social-psychological level for those concerned, in a context in which the studio 'suit' has often been cast as a despised, philistine figure, only interested in the most crass forms of profitability and as part of a 'soulless' machine that stifles creative talent (a characterisation widely in play today as well as often across the history of Hollywood).

The role of prestige and status, alongside more material sources of wealth or reward, has long been acknowledged in various sociological or related traditions that might be invoked here, including the work of figures as different as Max Weber and Georges Bataille. Far from all behaviour – individual or collective – is driven by economic rationality, an issue also widely debated at a more pragmatic level within disciplines such as social psychology and the study of business and management. Studies of the self-images of employees of companies with poor reputations, for example, indicate a range of 'taint-management' strategies (including the cultivation of a stance of cynical distance from the corporate image) used in the construction of more positive identities, a process that might easily be imagined at work among some studio executives.[86]

Medved's argument about the desire of members of the Hollywood community for status and prestige need not entirely be dismissed, but can be understood as part of a more complex situation in which commercial and less commercial – or less obviously commercial – motivations can simultaneously be involved. The importance of status, and of a sense of identification with more creative figures such as filmmakers and stars, is also acknowledged by Edward Jay Epstein – notably so in a work focused primarily on the pragmatic economic nuts and bolts of the functioning of the contemporary studios as 'clearinghouses', the primary roles of which are the collection and allocation of fees for the use of the intellectual properties they control. An important part of the studio environment, for Epstein, even in this conglomerate-era business world, is the sense of community that is involved, one in which executives constantly mingle, socially as well as professionally, with stars, directors, producers and agents:

> If studio executives only made films that maximized the amount
> of money in their clearinghouses, they would do so at the serious
> risk of losing their standing in their community and, with it, their
> connection to the people, events, honors, and opportunities that
> brought them to Hollywood in the first place. With such a personal
> investment in their status and solidarity with the stars, directors,
> power brokers, and other doyens of Hollywood, they have concerns
> that go beyond the economic logic dictated balance sheet of the
> clearinghouses.[87]

While sources of prestige such as awards can be translatable into economic returns, as suggested above, Epstein argues also for the importance of status of this kind in its own right, a view for which he finds support from the legendary Hollywood figure Lew Wasserman, the former agent widely viewed to have been one of the architects of the studio system of the post-classical era.[88] One of the factors cited here, by both Epstein and Wasserman, is the importance of critical success and awards to the *morale* of those involved – either individually or collectively – in addition to any further rewards they might reap at the box office.

If a key dimension of the status of executives entailed in relationships such as these is a matter of their position within the Hollywood community – a form of social capital, alongside the economic and cultural – this can also be understood in more pragmatic terms, as is implied in the quotation from Epstein above. Their standing with key filmmakers, performers or other power brokers such as agents is a major factor in their ability to function in core commercially oriented terms, from which Epstein suggests a related factor that might sometimes encourage their involvement in less financially attractive productions. While executives have to consider the costs of giving the green light to such films, Epstein argues, they also have to consider the potential costs to themselves of *not* doing so, particularly through the risk of alienating producers, directors and stars whose services the studio might require in the future. This is, again, put in terms that are not just matters of rational calculation but that involve a sense of the potential to cause damage to 'the social fabric', a point on which Epstein cites the backing of the former head of Warner Communications, Steve Ross, another figure indentified as one of the creators of the contemporary Hollywood infrastructure (that Epstein finds agreement between these arguments and the opinion of major figures such as Wasserman and Ross adds considerable weight to his case).[89] As Epstein quotes one 'top agent': 'Whatever the financial calculus, it takes a truly brave studio head to reject the movies of stars they value.'[90] An additional factor suggested by Epstein is the fact that the tenure of senior studio executives is often relatively brief and their departure typically followed by the signing of a multi-picture deal as a producer for the same organisation – an often far more lucrative situation, but one the success of which might be even more likely to depend on having maintained good relations with leading directors and stars by not having turned down their pet projects in a previous more powerful incarnation.

Notes

1   For one example of an over-statement of the 'disappearance' of such films, see Tino Balio, *Hollywood in the New Millennium*, Basingstoke: Palgrave Macmillan, 2013, p. 149

2   Brooks Barnes, 'Hollywood moves away from middlebrow', 26 December 2010, via nytimes.com

3   Geoff Boucher, 'Joseph Gordon-Levitt and Ellen Page embrace the "Inception" of smart projects', 11 July 2010, via latimes.com

4   Robert Thompson, *Television's Second Golden Age: From* Hill Street Blues *to* ER, Syracuse: Syracuse University Press, 1996, p. 12. For the study that first coined the term 'quality television', in relation to productions of the 1970s, see Jane Feuer, Paul Kerr and Tise Vahimagi eds, *MTM: Quality Television*, London: BFI, 1984

5   See Janet McCabe and Kim Akass, eds, *Quality TV: Contemporary American Television and Beyond*, London: I.B. Tauris, 2007

6   William Uricchio and Roberta Pearson, *Reframing Culture: The Case of the Vitagraph Quality Films*, Princeton: Princeton University Press, 1993

7   Uricchio and Pearson, *Reframing Culture*, pp. 55–60

8   Eileen Bowser, *The Transformation of Cinema*, Berkeley: University of California Press, 1990, p. 167

9   Bowser, *The Transformation of Cinema*, p. 256

10   Neil Gabler, *An Empire of Their Own: How the Jews Invented Hollywood*, New York: Anchor, 1988

11   Thomas Schatz, *The Genius of the System*, New York: Metropolitan Books, 1988, p. 406

12   Raymond Williams, *Culture and Society 1780–1950*, Harmondsworth: Penguin, 1961, p. 60. See also Larry Shiner, *The Invention of Art: A Cultural History*, Chicago: University of Chicago Press, 2001

13   Leo Lowenthal, 'The Debate over Art and Popular Culture: Synopsis' in Lowenthal, *Literature and Mass Culture*, New Brunswick: Transaction Books, 1984

14   Ibid., p. 19

15   Ibid., p. 20

16   Robert Allen and Douglas Gomery, *Film History: Theory and Practice*, New York: McGraw-Hill, 1985

17   Allen and Gomery, *Film History*, p. 98

18   Ibid., p. 98

19   Ibid., pp. 98–9

20   Richard Koszarski, *An Evening's Entertainment: The Age of the Silent Feature Picture, 1915–1928*, Berkeley: University of California Press, 1990, p. 319

21   Ibid., p. 320

22   Richard Maltby, 'The Production Code and the Hays Office' in Tino Balio, ed., *Grand Design: Hollywood as a Modern Business Enterprise, 1930–1939*, Berkeley: University of California Press, 1993

23   For a discussion of distinctions made between the terms 'quality' (used in this case by critics) and 'prestige' (used somewhat differently within industry discourse) in a different context – that of British productions of the 1940s – see John Ellis, 'The quality film adventure: British critics and the cinema' in Andrew Higson, ed., *Dissolving Views: Key Writings on British Cinema*, London: Cassell, 1996

24   Balio, *Grand Design*, p. 179

25   Robert Kapsis, *Hitchcock: The Making of a Reputation*, Chicago: University of Chicago Press, 1992

26   Maltby, 'The Production Code', p. 63

27   Thomas Leitch, *Film Adaptation and Its Discontents: From* Gone with the Wind *to* The Passion of the Christ, Baltimore: Johns Hopkins University Press, 2007, p. 155

28   Thomas Schatz, *Boom and Bust: American Cinema in the 1940s*, Berkeley, University of California Press, 1997, p. 369

29   Chris Cagle, 'Two modes of prestige film', *Screen*, vol. 48, no. 3, autumn 2007, p. 293

30   Ibid., p. 297

31   Robert Ray, *A Certain Tendency of the Hollywood Cinema, 1930–1980*, Princeton: Princeton University Press, 1985, p. 144

32   Shyon Baumann, *Hollywood Highbrow: From Entertainment to Art*, Princeton: Princeton University Press, 2007, p. 3

33   Baumann, *Hollywood Highbrow*, p. 46

34   Howard Becker, *Art Worlds*, Berkeley: University of California Press, 1982

35   Baumann, *Hollywood Highbrow*, p. 3

36   Ibid., p. 3

37   Ibid., p. 18

38   François Truffaut, 'A certain tendency of the French cinema' in Bill Nichols, ed., *Movies and Methods*, vol. 1, Berkeley: University of California Press, 1976

39   See Jim Collins, *Bring on the Books for Everybody: How Literary Culture Became Popular Culture*, Durham: Duke University Press, 2010, pp. 127–8

40   For a similar argument in relation to television, see Michael Z. Newman and Elana Levine, *Legitimating Television: Media Convergence and Cultural Status*, New York and London: Routledge, 2012

41   Baumann, *Hollywood Highbrow*, p. 109

42   For the broader economic background to this, see David Hesmondhalgh, *The Culture Industries*, London: Sage, 2007

43   Ibid., p. 196

44   For more on this, see Geoff King, *American Independent Cinema*, London: I.B.Tauris, 2005, Chapter 1

45   Yannis Tzioumakis, '"Independent", "Indie" and "Indiewood": Towards a periodisation of contemporary (post-1980) American independent cinema' in Geoff King, Claire Molloy and Tzioumakis, eds, *American Independent Cinema: Indie, Indiewood and Beyond*, London: Routledge, 2013.

46   Jeffrey Sconce, 'Irony, nihilism and the new American "smart" film', *Screen*, vol. 43, no. 4, winter 2002

47   Geoff King, *Indie 2.0: Change and Continuity in Contemporary American Indie Film*, London, I.B.Tauris, Chapter 1. See also, for example, Claire Perkins, *American Smart Cinema*, Edinburgh: Edinburgh University Press, 2012

48   Stephen Prince, *A New Pot of Gold: Hollywood Under the Electronic Rainbow, 1980–1989*, New York: Charles Scribner's Sons, 2000, p. 369

49   Michael Medved, *Hollywood vs. America*, New York: Harper, 1993, p. 3 (first published 1992)

50   Ibid., p. 10

51   Ibid., p. 26

52   Irene Taviss Thomson, *Culture Wars and Enduring American Dilemmas*, Ann Arbor: University of Michigan Press, 2010

53   For example, Jeffrey Kuhner, 'Hollywood's culture of death', 22 February 2009, via www.washingtontimes.com. For an account that makes *Hollywood vs. American* appear almost restrained, see Michael Vincent Boyer, *The Hollywood Culture War: What You Don't Know CAN Hurt You!* Xlibris Corporation, 2008

54   Theodor Adorno and Max Horkheimer, 'The culture industries' in Adorno and Horkheimer, *Dialectic of Enlightenment*, London: Verso, 1997

55   Pierre Bourdieu, 'The field of cultural production, or the economic world reversed' in Bourdieu, *The Field of Cultural Production*, London: Routledge, 1983

56   Medved, *Hollywood vs. America*, p. 292

57   James English, *The Economy of Prestige: Prizes, Awards, and the Circulation of Cultural Value*, Cambridge, Mass.: Harvard University Press, 2005, p. 11

58   English, *The Economy of Prestige*, p. 153

59   Ibid., p. 153

60   Ibid., pp. 74–9

61   Claire Monk, *Heritage Film Audiences: Period Films and Contemporary Audiences in the UK*, Edinburgh: Edinburgh University Press, 2011

62   Lawrence Levine, *Highbrow/Lowbrow: The Emergence of Cultural Hierarchy in America*, Cambridge, Mass.: Harvard University Press, 1988

63   See King, *American Independent Cinema* and *Indiewood, USA: Where Hollywood Meets Independent Cinema*, London: I.B.Tauris, 2009.

64   David Andrews, *Theorizing Art Cinemas: Foreign, Cult, Avant-Garde, and Beyond*, Austin: University of Texas Press, 2013

65   Collins, *Bring on the Books for Everybody*

66   Ibid., p.178

67   For more on these processes, see King, *Indiewood, USA*, p. 13

68   Morris Holbrook and Michela Addis, 'Art versus commerce in the movie industry: A two-path model of motion-picture success', *Journal of Cultural Economics*, vol. 32, no. 2, 2008

69   Holbrook and Addis, 'Art versus commerce', p. 102

70   Dwight Macdonald, 'Masscult and midcult' in *Masscult and Midcult: Essays Against the American Grain*, New York: New York Review of Books, 2011, p. 35 (originally published 1962)

71   Macdonald, 'Masscult and Midcult', p. 35

72   Ibid., p. 36

73   Ibid., p. 35

74   Janice Radway, *A Feeling for Books: The Book-of-the-Month Club, Literary Taste, and Middle-Class Desire*, Chapel Hill: University of North Carolina Press, 1999, p. 152

75   Paramount executive Walter Wanger, quoted in Gabler, *An Empire of Their Own*, p. 204

76   See King, *Indiewood, USA*, pp. 200–2

77   Paul DiMaggio and Paul Hirsch, 'Production organizations in the Arts', *American Behavioral Scientist*, vol. 19, no. 6, July/August, 1976

78   Robert Pekurny, 'Coping with television production' in James Ettema and D. Charles Whitney, *Individuals in Mass Media Organizations: Creativity and Constraint*, London: Sage, 1982

79   William Goldman, *Adventures in the Screen Trade: A Personal View of Hollywood*, London: Abacus, 1983, p. 39

80   Joseph Turow, 'Unconventional programs on commercial television' in Ettema and Whitney, *Individuals in Mass Media Organizations*, London: Sage, 1982.

81 John Thornton Caldwell, *Production Culture: Industrial Reflexivity and Critical Practice in Film and Television*, Durham & London: Duke University Press, 2008
82 Caldwell, *Production Culture*, p. 242
83 Ibid., pp. 243–4
84 Ibid., p. 244
85 Ibid., p. 244
86 Numerous such examples are cited in Sanne Frandsen, 'Organizational image, identification, and cynical distance: Prestigious professionals in a low-prestige organization', *Management Communication Quarterly*, vol. 26, no. 3, 2012
87 Edward Jay Epstein, *The Big Picture: Money and Power in Hollywood*, New York: Random House, 2006, p. 131
88 Ibid., p. 145
89 Ibid., p. 146
90 Ibid., p. 146

1

Markers of quality and contemporary Hollywood strategy

It is useful at this point to consider in broad terms some of the dimensions in which quality is marked in the kinds of films examined in this book and some of those cited above. What follows is an initial sketch of some of the key factors considered in greater detail in the subsequent case studies. Two main grounds of definition exist for markers of quality, although these function in dynamic relationship to one another rather than as separate dimensions. One consists of points of similarity to other works or broader realms of production that claim, or are generally accorded, higher cultural status. The other is the establishment, implicitly or otherwise, of an impression of difference from that which is associated with the 'lower' realm of the Hollywood mainstream, constituted by the characteristics – textual and otherwise – attributed to what is perceived to be more routine or core studio output. One can be viewed as the making, on some level, of a positive claim; the other as a negative marker of distinction. Both operations might be in play simultaneously.

It is important to be clear from the start that what are involved here are processes of distinction that operate in relation to prevailing or received notions of what constitutes 'higher' or 'lower' quality. These hierarchical conceptions are liable to exist in exaggerated, invidious and over-simplified form (for example, the widespread attribution to blockbuster-scale Hollywood productions – or 'the mainstream' more generally – of degrees of aesthetic crudeness, standardisation or simplicity that are far from always substantiated by close analysis). The notion of the 'mainstream' – against which quality, art or indie distinctions are made – is best understood as a relative concept, one that implies (usually valorised) alternatives of one kind or degree, and that only exists discursively as the product of such a dynamic. Specific textual and extra-textual characteristics can be associated with the mainstream in contemporary Hollywood, as outlined below, but the manner in which these are customarily articulated is the product of a number of long-standing discursive contexts of the kind examined further in this chapter. I begin with a list of potential positive markers of quality, combined with, and in some instances followed by, an outline of some elements of the negative other against which these characteristically are defined. I then return to the question of the place of the quality film within contemporary studio strategy, before outlining the main approaches taken to the case studies that comprise the rest of the book (the basis on which these were chosen is explained towards the end of this chapter).

Markers of quality: an initial sketch

As has already been seen in many historical examples, source material can be one key supplier of quality associations, the most obvious instances being films adapted from canonised literary texts. These tend to figure less prominently, however, in studio productions of recent decades. The overt 'classic' literary adaptation is an arena that has tended to fall into the orbit of the speciality divisions more often than that of the main studio arms (an example from the latter is Warner's *The Great Gatsby* [2013]). The same is true generally of studio adaptations of more contemporary serious 'literary' fiction, which are less common in general, the principal domain of which has also been either the indie or Indiewood sectors. Where studios have been the sources of such productions, these are likely to include strongly mainstream-emotional hooks, as in cases such as Warner's *Extremely*

Loud and Incredibly Close (2011) and Fox's *Life of Pi* (2012), each of which features a central emotive performance by a child or young performer.

More frequent sources for the contemporary studio quality film probably are works of genre fiction that claim a somewhat higher status than is the norm in their own realm, products that are in this respect situated in a manner similar to that of the films themselves, as can be seen from some of the examples considered in detail in the chapters below (particularly Chapter 4). A subversion, or more subtle questioning or mixing of genre components, can be another more general source of quality resonances, a prominent factor also in many canonised examples of quality TV. Here, too, however – or in films based on original screenplays or other sources – an appeal is often made to the literary in more general terms, relating to particular narrative qualities and their broader associations with the type of fiction liable to be accorded higher cultural status.

Source material can also be an important factor in the marking of quality more broadly than in relation to literary texts. Reference to what are understood to be 'real world' issues – whether directly or through adaptation of other sources – is another widespread marker of quality, as seen in the historical social problem film and its more recent equivalents, a framework of relevance to the examples examined in Chapters 3 and 5. A broad opposition is established here between the valences of that which is understood to exist more or less in the realm of fantasy – whether all-out overt fantasy, at a generic level, or in a general unlikeliness of material or its treatment elsewhere – and that which is considered to have a more immediate relationship to plausible materials or perceived realities of the external world. We are here clearly in the realm of the substantive content of narrative material. The clearest markers of quality might be found in this case in particular (realist, although this is a term that brings its own complications) treatments of material such as politics or serious social issues (also a key component in most definitions of art and indie cinema, alongside formal innovation or experiment). This is especially the case when these include a critical attitude towards dominant institutions. The latter tends to be limited, at best, however, in studio quality films of any period, within which any critique of an overtly political nature is rare. More likely is an implicit questioning of mainstream Hollywood norms such as the presence of less-than-entirely sympathetic/heroic central characters, as found in a number of the examples examined in this book. This leads us more generally into a consideration of serious modality as a marker of quality, in the presentation of material – both the material itself and its manner of articulation – in a way that suggests that we are meant to treat it as having implications for our understanding of matters of substance beyond the world of the screen. Just as a particular range of modality markers can encourage the viewer to take material un-seriously in various ways in comedy, other markers encourage us to respond in the opposite direction.

While markers of broad comedy encourage a distanced response to the action on screen (slapstick violence, for example, that does not seem really to hurt the characters in any serious way), markers of seriousness encourage a stronger level of implication on the part of the viewer in both what happens within the diegetic universe and what it might tell us about the world beyond. The serious is thus established in opposition to the 'escapist' (that which distracts us from realities), a major marker of quality in many cases (the literary adaptation is likely to stake a similar claim to such seriousness). From this it follows that seriousness-as-quality often entails a darker or more downbeat view of the world than that which is associated with escapism. Pessimism is more likely to be accorded quality status than optimism, particularly in more recent formulations of quality, on the grounds that it might involve an embracing of the complex, difficult and challenging dimensions of life. A dark seriousness is again associated with notions of realism, of confronting what might often appear to be intractable problems, as seen in some of the postwar examples cited in the Introduction. This would usually be articulated in opposition to notions of escapism as defined by the provision of easy, comforting, but essentially illusory simplifications, wish-fulfilments and idealisations – ways of avoiding anything more challenging or uncomfortable (qualities widely associated with the Hollywood mainstream, including the individual-based outcomes of many social problem films).

This is another point of difference from the historical variety of quality rooted in notions of moral uplift – the latter being one that can entail an idealisation of social or other relations, as opposed to

an emphasis on harsher and more critical realism. All such judgements are, of course, premised on particular ideological positions,
as suggested in the Introduction. Wish-fulfilment and idealisation
as found in Hollywood are often conservative in implication when
viewed within the context of the inequalities of capitalist, patriarchal
or otherwise divided societies. A darker-toned realism is positioned
implicitly as highlighting the downside of prevailing regimes of
wealth and power (this was, again, a key dimension of some postwar art cinema). The different valuation of such qualities is also more
deeply ingrained in the history of Western cultural production. Not
least of the grounds for such assumptions would be the long-standing
influence of the hierarchical opposition offered by Aristotle between
comedy and tragedy; the latter being valorised as a form superior to,
and of greater consequence than, the latter.

These issues of potential seriousness, darkness and pessimism of
content have numerous ramifications at the formal level, in the particular textual qualities through which they are signified or highlighted. Quality at the level of narrative might be marked, variously,
through slower narrative pace and development or greater complexity of plotting. These are markers of distinction widespread in the
American independent and art-film sectors that are also applicable to
several of the examples examined in this book. Narrative might, in
general, be marked as subtle, low-key or nuanced in character – and/
or more demanding – requiring closer attention from the viewer than
is normally expected in Hollywood. A sense of drift might in some
cases replace dynamic, character-driven action; or, on the contrary,
narrative and/or dialogue might be more rapidly paced and 'smarter'
in quality. Characterisation, in particular, might be more ambiguous,
presented as more psychologically in-depth, lacking the relatively
clear-cut distinctions between 'good' and 'bad' more typically associated with Hollywood and again requiring more cognitive work on
the part of the viewer and implying a more complex view of the
world – a quality often associated with art cinema. A notable feature
of many of the case studies examined in this book is the presence of
central characters who offer in some ways awkward or uncomfortable
sources of allegiance (also sometimes providing grounds for distinction at the level of critically vaunted performance).

The viewer might also be denied the fantasy-pleasurable closure provided by the canonical notion of the 'happy ending', a key ingredient in the wish-fulfilment escapism often associated with Hollywood films, or some of the more predictable dimensions of genre. An over-simplified notion of the happy ending is a good example of the kind of negative quality widely taken to be a core component of the Hollywood norm by both general and academic commentators, as James MacDowell demonstrates, rather than having usually been thought in need of substantiation as a concept in any detail.[1] It is precisely the nature of such characterisation as a taken-for-granted *assumption* that gives it so much power as a negative basis against which more positively to value other approaches, including some of those employed in the case studies examined in more detail below.

A mood of darkness and pessimism can be figured literally in other formal dimensions, most obviously lighting or its relative absence. This is another dimension in which subtlety and nuance often serve as markers of quality: in lighting, camerawork and/or editing regimes. Markers of quality here might include that which suggests a 'classical' or elegant framing and *decoupage*. Camera movement might be less insistent than has become characteristic of many contemporary studio features, and editing slower and more restrained. Potential negative points of reference here would be the form of 'intensified continuity' identified by David Bordwell as a widespread tendency in the Hollywood of the twenty-first century, or the forms of glossy 'shallow' imagery diagnosed by other commentators and attributed to various influences including those of advertising and music video – formats often ascribed a lower cultural status.[2] It is notable that the classical, in this context, can become a marker of relative quality against which certain other formal approaches are set, given its status for many more radical practices (including modernist tendencies in some examples of art cinema as well as the avant-garde or the experimental) as an index of conformity *against* which to react. The studio quality film tends not to be formally distinctive in more overtly marked ways, unlike some more innovative examples from the indie or art-film sectors. It is largely classical in terms of its framing and editing regimes (as, indeed, are many examples of indie film), although with scope for some exceptions.

The implication of Bordwell's account is that many contemporary films have become *over*-insistent, camera movement in particular being used excessively (during dialogue sequences, for example) rather than being reserved for the heightening of particular moments. The result, it is implied, is a lack of discrimination and nuance. A valorised alternative, for Bordwell, is the more subtle framing, staging and *mise-en-scène* found in the work of art filmmakers such as Mizoguchi Kenji, Theo Angelopoulos and Hou Hsiao-hsien – a style that often includes the use of long takes during which the viewer is required to be patient and to work to find particular moments of significance, as opposed to having everything insistently spelled out in the more typically Hollywood manner.[3] Bordwell is careful to frame his argument as one in favour of more variety than he finds in the contemporary Hollywood mainstream, including – but not necessarily limited to – these alternative approaches. But a clearly hierarchical impression emerges from the distinctions he makes between the two and the grounds upon which these rest. The quality film is likely, typically, to occupy a position somewhere between the poles offered by intensified continuity and the art-cinema styles of the likes of Mizoguchi, Angelopoulos and Hou.

A consistent negative reference point in many of these debates is a notion that media such as popular television and music video – and films influenced by such forms – are designed to appeal to either particular classes of viewers or a wider society afflicted by a 'limited attention span', a prevalent discourse in media accounts of recent/contemporary American/Western society. This has become, as Michael Newman suggests, something of a self-fulfilling prophecy, the notion of such limitations among viewers having gained currency among creative workers in the media industry regardless of its highly questionable basis as a cultural diagnosis (one based, Newman suggests, almost entirely on anecdotal evidence).[4] The discourse surrounding this conception, the consolidation of which Newman dates particularly to the 1970s and 1980s, provides the underpinning for numerous quality/non-quality distinctions. The former is regularly characterised by the 'sustained' attention required by literary forms such as the novel (and the novelistic elsewhere) and the latter by generally lower-status forms (when characterised in broad and sweepingly negative terms)

such as television, music video and short-form online outputs such as
YouTube videos.

A plausible explanation for the strength and persistence of this discourse is that it provides a means of reasserting ideological distinctions
'in the face of disrupted power dynamics and the breakdown of social
distinctions'.[5] This is a context relating to one era that shares many
broad features in common with those of the earlier development of
popular culture in general, and the film medium in particular, cited
above. In this iteration:

> It reasserts the superiority of adult culture (longer-form, more con-
> templative) over youth culture (faster-paced, more distracting) and of
> a traditional establishment culture (print culture, the culture of edu-
> cational institutions) over a threatening emergent culture (electronic
> visual culture, educational TV, myriad cable and satellite channels).[6]

An element of reflexivity is another marker of some instances of quality, one of the ingredients identified by Thompson and others in the
case of quality television. Varying degrees of self-awareness expressed
by the text – explicit or more implicit internal reference to the kinds
of qualities that it embodies – offer further evidence of claims to
a more sophisticated approach than that usually associated with the
mainstream; one in which the viewer is offered a 'knowing' position,
to some extent, superior to that of 'ordinary' Hollywood viewers
assumed to be carried blithely along by textual mechanisms of which
they remain largely or entirely unconscious. At the more radical end,
this might be something like the alienation effect associated with the
theatre of Bertolt Brecht, designed to create a distanced and analytical
perspective on the material. Even at the quality end of the Hollywood
spectrum, however, any such dimension is likely to be much less (if at
all) disruptive of more mainstream processes of engagement (a quality more likely to be found in some works of art cinema). A similarly
'knowing' attitude might also be found, however, in some forms that
are not usually viewed as part of the quality tradition, including broad
varieties of parody.

If the notion of the mainstream against which quality is usually
defined includes some of the characteristics cited above – from broad

notions of escapism to specific ingredients such as certain kinds of happy ending or the camera movement and cutting associated with intensified continuity – these can be elaborated further in various ways. If quality suggests associations with extra-economic 'artistic' dimensions – even if it can have its own kinds of commercial appeal or longer-term motivation – its conventional opposite is Hollywood at its most narrowly business oriented. This would be the studios at their most nakedly commercial, a world in which what counts is assumed to be not so much films in themselves, but their status as product that can be exploited in various forms by studios that exist as parts of broader conglomerates, the main focus of which is on the creation of profitable brands and franchises. The takeover of the studios by larger corporations, a process begun in its contemporary form in the 1960s, is a key marker of this general status. This is a Hollywood charac-terised by the centrality of market research and marketing, activities often seen from a critical perspective as unduly interfering in, and thus undermining, the creative process. A particular emphasis is expected to be put on the lowest-common-denominator factors likely to give its products the widest possible audience appeal across the globe and the greatest potential for tie-in deals with (downmarket) consumer products such as children's breakfast cereals and burger chains.

The very extent to which certain ingredients are deemed to be able to reach a global audience regardless of language – particularly action, spectacle and star presence – would in itself suggest their lower-quality nature in a schema in which language is likely to be seen as a key dimension of more intellectual potential. Allied to this is the extent to which the studios are seen primarily as targeting a teenage or under-25 rather than a more adult constituency. The term 'adult' is itself often used as a signifier of quality, as in 'adult drama' – a term used in some journalistic examples cited in this book – when employed in opposition to explicit or implicit notions of the 'juven-ile'. 'Drama' itself can also signify similarly, when used to suggest a distinct category, one that often implies 'serious drama', rather than to identify a modality employed more widely in non-comic fictional narrative. The manner of release is a key signifier in itself, as suggested in the Introduction. The large-scale openings accompanied by heavy advertising characteristic of blockbuster productions are markers of seemingly unmitigated commercial activity and, implicitly, a form of consumption based on persuasion and sheer pervasiveness. This is opposed to the notion of any more discriminating exercise of choice, taste or organic processes of discovery, such as those often associated with the indie, cult or art-film sectors and their viewers.

A good example of how some of these qualities are interpreted can be found in the terms in which this is put by Epstein in *The Hollywood Economist*, a text that offers useful analysis of the manner in which the studios operate and how they earn their income (chiefly through their domination of distribution and the charging of fees of various kinds that provide healthy income even where there is an absence of net profit).[7] The gist of the argument, as far as quality is concerned, is that Hollywood has been 'dumbed down' as a result of its focus on younger viewers, who are considered to be the easiest to target through mass TV advertising (tending to favour relatively easily identified programming). As a group they are considered the most appealing to theatres on the basis of their tendency to consume large volumes of popcorn, fizzy drinks and other products from concession stands that generate the bulk of profits for cinema chains. As far as the exhibition business is concerned, films are understood to serve primarily as vehicles for the sale of such goods, the cultural associations of which are clearly at the lower end of the scale. Such viewers are also seen as the heaviest consumers of tie-in or merchandising products such as fast food and video games, the dominant associations of which occupy a similar cultural position.

The point here is not to dispute the pertinence of much of this analysis, but to note its contribution to the broader sense of how mainstream Hollywood practice tends to be situated. The language adopted by Epstein adds to the impression, his account referring on several occasions to such viewers being 'herded' to the cinema by advertising planted in the TV programming on which they 'graze' (as in the notion of limited attention span cited above).[8] The simplistic and unjustified characterisation of the consumers of popular culture as herd-like – by implication, animalistic and undiscriminating – is familiar from accounts of the earlier historical period examined by Raymond Williams and Leo Lowenthal. That negative associations of these kinds can matter to the studios is suggested by a strategy adopted by the Warner division New Line when it sought to claim higher cultural status than usual for blockbuster-scale productions for the second instalment of its *Lord of the Rings* series: *The Two Towers* (2002). The branding strategy included moving from a major tie-in deal with Burger King ('Frodo Fries') to one with Verizon Wireless. As Paul Grainge suggests, this involved seeking 'to consolidate its core audience – the high-spending, technology-proficient youth demographic – in ways that also sought to lose associations that could stigmatize the trilogy's bid for cultural (in particular Oscar) status'.[9]

If the source material associated with quality might include the literary adaptation, more ambitious genre fictions or real-world material with serious social resonances, the sources most favoured at the mainstream end of the scale are those of the most effectively pre-sold products of popular culture. Unsurprisingly, these are often the kinds of sources that tend to occupy positions low in the prevailing cultural hierarchy (regardless of whether we might think this position is deserved or not). This is often because of their association with a teenage constituency, notably the comic books that have provided the basis for large numbers of recent blockbuster-scale productions. Even lower status might be ascribed to adaptations of video games, on the basis of the position games are ascribed in broader hierarchies, the 'low' genres with which they are often associated (action, horror, war, fantasy, etc.), and the widespread perception that commercially distributed games are more suited to the realm of action/spectacle than that of 'more respectable' or sustained narrative or thematic development. The issue, again, is not whether or not such evaluations are merited, but their prominence within prevailing discursive regimes.

Similarly placed, or even lower down the scale, might be adaptations from non-narrative based sources associated with younger people such as theme park rides (the *Pirates of the Caribbean* series [from 2003]), toys (*Transformers* [from 2007], the *GI Joe* franchise [from 2009]) or traditional games (*Battleship* [2012]). Low status is also ascribed in most cases to sequels to other films or franchise properties, particularly when viewed as non-original spin-offs motivated only by profit (likely to be situated lower in prevailing hierarchies than series based on serially produced originals in other media). This is a form that perhaps achieves reputational nadir in cases of toy-based sequels such as those in the *Transformers* franchise (see Figure 1.1). Company names can, on occasion, indicate quality in the contemporary period, one in which major studio labels do not usually signify greatly in their own right. The strongest example is probably Pixar, which gained the status of a marker of the best in Hollywood animation. Such names can also indicate the opposite, as in the likely connotations of any film bearing the label of the toy company Hasbro as co-producer.

The basis on which such material is denigrated, in prevailing critical hierarchies, offers another point of continuity with the longer tradition of the development of notions of art and culture examined by Raymond Williams. At play in the positioning of such productions, among other potential influences, is a long-standing Romantic opposition between the notion of autonomous artistic genius, as a source of genuine creativity, and the world of industrial manufacturing; a contrast situated within a wider series of oppositions between that which is characterised as either organic or mechanical (the latter being one of the earliest grounds for the potentially low status of photography and moving pictures). The contemporary notion of 'art' as a separate and higher realm was created, Williams suggests, as part of a broad response to industrialisation. The latter included an increased subjection of art and literature to the rules of the market, against which the Romantic position was asserted. Art and culture, in this context, became established as existing in antithesis to the realm of the market – an opposition that has continued to structure much of the discourse around notions of art and creativity within industrialised media such as Hollywood cinema.

Williams cites an early document of English Romanticism, from 1759, in which the opposition is figured rhetorically in terms that still seem resonant today, and in particular relation to the distinction between work of artistic leanings and the contemporary Hollywood mainstream. An original work, for this writer, Edward Young, 'may be said to be of a *vegetable* nature; it rises spontaneously from the vital root of genius; it *grows*, it is not *made*'. Non-originals or imitations, by contrast, 'are often a sort of *manufacture*' wrought 'out of pre-existent materials not their own'.[10] The valorisation of that which is considered to be organic in nature – particularly through the creation of an

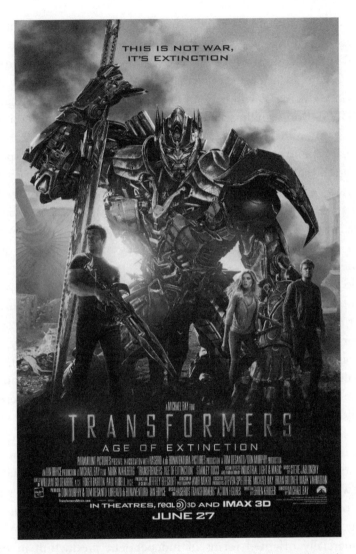

Figure 1.1. Low in the cultural hierarchy: selling the unsubtle toy-based franchise blockbuster, as manifested by the fourth in the *Transformers* series © Paramount Pictures Corporation

impression of 'organic unity' and coherence, rather than of artificially confected manufacture – is another part of this discourse that can also be traced to more distant historical roots, as far back as the work of ancient Greek thinkers such as Aristotle and Plato (this discourse is considered further in Chapter 6). The notion of a kind of organic process of origination – often centred on the creativity of the individual auteur, contrasted with that of studio 'production by committee' – retains its place today in the discourses surrounding art, indie or quality cinema, as will be seen in some of the case studies that follow. The notion of industrial manufacture and imitation, as a basis of lower status, remains equally heavily in play in the typical characterisation of the mainstream. The same can be said of the more specific accusation that certain kinds of works are wrought from 'pre-existent materials' – the various sources of pre-sold appeal, including those cited above and generic templates more generally – that are viewed, implicitly if not explicitly, as being assembled in an inorganic manner rather than as a result of any inherent belonging (i.e. 'not their own').

The mainstream against which quality is defined in Hollywood would also include particular swathes of genre territory (as well as, potentially, the very notion of the generic), especially the genres of lower established repute such as action, broad comedy, violent crime, horror and other forms of escapist fantasy. These are in many cases associated with the realm of the body (and of the lower classes), traditionally positioned lower in established cultural hierarchies than that of the mind (the domain often associated with the more cerebral middle- or upper-class aspects of art or quality traditions). The possibility also exists for quality to be asserted through particular subversions or complications of such frameworks, but the opposition itself remains deeply ideological in character. In some cases, such material is viewed as too 'disreputable' for the major studios themselves, which have tended to be quite squeamish in their concern for their own repute, an attitude that has created numerous opportunities for more commercially oriented forms of independent production in genre territory such as horror and lower-budget action cinema.

As far as form is concerned, the kinds of qualities cited above would be grouped with others labelled as 'crude' or over-emphatic and/or designed for those of supposedly limited attention span (as opposed to the subtle and nuanced that require closer attention). The critical verdict on such material is usually that it puts too much emphasis on the provision of spectacle and various forms of audio-visual 'impact', and is over-reliant on special effects. While the quality of effects themselves might often be appreciated (at the level of how convincing they can become, or how seamlessly integrated with live action or real locations), the idea that they unduly dominate many mainstream productions (usually, greatly exaggerated) is a familiar component of discourses surrounding notions of the mainstream and the grounds on which it is distinguished from a range of higher quality alternatives. Effects also tend to be associated with the lower-status realm of the 'illusory' – as part of the escapist fantasy of popular culture – as opposed to that which is considered to be either more realistic or more seriously 'artistic' (this despite the fact that they can be deployed in very different contexts, including the creation of strong impressions of realism). The digital manipulations associated with contemporary visual effects, along with the digital more broadly, have also been denigrated on the basis of their supposed undermining of the indexical relationship to reality that is often assumed (somewhat simplistically) to underlie photographic production on celluloid.[11]

If certain varieties of narrative carry higher cultural associations than others, as suggested above, narrative itself tends to be valorised when counterposed to spectacle and the widespread deployment of special effects often associated with Hollywood at its most corporate, commercial and franchise-oriented. The roots of this opposition can again be found in broad prevailing distinctions between that which is customarily associated with the realms of mind and body (and their associations with particular classes, or genders), and in more specific discourses of the kind identified by Williams and Lowenthal. Investment in narrative – even in mainstream and often clichéd forms – suggests at least some commitment to the realm of the literate, the logical or the making of cognitive sense. Spectacle, in contrast, is often associated with the lower and supposedly less discriminating realm of physical sensation and limited attention span, as manifested in Hollywood by the vicarious impact created by some forms of intensified continuity or what I have elsewhere termed an 'impact aesthetic' established by devices such as rapid cutting, camera movement and the propelling of objects towards the viewer in certain kinds of action sequences.[12] The roots of such oppositions can also in some respects be traced back to sources from classical philosophy, figures such as Plato and Descartes providing the kind of reference

points here that are supplied by Aristotle in the case of the valorisation of the tragic. Their prevalence in subsequent dominant cultural
formations can be ascribed in part to their capacity to have func-
tioned for many generations as markers of elite power and prestige,
the stuff of 'the mind' requiring educational and other resources of
cultural capital more exclusive in their availability than the satisfaction
of more bodily-oriented pleasures.[13]

Such broad and diffuse points of reference can also be related
to the more specific historical context elaborated by Williams and
Lowenthal, the period within which articulations of artistic value
gained a particular saliency and cultural prominence that appears
more directly to shape the prevalence of such discourses today; that
is to say, as they relate to the specific issue of the manner in which
oppositions are constructed between higher and lower cultural forms
in an era of mass forms of communication. The verdict of Goethe,
cited by Lowenthal, on certain aspects of the popular culture of his
time – particularly the theatre – resonates quite strongly, for example,
with the negative valuation of the spectacular dimension of contemporary Hollywood cinema. The purpose of art for Goethe, Lowenthal
suggests, is the encouragement of imagination and contemplation,
qualities that remain to the fore in more recent attributions of quality.
Goethe believes, for Lowenthal,

> that the more a given work of art occupies the senses of the audience,
> the less scope is left for the imagination; in this respect, the impact
> of a bad book is infinitely less than the impact of a bad spectacle that
> appeals simultaneously to the eye, and the ear, and that reduces the
> spectator to almost complete passivity.[14]

A similar verdict was delivered by William Wordsworth and numerous
other critics. Concerns were expressed about the qualities that were
encouraged in literary forms such as novels and plays as they sought to
reach larger audiences during the eighteenth century, across a wider
social spectrum than had been the case in the past.[15]

A central target was a trend towards increased sensationalism in
popular works, including sentimentality and an emphasis on sex, crime
and violence, tendencies that only increased when the first truly mass

audiences were created in the nineteenth century. Institutions such as theatre and opera were accused of over-reliance on spectacle and stage effects, at the expense of plot, in a manner that further underlines the degree to which discourses established or heightened in this period remain in play today. That the studios have some investment in seeking to position their products on the more positive side of this equation, even in cases of highly mainstream blockbuster scale, is suggested by some of the discourses mobilised in relation to the adoption of new 3D formats since 2005. As Ariel Rogers suggests, an effort was made by executives to associate this iteration of 3D with a narrative-oriented sense of *immersion* in the fictional world on-screen, while downplaying the role of *emergent* effects – objects thrust out into the space of the viewer – the resonances of which are those of lower-cultural fairground-style spectacular attractions.[16] If 3D is another dimension often associated with lower status – as either a 'cheap' gimmick, a source of lowered image quality, or something motivated almost entirely by commercial concerns of one kind or another – this is another area *within* which hierarchical distinctions can be made. Lowest on the scale would be examples in which 3D is viewed as an opportunistic retrofitted conversion in post-production (and so not even the 'genuine' article); higher would be its use in otherwise more critically lauded examples with quality associations of other kinds such as *Pi* (literary source) and *Hugo* (2011, noted auteur director, Martin Scorsese).[17]

The above sketch is based on a relational understanding of quality, situated within the broader historical context in which, as Williams suggests, notions such as art and creativity gained some of their key contemporary resonances, separated out from other aspects of culture that tended to be denigrated as a result, and used in the same sense in which the term has been employed in relation to certain established forms of television. What, then, of claims made on the basis of the supposedly 'universal' nature of some valued aesthetic qualities: those such as 'beauty' and 'harmony', for example, that might be added to the list of valorised terms included in this section? The aim of this book is to examine a particular usage, one that is institutionalised within established discourses. It is hard, however, to avoid at some point coming up against evaluative arguments that claim the status of more than just positions within an essentially relativist and materially determined hierarchy. If quality is usually taken to mean the 'doing of particular kinds of things' – in the sense that is the primary focus of this book, as opposed to the 'doing of something particularly well' – the latter meaning of the term is also worthy of some consideration, even from a position that rejects any claims rooted in notions of absolute or universal aesthetic merit. It might well be argued that some individual filmmakers, for example, are more skilled than others, or that some individual works are more finely wrought than is the norm in Hollywood. But this does not necessarily entail the type of production that makes claims to higher cultural status of the kind considered above, although some similar oppositions might remain in play. This issue is addressed in the final chapter of the book in relation to the competing claims to various forms of quality found in, or in discourses surrounding, the work of Stanley Kubrick and Steven Spielberg. In all cases, however, I would argue that quality is only ever asserted in terms of some specific reference point – usually far from neutral at the ideological level – rather than being a quantity that can be understood to exist only on its own terms.

To a large extent, what is involved in many of the distinctions articulated in this chapter is part of a broader opposition – already implied on several occasions above – between conventional understandings and institutionalised practices associated with the realms of 'art' and 'entertainment'. In the case of the Hollywood quality film, however, what we find tends to inhabit a place somewhere between the poles suggested by such terms. This space can itself be a broad one, including the realms of indie and Indiewood film as well as that of quality production from within the main studio divisions. The most commercially mainstream studio films are clearly engineered quite deliberately, through many decades of evolution, to appeal to the widest possible audience – or to the particular audience segments believed at any time to be the most fruitful Hollywood constituency. The quality film likewise appears to be designed to achieve a particular kind of appeal that might in some cases be a degree more specialised, but that is also usually intended to be capable of achieving broad circulation – generally by combining markers of distinction of the kind outlined above with more familiar/mainstream grounds of appeal.

Contemporary Hollywood strategy

How, then, might we explain contemporary examples of the Hollywood quality film in relation to broader studio strategies? The suggestions offered by the press sources cited at the start of this book are predicated on the existence of an upsurge of such films in one year: 2010. Evidence does exist to support this conclusion. A list of all releases in the US in this year confirms the persistence of plenty of the kinds of films that would conventionally be located at the *opposite* end of the spectrum from quality – four of the top five box office grosses being achieved by sequels in the *Toy Story*, *Iron Man*, *Twilight* and *Harry Potter* franchises (whatever relative quality distinctions might be made on some grounds among such products).[18] A number of films with identifiable quality associations are also found in the top 50, however, including *Inception* in the top ten (number six). The presence of *Inception* here can be explained by the location of any such features in this case in the context of what remains a large-scale and spectacular blockbuster, as examined in Chapter 2. Other studio main division films with reasonably clear quality resonances to be found in the top 50 are *True Grit* from Paramount (sold on the basis of its status as a remake of a well-known original by the high profile Coen brothers) at 13, and *The Social Network* at 32. A case might also be made for Martin Scorsese's *Shutter Island* – another Paramount production, starring Leonardo DiCaprio – at 20. Also well placed in the top 50 are the Indiewood releases *The King's Speech* from Miramax at 18, and *Black Swan* from Fox Searchlight at 25. This might seem a relatively moderate presence but is noticeably different from the top 50s of the preceding five years.[19] It is hard to identify any studio films with clear quality credentials in the equivalent lists from 2005 to 2009, most of which years include two or three such films each at best and all from the speciality divisions rather than the main studio arms.

How this might be explained is less clear-cut. The suggestions offered by the press sources cited in the Introduction are somewhat speculative and not very convincing. The statement that a move towards quality could be seen as a response to general uncertainty about the marketplace seems less plausible in the contemporary context, despite Turow's argument about the broader connection between

innovation and conditions of change or threat. Whatever the periodic ups and downs of individual studios – and wider concerns about
issues such as how most effectively to handle a transition to a more
online-based world of post-theatrical business – the broader basis of
corporate-owned Hollywood appeared generally to be relatively stable in this period, as manifested in part by the consistent presence of
successful large franchise products at the top of the yearly box office
lists. The studios might also be expected to turn towards more familiar
star and/or franchise material in times of relative downturn or uncertainty, as opposed to the more radical opening that was created by the
much larger crisis that characterised the period of the Hollywood
Renaissance. And, as suggested above, stability itself in the film business might be seen to be as likely as its opposite – or perhaps more
likely – to create space for relative and occasional innovation of the
kind found in the films examined in this book.

The alternative notion, that the studios might have been held to
a higher standard than was the case in the recent past as a result of
factors such as the prevalence of social networking and its ability to
undermine marketing, also seems less than convincing. The basis of
the argument about social media made in *The New York Times* was
the disappointing performance in 2010 of heavily marketed 'tried and
true' (i.e. non-quality) productions such as *The Wolfman*, *The Tourist*
and *Sex and the City* compared with the success of 'gambles on original concepts' such as *Inception* and *The Social Network*. But the conclusion remains speculative, as is perhaps inevitably the case with this
kind of reporting.[20] Press coverage of such trends in the quality arena
tends to over-state their extent, often through a cyclical process of
diagnoses that shifts between two rhetorical extremes that might not
best reflect the reality of ongoing studio practice.

The first part of such a cycle amounts to regular declarations of
the 'abandonment' by Hollywood of more serious 'adult' production,
a phenomenon usually blamed on the release of what are seen as
excess numbers of franchise films, sequels or others of lower cultural
standing. This is then followed by occasional bursts of excitement,
or puzzlement, at what appears to be a break from this pattern, as
was the case in 2010 (another piece in *The New York Times* by the
same author declared that 'something extraordinary has happened this

fall')[21]. A similar reporting of a 'resurgence' of 'the grown-up side of Hollywood, in some quarters at least', 'the kind of pictures that only a few years ago appeared headed toward extinction', came in 2011 in relation to a Sony slate that included *Moneyball* and *The Ides of March*.[22] Another example of this occurred at the end of 1999, the year of at least partially quality-oriented studio films including *Fight Club*, *Three Kings* and *American Beauty*.[23] This is a phenomenon of interest in its own right, as part of the process through which Hollywood is situated discursively – and often rhetorically – in relation to notions of quality or its opposite. The reality is probably that somewhat more continuity exists than is implied by such accounts, even if some years might see more quality films, or quality successes, than others, and if the general hospitality of the studio environment to such films might change in relative degree as a result of specific developments in the overall movie economy. An over-statement of how 'low' Hollywood is often said to have sunk – see, for example some of the reporting around the time of the release of *Battleship* in 2012 – creates an impression that studio production is of such an unambitious nature that *anything* perceived to be relatively challenging or original appears to stand out further from the norm than might really be the case. The issue might be less one of Hollywood's abandonment and occasional return to 'adult' films than one relating to the disproportionate level of attention gained by certain films of this kind that achieve particular success or critical prominence, or both.

Particular factors might still encourage more quality films to appear at some times than others, as was seen in the historical sketch provided above, including the simple fact (and basic Hollywood strategy) that successful examples might prompt the production of others of a similar kind. The perceived upsurge of 1999 was associated by many commentators at the time with developments in the independent and Indiewood spheres, some of the more prominent successes of which were seen as encouraging the studios to increase their investments in this arena, either via their speciality divisions or more directly though their main production and distribution arms. There might also be particular reasons for quality or other below-blockbuster-level films facing a greater-than-usual squeeze in some periods, as a result of wider industry context or strategy. One study of studio output from

2006 to 2012 concluded that profit margins were higher at the end of the period than at the beginning, largely as a result of a significant reduction in the number of releases (a drop of 69 titles, or 34 per cent, to 134 in 2012).[24] This entailed an increase in the already-substantial focus of resources on blockbuster 'tentpole' and franchise productions, at the expense of other types of film. *Variety* concluded: 'As Hollywood's creative community can attest, the midrange budget studio pic is fast becoming an endangered species.'[25]

This verdict might be another example of the tendency to exaggerate the situation one way or the other, assuming that such films are not likely ever to disappear altogether (and four of the six main case studies in this book appeared in this period). The mid-budget category is one within which most quality films would be expected to fall – among other star- and/or genre-led films of lower-than-blockbuster scale – and one that has often been viewed as under threat as a result of increased focus on large-scale franchise productions. Another often somewhat rhetorical account of a supposed dearth of scope for anything other than franchise tentpoles (and very low-budget non-studio productions) is offered by the producer Linda Obst in her 2013 book *Sleepless in Hollywood: Tales from the New Abnormal in the Movie Business*.[26] This is also grounded in specific developments in the studio economy, however, principally a decline in DVD sales in the latter part of the 2000s and uncertainty about how this crucial part of the business might be replaced. The verdict of senior executives cited by Obst is that the response was an increased reliance on the growth of overseas markets, and thus a privileging of potential overseas performance in the process of deciding which films to green-light – a basis generally unlikely to favour riskier or less obviously mainstream material – along with a general financial contraction and concomitant reduction in the space available for more creative projects. A studio reorientation in this direction was further encouraged, Obst suggests, by the recession of the late 2000s and the Hollywood writers' strike of 2007–08, each of which encouraged a reduction in the scope for production beyond the realm of the most reliably pre-sold franchises or other perceived sources of insurance such as the involvement of A-list stars and directors. Circumstances such as these are likely to have increased the difficulties for those seeking to pursue less obviously commercial material, even if the extent to which this is the case might sometimes appear to be exaggerated. That some such films continued to appear at this time might, therefore, seem all the more significant and in need of the kind of explanation sought by this book.

A significant component of the support that persisted for quality films in this period can be attributed to the role played by independent financiers, working in partnership with the studios. These constituted an increasingly important dimension of general studio strategy in the early decades of the twenty-first century, the names of investor companies such as Relativity Media, Legendary Pictures and the longer-standing Village Roadshow becoming familiar parts of movie bank balances and opening title sequences (in some cases, combining investment partnerships alongside the majors with expansion into production and/or distribution operations of their own). While funders such as these invested in blockbusters, they were also credited with maintaining funding for the mid-budget productions required by the studios to fill their distribution pipelines, enabling them to produce more films than would otherwise be the case. It is striking that deals with such companies were in place for all but one of the case study examples examined in this book: Legendary with *Inception* at the larger scale; Relativity with *The Social Network*; Village Roadshow with *Mystic River*; and the equity fund Virtual Studios with *The Assassination of Jesse James* and *Blood Diamond*. The exception is *A.I.*, a film that already had the support of two studios.[27] A notable example of an investor associated particularly with films from the quality end of the spectrum in this era is provided by Megan Ellison's Annapurna Pictures, a contributor to titles such as *Zero Dark Thirty* (2012, Kathryn Bigelow) and *American Hustle* (2013, David O. Russell) – both with Columbia – as well as the independents *The Master* (2012, Paul Thomas Anderson) and *Her* (2013, Spike Jonze).

One of the initially more plausible suggestions in the press reporting cited above is that the existence within the studios of some of the quality films of the period around 2010 might be explained by the closure of a number of speciality divisions two years earlier. This might appear to provide a neat and tidy explanation. If at some level the studios remained committed to the production of prestige-grabbing quality films – even in difficult times – for some combination of commercial reasons and those potentially relating to prestige in its own right, it might make perfect sense for those which closed down their speciality divisions to include more such films within the slates of their main operations. Is it, then, coincidence that the bulk of the films included as case studies in this book were released by Warner Bros, one of the studios that had closed its speciality wing, Warner Independent Pictures (WIP), in 2008? The films were not chosen on this basis, but to illustrate particular tendencies within contemporary quality production more generally. It might be considered striking, however, that so many turned out to be from a studio that underwent this process. That Warner figures centrally in this study also provides a good test of the extent to which space can be found for degrees of quality within the studio system more generally, given its reputation since the late 1980s as the quintessential embodiment of Hollywood at its most corporate.[28] It is not the case, however, that most of the films examined here were likely to have been speciality releases in other circumstances. For one thing, most were pre-2008 releases, including the film that at the textual level might have most in common with other speciality releases of the time: *The Assassination of Jesse James by the Coward Robert Ford*. Others, regardless of whether they were released before or after the closure of WIP, would have been unlikely candidates for speciality division release: the blockbuster-scale *Inception* and the star- and/or star-director-led *Mystic River*, *Blood Diamond* and *A.I. Artificial Intelligence*.

We might, then, ask why *The Assassination of Jesse James* was not a WIP production and/or release, a question addressed in Chapter 4. The remaining case study example, *The Social Network*, was released by Columbia Pictures, a division of the Sony empire. Sony was one of the studios at the time to have maintained its speciality division, Sony Pictures Classics (SPC), but this was always a smaller-scale and more art-cinema-oriented subsidiary than the others, and would be much less likely to be associated with a work of this kind, the specifics of which are examined in Chapter 3. An additional factor to be considered here, then, is the particular strategy associated with one division or another. The other two speciality divisions to remain successfully in place after 2008 were Fox Searchlight and Focus Features (a division of Universal), each of which was associated with the more commercial end of the Indiewood spectrum than either WIP or SPC. It might be the case, therefore, that we would expect studio quality films of the post-2008 period to be less likely to be associated with Fox or Universal, given the continued existence and stability of speciality divisions that had successfully handled relatively substantial Indiewood features. One of the reasons for the closure of some of the divisions appears to have been the failure of the studios involved to establish clear lines between subsidiary and parent. The fact remains, though, that the contemporary studio quality film, as defined in this book, is not coterminous in its actual qualities with those associated with the speciality divisions. It often includes factors that appear more oriented towards the commercial mainstream than those usually characteristic of the output of the subsidiaries. The distinction is far from absolute, and it might be hard to tell the difference between some examples from either side of the line, or to explain in every case exactly why a film falls into one category or the other. Some leeway remains within either arena. But differences can be identified in many cases, including most of the case studies examined in detail in this book.

There may well not be any specific strategy leading to the production of quality studio films that can be pinned down with any certainty in a particular period such as that which is the main focus of this book. We might be able to argue for the broad value of an element of prestige in studio release slates, for reasons examined above, without necessarily being able to identify an immediate explanatory context relating to an overall studio strategy in any individual or collective instance. The picture might not always be as clear-cut as is suggested by Allen and Gomery, for example, in the case of *Sunrise* and Fox in the early 1920s, or in the more obvious commercial motivations for the pursuit of the quality strand in American television as a result of particular changes in the broadcast landscape in recent decades.

The declared motivations of senior studio figures are certainly best treated with scepticism, although they also provide evidence of the saliency of notions of quality at a discursive level. One of the *New York Times* features cited above quotes Amy Pascal, co-chair of Sony Pictures Entertainment, for example, suggesting that the studio thinks that 'the future is about filmmakers with original voices', going

on to add that 'Original is good, and good is commercial.'[29] It is hard
to take a statement of this kind at face value but it is notable that such
a figure should consider it necessary to identify with the notion of
'original voices', when voices of that kind could hardly be said typically to represent studio output. This tells us something about the
broader currency of such notions and a context in which Hollywood
usually has to defend itself, implicitly or explicitly, against charges that
it represents more or less the opposite of the original. The 'original is
good, and good is commercial' formula is a typical rhetorical attempt
to square the circle, one that again might be judged to fly in the face
of the reality of the majority of studio output but that also seems significant in the expression of what appears to be a desire to attempt to
claim such ground.

Particular, local circumstances are examined in the case studies that
follow. These might relate to the specific aspirations of individual studios at one moment or another (the quotation from Pascal comes in
a piece partly focused on the significance of the release of *The Social
Network*). The role of powerful directors and the presence of stars
remain central factors, as will be seen in all the examples examined in
this book. The figure of the individual filmmaker can play an important role in two dimensions. First, for those with sufficient clout, in
being able to get certain kinds of films produced that might otherwise
not receive studio backing. Second, in acting as a key component, in
many instances, of the discursive basis on which ascriptions of quality
are made to the resultant work.

The manner in which these and other figures are able to support
work with quality associations might be less to do with broader studio strategy of the kind that is implied in press coverage than the fact
that some space can exist within the system when the right components are in place at a particular moment. The explanation might in
this sense be a negative one, at least in part, according to which the
supporters and creators of quality films are able to take advantage of
the fact that studio operations are far from entirely closed or 'rational'
business systems – as suggested in some of the broader media studies
cited in the Introduction – even when facing financial difficulties. The
fact that such space can exist should itself not be over-stated, however, given the extent to which it usually remains conditional on the

possession by certain figures of large resources of commercial clout, often working on relatively small budgets by Hollywood standards. A desire to attract such figures to a particular studio might be one of the more obvious explanations for the presence of some quality films, but this still leaves open to question the exact motivations that might be involved. These are likely to include clearly commercial motives, either in the immediate box office expectations associated with what an individual star or director (or some combination of the two) brings to a project, or as a way of indulging such figures in some cases that might be considered to be 'vanity' projects in the hope of developing a relationship that results in subsequent pay-off in the shape of their services in more obviously commercial future material. Prestige in its own right might still be a factor, however, including the possibility that the vanity project might also have a certain appeal to some figures at the executive level for the kinds of reasons considered in the Introduction.

The remainder of this book explores these issues in relation to a series of case studies of individual films, as identified above. A limited number of films are considered in detail but these can be taken to represent some broader tendencies within the Hollywood of recent decades, situated within the longer history of the studio quality film outlined in the Introduction. These are examined at a number of levels, although the exact balance between these varies from one chapter to another, some of the reasons for which are given below (these include the practical limits on space, which mean I have not been able to examine all dimensions at equal length in each chapter). Most chapters begin with close textual analysis of the film or films included, identifying features that make claims to quality status through the kinds of culturally sanctioned resonances outlined above, and examining exactly how far these represent breaks from the Hollywood norm and how they might be balanced by elements that lean more towards dominant industry convention. Specific textual features are considered in the context of the broader discourses of quality and its perceived opposites suggested above.

I have chosen deliberately not to focus solely on studio films that fit most clearly and unambiguously within the quality realm (such as *The Social Network* and *The Assassination of Jesse James*), but to include some (such as *Inception* and *Blood Diamond*) that display more mainstream-conventional dynamics in larger quantity in order further to analyse the manner in which such dimensions can be combined or interrelated and to highlight the essentially relative and contestable nature of quality distinctions, within the studio context or elsewhere. The films were selected partly on the basis of my initial reading of their textual characteristics. I have not relied only on my own interpretation, however, the location of each production within this realm having been supported (even if sometimes also contested) by aspects of the critical discourse surrounding each title on release. I have also chosen to focus only on a small number of case study examples, to permit their analysis in close detail at several different levels, rather than to attempt a wider survey of the number and variety of films that might be included in this territory, as would be desirable if space permitted (a brief sketch of a broader range of examples is provided in the Conclusion). While not selected on the basis of being representative in any scientific manner, I believe the examples to be reasonably characteristic manifestations of at least some of the quality associations outlined above. Other films could have been chosen to illustrate some of the same or related tendencies.

The rationale for the choices is as follows, in chapter order. *Inception*, the subject of Chapter 2, was chosen to illustrate the potential for claims of quality to be made on behalf of a spectacular summer blockbuster – the type of film usually associated with the opposite end of the scale – particularly on the basis of its relative complexity of narrative. As such, it offers a useful location to examine the manner in which such claims can be both made and subjected to contest – the latter throwing into light the basis on which such claims rest – for which reason this chapter devotes more space than others to an examination of the terms in which this debate was conducted by critics. *The Social Network*, examined in Chapter 3, offers an example from the same year of what can be seen in some respects as a more traditional variety of quality film, in its leanings towards aspects of the well-established and polished 'heritage' format, in combination with its association with the particular qualities of writing and imagery brought by its high-profile screenwriter Aaron Sorkin and director David Fincher. This is an example also of quality as signified by particular types of approaches to highly contemporary 'real world' issues and of the bio-pic, a long-standing prestige format.

If quality is often marked in the studio film by particular kinds of treatments of material from genre fiction, as suggested above, two examples of this provide the case studies in Chapter 4: *The Assassination of Jesse James by the Coward Robert Ford* and *Mystic River*. These are chosen to provide relatively less and more mainstream-leaning examples of this kind of adaptation, which also helps to illustrate the variable nature of the industrial relationships through which such work is produced – in this case two instances involving the same studio in which the outcome was rather different. The examination of the visual qualities of *The Assassination of Jesse James* also provides an opportunity for a more extended consideration of some issues relating to the status of the 'classical' – including its historical artistic reference points – as a marker of quality. As well as demonstrating the manner in which dark and emotive material might be received in the quality sphere of 'tragedy', rather than being allocated the lower status of 'melodrama', *Mystic River* serves as a good example of the kind of quality film that offers a strong vehicle for the kind of performance likely to score in the prestige stakes in the form of best actor awards.

The focus shifts somewhat in Chapter 5, in which *Blood Diamond* is examined as a contemporary manifestation of the social problem film, a vehicle through which to examine the manner in which such films mix elements situated as 'educational', in some way, with more familiar Hollywood routines. The prominence of this dimension leads to a stronger focus on the political/ideological nature of the work than is the case in the rest of the book. Like *Inception*, this film was chosen as an example that combines some claims to quality status, at the level of subject matter and treatment, with stronger leanings towards the mainstream-conventional than are found in the other case studies. More space than elsewhere is devoted here to some consideration of the treatment of similar issues by additional films located in the indie or Indiewood sectors, the aim being to indicate some of the relative degrees of different positioning found each side of the studio line.

A.I. Artificial Intelligence is employed in Chapter 6 as a framework through which to begin to address a number of issues relating to different dimensions of quality, some of which have been indicated above. This is achieved initially through an examination of its status as a product of two figures with contrasting reputations: Steven Spielberg and Stanley Kubrick. If the principal focus of the book is on notions of quality in the sense of the pursuit of material that is accorded a superior position in prevailing cultural hierarchies, the consideration of Spielberg in this chapter includes examination of claims made for some of his work on the basis of a particularly skilled deployment of approaches designed for popular appeal in its own right. The latter is a reading that rests on the employment of notions of coherence and organic unity as measures of value, concepts that open up a range of questions about established critical traditions in which such qualities have been valorised.

One approach that does not feature other than occasionally in this book is a reading of the films in broader cultural-symptomatic terms, a dimension largely beyond the main area of focus. Such a reading would be possible. The presence of somewhat less conventional central heroic figures in a number of the examples (*The Social Network*, *The Assassination of Jesse James*, *Blood Diamond* and to some extent *Mystic River*) could, for example, be diagnosed as a symptom of some aspects of the broader social-political context, as has been suggested of similar examples, in greater number, during the Hollywood Renaissance (also not without earlier precedents in studio history). Whether or not such figures are sufficiently prevalent in the contemporary period to bear such a reading remains open to question but is a topic potentially worthy of further consideration. This is not an issue pursued in this book, however, partly for reasons of space, but also on the grounds that the quality strand is a minority one and, as a result, perhaps less well suited to a broadly symptomatic reading of this kind.

One marker of quality might be for films specifically *not* to be viewed as symptomatic of mainstream social currents but to offer a more distinction-marking critique of these. The difference between the two is likely to be far less clear-cut within the studio realm, however. A more nuanced reading at this level might expect to find a variety of currents potentially in play, the nature of which might vary to some extent across the mainstream/alternative spectrum. A symptomatic approach might seem more apt in the case of a more mainstream example such as *Inception* – which is considered in relation to a number of such readings of the 'puzzle' film in Chapter 2 – although these are found to be somewhat sweeping and speculative and less helpful in understanding the bases of the existence of the film, for my purposes, than more proximate, industrially grounded explanations. Each case study includes examination of the history of the production(s) involved, seeking to explain how particular projects with quality resonances were able to come to fruition within their studio locations, and how these might be related to broader industrial strategies of the kind suggested here.

A key point worth emphasis at this stage is that notions of quality are never purely textual matters, or in any way intrinsic to the text as viewed in isolation.[30] Textual factors are central to the basis on which markers of quality distinction are attributed, but this process is one specifically of *attribution* rather than essence, a process that entails the (implicit or explicit) activation of particular discursive regimes. The presence of such regimes can be inferred *within* as well as beyond the text, however, given their power to shape the kinds of approaches likely to be adopted by filmmakers seeking effectively to position their work at one point or another within the available spectrum. If the text cannot be taken in isolation, ascriptions of quality do not rely solely on the immediate endorsements of external authorities such as critics or academics, those who constitute a dominant form of what Stanley Fish describes as an 'interpretive community'.[31] Quality can be built in at the textual level itself; textual forms can be interpreted as embodiments of established cultural value. As David Andrews suggests, in the related context of definitions of art cinema, some caution is advisable here, to avoid any danger of lapsing into essentialist assumptions about the relatively 'higher' status of particular forms. We must, he suggests, present our criteria clearly (as I have sought to do above) and 'demonstrate that those criteria have solid institutional precedents in the work of traditional gatekeepers', such as influential academic or other critical sources (as I seek to do both above and in the case studies that follow).[32]

The more specific discursive regimes within which the case study examples were situated on release are considered through examination of the responses of prominent critics (those likely to have greater than usual authority and reach, key members of the dominant interpretive community), and some other journalistic commentators, along with brief analysis of a wider range of viewer responses via 'customer reviews' posted on the website of the leading retailer, Amazon (the extent to which these are used varies from one case study to another, partly for reasons of space). In the case of critical reviews, the aim is to focus particularly on the manner in which quality components are highlighted, or sometimes contested, in relation to other dimensions of the films concerned. Viewer responses are examined primarily to establish how these relate to the qualities foregrounded in my own textual readings and those offered as interpretive frameworks by professional critics or other para-textual forms such as DVD commentaries and extras. They can also provide evidence, in some cases, of the mobilisation of cultural capital on the part of viewers, of distinction-marking on their own part. I make no claim to offer anything like a definitive consideration of viewer responses, however, which would require a book-length work in its own right, merely to offer some indicative impression of the manner in which Hollywood claims to quality are sometimes invested in, taken up, or rejected by parts of the audience. Responses from critics, viewers and other commentators play a key role, collectively, in the establishment of quality credentials, part of the discursive infrastructure through which reputations for such status are created, sustained or challenged.

The aim of this book is not to make evaluative claims about the kinds of approaches that might be said to constitute quality within Hollywood in any absolute or judgemental sense. Neither is it to impose my own tastes or opinions – not that the influence of these, or of my own socially situated viewing position more generally, can entirely be avoided, an issue to which I return briefly at the end of Chapter 6. The aim is to examine what kinds of qualities are accorded such status within dominantly prevailing cultural hierarchies, and how far these represent a departure from industrial norms. The intention is to deepen our understanding of the particular and more general studio strategies within which such production is located, and thus our appreciation of how Hollywood functions in this domain; but also to contribute to broader debate about the manner in which certain forms of cultural value are established and the wider historical and contemporary contexts within which such discourses are situated.

Notes

1   James MacDowell, *Happy Endings in Hollywood Cinema: Cliché, Convention and the Final Couple*, Edinburgh: Edinburgh University Press, 2013

2   See David Bordwell, *The Way Hollywood Tells It: Story and Style in Modern Movies*, Berkeley: University of California Press, 2006; on the supposedly 'shallow' style of 'high concept' films, see Justin Wyatt, *High Concept: Movies and Marketing in Hollywood*, Austin: University of Texas Press, 1994. For a less typical instance of positive valuation of the influence of such media on film, see Carol Vernallis, *Unruly Media: YouTube, Music Video, and the New Digital Cinema*, Oxford: Oxford University Press, 2013

3   David Bordwell, *Figures Traced in Light: On Cinematic Staging*, Berkeley: University of California Press, 2005

4   Michael Newman, 'New media, young audiences and discourses of attention: From *Sesame Street* to "snack culture"', *Media, Culture & Society*, vol. 32, no. 4, 2010

5   Newman, 'New media, young audiences', p. 593

6   Ibid.

7   Jay Epstein, *The Hollywood Economist: The Hidden Financial Reality Behind the Movies*, Brooklyn: Melville House, 2nd edition, 2012

8   See, for example, Epstein, *The Hollywood Economist*, pp. 139–40

9   Paul Grainge, *Brand Hollywood: Selling Entertainment in a Global Media Age*, London: Routledge, 2008, p. 143

10   Edward Young, *Conjectures on Original Composition*, quoted in Raymond Williams, *Culture and Society 1780–1950*, Harmondsworth: Penguin, 1961, p. 54

11   For more on each of these points, see Stephen Prince, *Digital Visual Effects in Cinema: The Seduction of Reality*, New Brunswick: Rutgers University Press, 2010

12   Geoff King, *Spectacular Narratives: Hollywood in the Age of the Blockbuster*, London: I.B. Tauris, 2000, Chapter 4

13   The hierarchical favouring of 'mind' over 'body' has not gone uncontested, however. A key source for those who have celebrated the 'lower' domains for their radical potential is Mikhail Bakhtin, *Rabelais and*

His World, Bloomington: Indiana University Press, 1984. For a critique of the devaluation of the qualities of popular art/culture, viewed as a consequence of the separation out of certain forms of 'higher' art examined by Williams and Shiner, see Richard Shusterman, *Pragmatic Aesthetics: Living Beauty, Rethinking Art*, Oxford: Rowman & Littlefield, 2000, Chapter 7

14   Leo Lowenthal, 'The debate over art and popular culture' in Lowenthal, *Literature and Mass Culture*, News Brunswick: Transaction Books, 1984, pp. 31–2.

15   Leo Lowenthal, 'Eighteenth century England: A case study' in *Literature and Mass Culture*

16   Ariel Rogers, *Cinematic Appeals: The Experience of New Movie Technologies*, New York: Columbia University Press, 2013, pp. 198–9

17   For analysis of the thematically expressive, and therefore higher-valued, usage of 3D in the latter, see Lisa Purse, *Digital Imaging in Popular Culture*, Edinburgh: Edinburgh University Press, 2013

18   I am using the list of releases for the year provided by Box Office Mojo, http://boxofficemojo.com/yearly/chart/?page=1&view=releas edate&view2=domestic&yr=2010&p=.htm

19   Also from yearly charts at boxofficemojo.com

20   Brooks Barnes, 'Hollywood moves away from middlebrow', *Variety*, 26 December 2010, accessed via nytimes.com

21   Brooks Barnes, 'With adult dramas raking in cash, "The Social Network" will resurface in theaters', *The New York Times*, Arts Beat, 5 January 2011, http://artsbeat.blogs.nytimes.com/2011/01/05/ with-adult-dramas-raking-in-cash-the-social-network-will-resurface-in-theaters/

22   Michael Cieply, 'Sony slate a big bet on dramas', *The New York Times*, 11 September 2011, http://www.nytimes.com/2011/09/12/ business/media/sony-pictures-bets-on-dramas-for-grown-ups. html?pagewanted=all

23   For analysis of two of these examples, see King, *Indiewood, USA: Where Hollywood Meets Independent Cinema*, London: I.B.Tauris, 2009, Chapter 4

24   Study by Nomura Equity Research, reported in Cynthia Littleton, 'Major film studios prosper on the margins', *Variety*, 16 April 2013, via variety.com

25   Littleton, 'Major film studios prosper'

26 Linda Obst, *Sleepless in Hollywood: Tales from the New Abnormal in the Movie Business*, New York: Simon & Schuster, 2013

27 For a useful account, see Marc Graser, 'Heavy hitters pick up slack as studios evolve', *Variety*, 24 February 2012, via variety.com

28 See, for example, Grainge, *Brand Hollywood*, pp. 109–10

29 Barnes, 'Hollywood moves away from middlebrow'

30 See Barbara Klinger, *Melodrama and Meaning: History, Culture and the Films of Douglas Sirk*, New York: Wiley, 2004

31 Stanley Fish, *Is There a Text in This Class? The Authority of Interpretive Communities*, Cambridge, Mass.: Harvard University Press, 1980

32 David Andrews, 'Towards an inclusive, exclusive approach to art cinema' in Rosalind Galt and Karl Schoonover, eds, *Global Art Cinema: New Theories and Histories*, Oxford: Oxford University Press, 2010

2

Inception and the 'quality' blockbuster

Inception (2010) offers a somewhat atypical starting point for the case studies that constitute the remainder of this book. In many respects it might be expected to be located quite firmly within the conception of the mainstream *against* which quality is usually defined. As a spectacular $160 million blockbuster released in mid summer on 3,792 screens, with spending on marketing estimated at another $100 million, *Inception* is a film on the scale of the largest of 'tentpole' pictures, a domain of central importance to the commercial fortunes of the major studio distributors. It was received in influential parts of the media as an example of quality production within the blockbuster realm, however, as seen in some of the sources cited in the Introduction. Despite its scale, cost and the display of a number of features typical of either the summer blockbuster or mainstream production more generally, *Inception* was viewed in some ways or to some extent as an exception to the rule. The main basis for this is its relative complexity of narrative design, widely seen as more challenging than usual for films of this variety. A number of other dimensions of the film also give it certain resonances of the kind of quality outlined above, including a general darkness of tone in some places, the central role of individual authorship attributed to the production, and a perceived degree of self-referentiality. It can also be considered, however, as an instance in which claims to quality status have been contested, in the critical discourse surrounding the film, on the basis of the way it mixes signifiers of quality and of more conventionally mainstream production. As such, it throws into sharp relief some of the key issues addressed by this book, hence its value as an initial point of departure.

This chapter begins with close analysis of the relative narrative complexity of the film, examining exactly how far this takes *Inception* from the typical characteristics of such productions, and the extent to which this dimension is combined with more conventional Hollywood ingredients including other aspects of its narrative design and the provision of certain varieties of spectacular attraction. As with the other case studies in this book, I also seek to offer an explanation for the existence of a feature that offers such a mixture of qualities, particularly at the level of proximate factors relating to the shaping of the production at Warner Bros. by its writer-director, Christopher Nolan, at a specific moment in his career. Exactly to what extent the film was embraced as a manifestation of quality, and how this was framed, is considered through examination of the discourses of prominent critics and a broader sample of viewer responses.

'A dream within a dream: I'm impressed'

First, then, to the complexity of narrative. Exactly how much of a challenge does the film offer to the viewer and to what extent does this constitute grounds for the attribution of the quality label? *Inception* can be understood in relation to the notion of the 'puzzle film', a category identified by a number of commentators and usually associated more strongly with work from the American independent sector or international art cinema.[1] The puzzle film can be understood as entailing a particular kind of greater-than-usual complexity of narrative, a variety in which an overt challenge is presented to the viewer to follow or work out the logic behind an initially confusing presentation of events. The puzzle, in such cases, might or might not entirely be resolved by the end of the film. In general, such films offer a significant, but by no means total, departure from the established norms of 'classical' or canonical narration. The latter is usually characterised by qualities such as clarity and communicativeness, among others, according to which the viewer is presented with a clearly comprehensible series of events in which little is concealed other than what might happen next (and even this is often largely predictable in broad terms).[2] The puzzle film, or films that include puzzling dimensions without necessarily being defined by them, can deny the viewer some of this clarity and communicativeness in various ways and to various degrees. The exact nature of events or their causes might not fully be spelled out, leaving the viewer either confused or required cognitively to work harder than usual to stay on top of the material. This can clearly be a way in which filmmakers can make claims to higher levels of quality, by setting higher demands. It also provides scope for viewers to exercise higher levels of cultural capital through their ability positively to appreciate such material.

There is no doubt that *Inception* qualifies for this status to some significant extent. It requires more work on the part of the viewer – if the details of the plotting are to be followed closely – than is typical of classical narrative in general or the particular kind of narrative framework associated with productions of blockbuster scale. But how far does this go? A useful place to begin is with the opening of the film, to consider what degrees of clarity or puzzlement are established from the start and how, when and to what extent the latter are resolved. This can be understood in terms that include the kinds of narrative enigmas posed by the film and the manner in which these are treated. This section then goes on to examine the broader structure of the film, with a particular focus on the nesting of dream experiences within dreams, and the potential ambiguity of the ending.

Inception begins with footage of the central character, Cobb (Leonardo DiCaprio), washed up on the shore, the images intercut with shots of two young children playing on a beach. The impression might be given at first that these occupy the same space and time, cuts between close shots of Cobb's face and the children implying an eye-line match and the light broadly similar in each case; sufficient cues are provided to link the two, initially at least, and to constitute what appears to be a deliberate subsequent encouragement of confusion. We then see Cobb being accosted by an Oriental figure with a gun (and nothing more of the children) and taken before an older Japanese character. We learn that Cobb was found in a delirious state, but asking for the older figure by name, and that he was 'carrying nothing but this' (a pistol, which seems conventional enough for such a movie situation) 'and this' (a small dark spinning top, which seems considerably more enigmatic). A number of initial questions are thus established, including: who are these two main characters, where has Cobb been washed up from, what is his relationship with the older Japanese man, what are his intentions, and what does the spinning top signify? Little of this is particularly unusual for the opening sequence of a mainstream Hollywood production (except perhaps the added confusion relating to the shots of the children). It is quite common for openings to plunge the viewer into a situation more or less *in media res*, without explanatory background information, and to establish a number of initial points of enigma. The question is: for how long is any of this sustained? In this case some is sustained, and further complicated, for a considerable part of the 148-minute running time of the film.

Some substantial hints are offered as the sequence continues and some of the main parameters of the narrative begin to be established. The film offers a number of what Roland Barthes terms 'partial' and 'suspended' answers to the enigmas it poses (the former defined by Barthes as increasing rather than reducing the desire for full revelation, the latter a stoppage of the disclosure).[3] The Japanese character picks up the top and says he knows what it is and has seen one before 'many, many years ago', adding that it belonged to 'a man I met in a half-remembered dream'. A cut follows to the face of Cobb, appearing suddenly to take note of what his interlocutor is saying, a cue that the viewer should also pay close attention. A marked shift then occurs, to a shot of a younger Japanese figure to whom Cobb is talking, and then back to Cobb in this other moment (he is dressed smartly here, to make clear the distinction from the earlier sequence). This immediately invites a question: is this, somehow, the *same* Japanese figure at an earlier time, when he was young, as seems to be implied, even if this would appear to be a logical impossibility given that Cobb remains much the same age as in the preceding sequence?

The exchanges that follow, between Cobb, the Japanese character later identified as Saito (Ken Watanabe) and a colleague of Cobb's, Arthur (Joseph Gordon-Levitt), establish some of the key narrative dimensions of the film in relation to the process of invading the minds of subjects while they are in dream states and Cobb's status as a leading practitioner of the art. Something of how this works is then dramatised in the revelation of the status of much of the material on screen to be parts of dreams or dreams-within-dreams. It is made clear that the second level of interchange between Cobb and Saito is taking place within a dream, when the dream world begins to fragment physically and we see some of the same characters in another level of reality from which the dream appears to originate. An added complication arises when a woman appears in this level of the narrative, identified by Cobb as Mal (Marion Cotillard).

The one dream ends but it then transpires that the level above it is also a dream and we are shifted up another level to a sequence on a bullet train, at which point it becomes clear that Cobb and his team have failed in an espionage mission. The viewer is challenged to some extent through these sequences by the shifts from one level of dream or reality to another, but the process is also telegraphed quite clearly (a number of devices are employed to achieve this effect, including repeated close-up shots of watches or clocks counting down in each level). The shifts of level here also prepare the viewer for the main plot that is to follow. What makes this part of the film remain quite puzzling, however, is the presence of other unresolved issues. How any of this relates to the opening sequence is unclear. The same goes for the status of Mal, to whom various (dark) enigmatic references are made, primarily by Arthur. It is this sense of throwing a great deal of material at the viewer at more or less the same time that is one of the most cognitively demanding aspects of the film, and thus a marker of quality (on the assumption that it is done deliberately, rather than the result of poor execution), as much as the offering of a series of nested dreams-within-dreams during this opening movement or in the bulk of the narrative that follows.

Figure 2.1. Bending reality: one of the Paris street special effects in *Inception* © Warner Bros. Entertainment Inc. and Legendary Pictures

Inception proceeds to establish that Cobb has been physically separated from his two young children, although the reasons for this are not elaborated. We also learn that the children's mother appears to be dead, which only adds to the puzzle relating to Mal. A core aspect of the plot is spelled out clearly when Saito recruits Cobb to attempt an act of inception – the active planting of an idea in the mind of a businessman who is about to inherit a large company – in return for a promise that Saito will be able to lift the blockage that prevents Cobb from returning home to America (the nature of which remains unclear). Cobb reveals that he has done this once before (although we are not given any details until much later). We then see Cobb in Paris to recruit a new dream architect, Ariadne (Ellen Page). Her introduction to how the process of dream construction works also becomes that of the audience. This is a standard expository narrative device, but the viewer is here again likely to become somewhat overloaded with relatively complicated material relating to issues such as how the subconscious of the dreamer relates to the artificially constructed dreamscape, exposition the viewer might or might not find entirely comprehensible in all its detail. Ariadne becomes a surrogate for the viewer on several subsequent occasions ('I'm just trying to understand') in which Cobb gradually, in instalments, explains aspects of the back-story involving himself and Mal.

The main plot of the film involves five primary levels of reality and dreaming. The action occurs while the top-level reality is set on board a long-haul flight to the US, during which the protagonists are under the influence of drugs that aide the dream-construction process. Within this is a dream level of action set in New York City, including an escape made in a van. Below this, with characters dreaming inside the van, is a setting in a hotel, from which another dream level takes us into a snowy outdoor landscape and a remote fortress building. Within the latter is a final level that involves the ruins of a dream world created in the past by Cobb and Mal. The exact logic of the process at work is not necessarily entirely clear at all moments and in every detail, but the broad parameters of this structure are quite readily comprehensible. Close intercutting from one level to another provides enough information to establish the logic of the various relationships between them, although, as with other aspects of the film, the sheer volume of this is sufficient for at least some points of confusion to be likely.

The most challenging component of the film is probably the dimension involving the emotional back-story about Cobb and Mal, an element that has a habit of cutting across and adding further confusion to other aspects of the pursuit from one level of dreaming to another. This remains the case despite the fact that this dimension is in itself quite conventional in marking a point of central character weakness or flaw. The fact that Mal is in fact dead, and therefore what we see of her has the status only of subconscious projection, is established 41 minutes into the film, and that Cobb is suspected of killing her (hence unable to return home) at approximately 50 minutes. A number of partial explanations of what was involved are provided, teasingly, at various points in the narrative. Much of the full story of what happened between the pair is spelled out at around the 80-minute mark (the fact that Mal killed herself, having become convinced that her reality was part of a dream world from which death was the only means of escape, and that she implicated Cobb in an attempt to force him to join her in the act of suicide). It is not until about 125 minutes, however, that we learn that Mal's fatal questioning of her reality status had originally been planted in her mind by Cobb, his previous experience with inception. A full explanation of the opening sequence does not come until close to the end of the film.

The final puzzle comes at the end, which leaves open the possibility that what appears to be a happy ending might remain the
imagined construct of another dream world. The central plot mission
apparently accomplished, Cobb goes unproblematically through US
customs and is in the process of being reunited with his children. The
initial shot provided here of the children – with their backs to camera,
back-lit in a nostalgic glow – is one we have seen as a kind of *leitmotif*
on several occasions during the film. This might make its reality status
here seem potentially questionable, given the dimension of the film
that relates to the intrusions of memories into the dream world. Cobb
sets his top to spin on a table as he walks outside to hug the children.
The camera pans across to the spinning top, the film having established earlier that it is Cobb's reality totem, an item known in its exact
qualities only to him and through which he can determine that he
occupies reality rather than being within the dream of someone else.
In a dream, Cobb earlier tells Ariadne, the top keeps spinning rather
than coming to rest. In the final shot of the film it continues to spin,
an abrupt cut to black and the main title being made before sufficient
time might have passed for it to be clear whether or not the top will
fall (it appears perhaps to be beginning to slow, but the cut intrudes
before we can be sure either way).

The cinematic signifiers leading up to this moment are those of
emotionally satisfying, melodramatic and mainstream-conventional
positive conclusion, an effect produced particularly by the upbeat
driving-and-building nature of the music that accompanies the
sequence depicting Cobb's passage through the airport. But the possibility is then introduced of this being undermined. Hints are provided
earlier, by Mal, that Cobb might have spent so much time in dream
worlds that he no longer believes in the existence of a single reality
and might thus have *chosen* to live in one particular dream. The viewer
who picks up on any or all of this is left with an enduring puzzle, a
'final twist' that might itself be something of a convention in this kind
of material but one that is perhaps unusual in its ambiguity rather than
in the definite articulation of some kind of reversal. In this respect
the ending differs from those of 'twist' films such as *The Sixth Sense*
(1999) or *The Others* (2001), in which a final revelation suggests a
radical reinterpretation of the reality status of the preceding events of

the film; or that of a more contemporary 'multiple realities' film such as *Source Code* (2011). The latter offers a freeze frame image at the moment that the protagonist is scheduled to die during the last in a series of re-enactments of the main plot situation. If it ended here, this would have more in common with the ending of *Inception*, but instead the footage comes back to life and proceeds towards a much more affirmative 'feel-good' (and therefore more mainstream-oriented) conclusion, in which the central character happily survives within an altered reality.

Inception offers plenty of overt exposition of the various processes entailed in the creation and navigation of the multiple dream levels, and of additional central plot points. The norms of classical narrative structure seem broadly to be obeyed most of the time, even if the volume of exposition is greater than usual. A reasonably clear cause/effect structure is generally in place, whether or not all elements of this might be apparent on a single viewing. Seeds are planted for various elements that develop subsequently and clear indicators are used to establish the distinct identity of each of the main dream levels (heavy rain in New York, the distinctive warm tones of the hotel interior sequences, the snowbound landscape, the artifice of the world created by Cobb and Mal). The challenge is primarily one of information overload, and might exist in many cases in the following of relatively minor detail (exactly what is vital in one level to ensure a particular development in another) as much as in grasping the broader dreams-within-dreams conceit.

Exactly how puzzling the film might be found by individual viewers is likely to vary, within the parameters set in this way by the text, and from one viewing to another. It is also important to bear in mind the potential significance of extra-textual sources of information. The narrative reading offered above tends to assume a first-time viewer coming to the film relatively cold, which is unlikely to be the typical experience, particularly for a film of this kind that gained more than usual media attention. For viewers primed by advance knowledge about the broad parameters of the narrative premise, some of the material might seem less puzzling than would otherwise be the case, or they might be prepared precisely to expect or look for sources of puzzlement and relatively sustained enigma. A general awareness of the manufactured dreams-within-dreams premise might be sufficient to encourage viewers to put some of the cognitive challenges effect-ively on hold for significant portions of the film. Neither should we assume that keeping up with every narrative detail need be a priority for every viewer, regardless of their prior knowledge. It is entirely possible for viewers to let the complexities of detail slide during the viewing experience, rather than constantly trying to follow the nar-rative in all its dimensions, particularly in a case such as this in which other sources of appeal – such as the forms of action and spectacle examined below – are also offered on a regular basis.

Whatever their individual orientations, viewers were certainly cued by critics to expect a greater degree of complexity than usual for mainstream Hollywood material. From the trade press (*Variety*: 'fiend-ishly intricate', 'challenges viewers')[4] to major 'quality' dailies (*Los Angeles Times*: 'Specifics of the plot can be difficult to pin down [...] can remain tantalizingly out of reach')[5] and broader-market publi-cations (*USA Today*: 'the most complex of any summer movie')[6], a clear consensus seems to be established on this point. A number of online resources were developed to help viewers who might strug-gle to follow all dimensions of the plot.[7] Some critics also noted the extent to which any demanding aspects of the narrative are balanced by more conventional material. As *The Washington Post* put it: 'Even at its most tangled and paradoxical, "Inception" keeps circling back to the motivation that has driven films from "The Wizard of Oz" to "E.T.": Cobb, finally, just wants to go home.'[8] Such an observation seems central to our understanding of the overall balance of qual-ities offered by the film. This point of focus – classically emotionally driven via Cobb's desire to be reunited with his children – is sufficient to provide broad-scale orientation for the viewer, even where it might not always be possible to follow the exact detail of every narrative step along the way. The same is true of the broader parameters of the con-spiracy plot, and the point can be made more generally that films that have puzzling or enigmatic elements can remain resolutely clear and classical in other narrative dimensions that tend to attract less atten-tion because of their employment of more familiar norms.

The viewer might also be cued by the film itself to expect to be challenged or to struggle to follow every element of the narrative.

Explicit reference is made at one point to the 'paradoxical archi-tecture' characteristic of the manufactured dreamscapes, a term that might be taken equally to apply to some of the architecture of the film itself, giving *Inception* something of the reflexive dimension some-times associated with quality production. Such commentary, along with references to the limited capacity of the waking mind, could be interpreted in more than one way. On the one hand, it might add to the more ambitious claims of the film in making the notion of complexity or paradox an underlying theme and as such a marker of quality untypical of the summer blockbuster. On the other, this might be taken as providing some licence to the viewer to *not* fully grasp all that happens on screen, on the basis that it might include paradox or too much for the waking mind of the typical moviegoer to pro-cess. Further ground is established here for the potential marking of points of distinction between the self-conceptions of some viewers and their perceptions of the capacity of others. Parallels can also be drawn between the whole process of dream construction dramatised in parts of *Inception* and that of filmmaking itself – a further source of implicit reflexivity that might, for some viewers, add to the quality resonances of the film.

The status of the film as more complex or challenging than usual can be seen as a selling point in its own right, by establishing it as distinct-ive and as a prominent ground for much of the media coverage, with potential to attract some audiences that might be less inclined to view more conventional action/spectacle-based blockbusters. There is a risk that this might also deter some potential viewers, although plenty of emphasis was also put on the more blockbuster-conventionally spec-tacular attractions of the film. Productions of this kind also encourage repeat viewing, whether in the cinema or on the small screen, in an attempt to gain greater understanding of the plot, a potential source of additional revenue. The advertising of home viewing releases often highlights this process, either via the additional opportunity to see the film itself or to take advantage of 'extra' features, in this case the promise of being able to 'go deeper into the dream' made in trailers for the *Inception* Blu-ray/DVD.

The film certainly offers rewards to those who go back for repeat viewing(s) and are able to pick up numerous hints that are unlikely to be clear without more than one pass. At its heart, though, *Inception* continues to obey a number of more typically or classically Hollywood norms, even if some elements might, in themselves, offer more cognitive challenge than is usual for productions of such solidly mainstream status, and even if the ending adds an ultimately unresolved conundrum. It has a main thematic plot (the 'inception' plan) coupled with a romantic/emotional sub-plot centred around the flawed male-lead character (his relationships with Mal and the children), and plenty of ways in which the one becomes classically conventionally entangled in the other. The film also offers a number of other more conventional blockbuster/action-movie appeals, including the central star presence and the provision of large-scale spectacle and action of various kinds.

Spectacular attractions

If its relatively puzzling narrative is one of the most prominent features of *Inception*, and a potential marker of quality, this dimension is closely rivalled – within the film itself and in critical discourses – by investment in large-scale spectacular attractions of the kind more commonly associated with the blockbuster realm. These can also be divided into elements that bring different cultural resonances, however, on more than one axis of distinction. We can distinguish between forms of spectacle broadly specific to this production (as markers of its more or less 'unique' selling point and of what is presented generally in productions of this kind as 'cutting edge' work in special effects), and more generic elements of spectacular Hollywood action. This distinction can, in some respects, be seen to embody the markers of respectively higher and lower cultural resonances within which notions of quality are usually located. This is not entirely the case, however, given the lower status often attributed to the realm of special effects in general and digital effects in particular, as will be seen further below.

The poster/cover/website artwork features the main protagonists standing in the middle of a city street. Behind them, approximately half-way up and at much the same height as DiCaprio/Cobb's head, the ground appears to tilt upwards at about 90 degrees, part of one of

Figure 2.2. Surreal dreamscape: the crumbling-building cliffs in
Inception © Warner Bros. Entertainment Inc. and Legendary Pictures

the 'bending reality' effects used inside the dreamscapes of the film. *Inception* offers a number of effects-based sequences of this kind, the most striking of which are the folding inwards of Paris streets (see Figure 2.1) and the crumbling cliffs of buildings at the edge of the world created by Cobb and Mal (see Figure 2.2). These images share some of the relatively 'intellectual' cultural resonances established by the 'mind-bending' dimension of the narrative, an approach signalled most explicitly in a visual reference to the work of the artist M.C. Escher in the form of an 'impossible' staircase used by Arthur in his induction of Ariadne into some of the tricks of their trade. The crumbling-building cliffs seem to establish a similarly distinctive resonance in their some-what surreal or nightmarish qualities, broadly suggestive of something closer to the realm of 'art' than that of popular culture.

More conventional sources of action-based spectacle include a number of chase and/or fighting sequences that occupy a very differ-ent position in prevailing cultural hierarchies, associated with some of the 'lower' generic realms outlined in the previous chapter. Markers of this status include the use of mobile camerawork and rapid cutting to evoke the intensity of gun battles and chases, a formal approach that fits with aspects of Bordwell's notion of intensified continuity or what I have termed elsewhere an 'impact aesthetic' designed to give the viewer a vicarious impression of immersion in the action.[9] This approach is clearly in evidence in sequences such as the chase in Mombasa and the gun battle on the streets of New York. Each of these employs conventional forms of unsteady camerawork, quick pans and faster cutting than is used in the bulk of the film, the camera also sometimes moving rapidly to follow characters in the thick of the action. These sequences do not use the full gamut of 'impact' effects, however, including the explosive outward projection of objects towards the viewer found in many films defined primarily by the action ingredient. They are, in that sense, more restrained than is often the case elsewhere, another detail that contributes to the overall balance between associations of quality and its perceived opposite. It is also notable that *Inception* does not employ an intensified style throughout. The majority of the film is shot and edited in a more leisurely and classical manner. The camera is often static, particularly in numerous dialogue scenes constructed in traditional shot/reverse-shot style, or tends to move only in a more subtle manner outside the major action sequences. What all of this signifies – if only subliminally – is a more restrained and 'classy' approach overall than is implied in Bordwell's characterisation of intensified continuity. Intensification is only used where merited by heightened action, rather than being employed indiscriminately – an 'everything but the kitchen sink' approach that generally serves as a marker of non-quality – as in the examples cited by Bordwell.

Within the shooting/chasing sequences, however, *Inception* retains some other central clichés of the lower-status action format. These include the obligatory unspoken truism that 'movie bad guys can't shoot', through which the action heroes typically win against implausibly unlikely odds. The film also on one occasion reverts to a typical action-movie comic one-liner to undercut the more serious implications of what is at stake for the characters, when Arthur struggles to deal with an assailant on an opposite rooftop during the New York action – only to be brushed aside by team-member Eames (Tom Hardy) with the dry comment 'You mustn't be afraid to dream a little bigger, darling', as he pulls out a grenade launcher that deals with the problem in one blast. It is notable that this detail was chosen for inclusion in one of the trailers for the film, a crowd-pleasing moment that represents the film at its most inclusive in audience appeal.

Forms of spectacle that might bring contrasting resonances are quite closely integrated in the film in some key sequences, particularly

Figure 2.3. Innovative explosion: the dream world bursts apart outside the café in *Inception* © Warner Bros. Entertainment Inc. and Legendary Pictures

on the occasions in which explosive action material is used in conjunction with the articulation of the connections between different dream levels. A link between the *Inception*-specific dimension and the more generic action-based form of spectacle is found on a number of occasions in which dream-constructed edifices are shaken or blown apart by explosions – the fireball-explosion being standard currency in lower-status action films – when their imaginary foundations are challenged. In the early sequence of shifts from one to another that begins in the Japanese setting, for example, it is a series of fireball-explosions in one level that marks the physical deterioration of the level below, providing a form of spectacle that plays a central role in the explanation to the viewer of how the different levels are connected. The same is true of the articulation of the relative situations in the multiple levels involved in the action climax marked on the uppermost dream level by the much-delayed, slow-motion crash of the van towards the water into which it falls from a bridge.

What we find in numerous cases is a mixing of the more and less distinctive resonances of spectacular attractions. When Cobb and Ariadne sit together outside a café, for example – she initially unaware that the location is inside a dream – the world they inhabit begins to fragment in a very particular spectacular fashion: slow-motion air-burst explosions outwards of objects ranging from the produce outside shops to the façades of buildings, effects that are marked as more subtle and innovative in character than typical action-movie explosions (see Figure 2.3). The effects signify both a certain kind of construct bursting at the seams, in a manner specific to the narrative framework, and a more familiar usage of effects to mark a heightened moment of physical impact. A similar combination of distinctive elements and much that is more conventional is found in extended fight sequences featuring Arthur in the hotel in zero-gravity conditions created by the downward plunge of the van in which this dream level is rooted; and in a sustained period of intercutting between this, the action surrounding the van (attacked by gunfire, overturned in a crash, etc.) and a lengthy series of chases and armed engagements in the snowscape.

That matters of cultural hierarchy can become complex, in the valorisation or otherwise of particular aspects of a film such as this, is also suggested by the resonances that accompany particular kinds of special effects. While the most eye-catching of the digital effects employed in *Inception* might be associated with the more distinctive 'mind-bending' dimensions of the film, a contrary pull is exerted by a tendency for the digital itself to be treated with suspicion and more traditional effects techniques to gain positive associations. Digital effects are often seen as a symptom of Hollywood at its lower-quality end, however convincing they might be, as suggested in the Introduction: as somehow 'shallow' and superficial sources of novelty; as thin, too artificial or inhuman in texture, tone or scale; as a threat to notions of more organic, real, material, hands-on craftsmanship, or to any notion of an indexical relationship to an original underlying reality. This is a discourse that can be viewed in broader historical terms, like most of those that underpin notions of quality/non-quality, in this case in the context of long-standing concerns about the threat of mechanisation to human craft-scale production. The industrial machine age appears partially to be included in the domain for which nostalgia is expressed in this instance, as against the more intangible realm of computer-generated or manipulated imagery (similarly nostalgic investments are often expressed, after their general passing within the industry, in the physicality of editing or projection on celluloid). A notable part of the discourse surrounding *Inception* in the media and in the para-textual extras supplied with the DVD/Blu-ray release is an emphasis on the extent to which what are often described as 'old school' physical effects were employed in the film, despite the reliance on computer-generated images (CGI) in some key sequences. This can be read as another claim to relative quality status, particularly in the way it is framed by some commentators.

A feature in the *Los Angeles Times* interprets the use of physical in-camera effects as 'a classic approach to filmmaking and craft', referring to this as 'the high-stakes pressure of capturing action in the real world where there's no keyboard and "escape", "back" or "delete" buttons'.[10] It is a point of pride for Nolan, the piece continues, 'for him to resist what he views as Hollywood's new over-reliance on pixel magic'. The terms in which this is expressed, here and in other accounts, seem significant, with a range of negative signifiers used in relation to the use of digital effects. The impression created is one in which CGI is too easy and malleable, where decisions need have no consequences (the availability of all those 'undo' buttons) rather than having to be followed through on the ground (and, it is implied, therefore having to be of higher quality in the first place).

Such discourses can clearly be self-serving on the part of film-makers and their collaborators, keen as they are to maintain strong impressions of their own individual agency as opposed to being seen as over-reliant on computer-generated effects, the use of which seems sometimes to be treated, rhetorically, as tantamount to cheating (despite the amount of creative input they require in their own right)[11]. Much is made in the DVD/Blu-ray extras, and in some journalistic coverage, of the concern to do as much as possible physically, in-camera, on large-scale sets – an approach offered as a guarantor of supposedly greater authenticity in the images that result. The number of visual effects shots used in the film was put at about 500, a total compared in favourable terms by effects supervisor Paul Franklin to the 1,500 to 2,000 he suggests is more typical of the film's contemporaries in the spectacular blockbuster domain.[12]

As Jonathan Gray suggests, paratexts such as these – those which frame texts either before, during or after the time of viewing – can play an active part in the attempt to create quality 'artistic' resonances, contrary to those normally associated with blockbuster-scale productions of this kind. He identifies a very similar process – in very much the same terms, including an implicit appeal to the 'organic' rather than the technical/CGI – in the numerous extras provided on a 'premium' DVD release of the second instalment of the *Lord of the Rings* series.[13] The notion of such films having this additional value, positioned as superior to the general run of studio production or spectacular blockbusters in particular, may be especially appealing to those most likely to be heavy consumers of spin-off features of this kind – viewers it seems reasonable to expect to be those with greater than usual personal investment in any individual example. In the case of *Lord of the Rings: The Two Towers* (2002), Gray suggests:

> The DVDs foster an intimate bond between cast, crew, and audience, one that combines with their construction of the DVD audience as discerning and requiring art aficionados, cloaking the entire circuit of product, text, and consumption in an aura of artistry and excellence.[14]

This suggests potential for a quite substantial commercial basis for the pursuit of claims to quality of this kind within and around some blockbusters-scale productions, particularly relating to the returns available from 'special edition' DVDs.

Inception offers an interesting case for consideration in debates about the relationship between narrative and spectacle more generally in the contemporary blockbuster. The spectacular blockbuster has often been accused of surrendering narrative to spectacle – a key component of its conventionally low standing – a viewpoint against which I have argued at length elsewhere.[15] The typical blockbuster, even in its most maligned form, in examples such as the *Transformers* sequels (2009, 2011, 2014, etc.), combines its spectacular action and special effects with considerable measures of classical-style narrative, often more of the latter than might seem necessary to the effective delivery of spectacle.[16] *Inception* is an exception in the relative complexity of its narrative material, but still mixes the two dimensions in a manner that can be seen as part of the core blockbuster recipe in which the two are, typically, mutually supportive rather than one working against the other. It seems highly likely that the action-spectacular dimensions were a key factor in the green-lighting by one of the majors of a film of this kind of budget and prominence that displays the degrees of narrative complexity outlined above (notwithstanding the fact that the spectacular elements would be a source of much of the budgetary expense). But how else might this be explained? At this point we need to examine the production context of the film in more detail.

Production context and 'auteur' associations

Another factor that balances the puzzle dimension of the film in more mainstream-commercial terms is the presence of DiCaprio as star. His name is given billing in quite large typeface above the title in poster and DVD-cover artwork, in which his full-length figure is presented front and centre, along with other members of the cast, suggesting that he was viewed as a key component of the film from a marketing perspective. Stardom remains a central plank of contemporary Hollywood, an important basis for many of its most prominent productions and, arguably, of even greater centrality to some quality films that might otherwise struggle to find a place within the confines of the studio system, as will be seen in some of the other case studies in this book (including the presence of DiCaprio in *Blood Diamond* in Chapter 5). If DiCaprio had the status of major box office draw at the time of the production of *Inception*, his career is one that could be seen as having mixed cultural resonances, including relatively early indie roles in films such as *What's Eating Gilbert Grape* (1993) and *The Basketball Diaries* (1995) before coming to wider attention in *Romeo + Juliet* (1996) and then achieving superstar status with *Titanic* (1997). Between *Titanic* and *Inception* many of his roles were in films that might be located towards the quality end of the Hollywood spectrum, partly via his association with the work of Martin Scorsese – a still widely venerated figure with an auteur reputation – in *Gangs of New York* (2002), *The Aviator* (2004), *The Departed* (2006) and *Shutter Island* (2010) (the latter with a more bleak puzzle/altered-reality plot). Such resonances can figure importantly in the shaping of a particular star-brand image of this kind, for reasons specific to the currency of stardom that can contribute significantly to the broader quality resonances of the films involved.

If the spectacular dimension, and the presence of a major star such as DiCaprio in the lead, between them go a long way to making *Inception* seem less of an exception to the blockbuster norm than would otherwise be the case, further explanation might still be required if we are to understand the existence within Hollywood of an example of quite this kind. Why, for example, should one of the studios take the risks that might be associated with the more challenging dimensions of the film, when similarly star-led thrilling/spectacular material might elsewhere be generated without any such complications? Another significant factor in making the project a less obvious bet for large-budget treatment was the fact that it had no direct relation to any existing franchise property with pre-sold name recognition, a key dimension of the contemporary blockbuster recipe. This might be further ground for the film to be located at least relatively closer to the quality end of the spectrum: positively, on the basis of its greater degree of originality of concept, and negatively in avoiding the lower associations that tend to accompany franchise or serial production in most cases.

The film does appear to have been seen as a potential risk ahead of its release. According to the *Los Angeles Times* – a press source of some authority on Hollywood – for Warner and its financing partner, Legendary Pictures, *Inception* 'represents a gamble at a time when Hollywood shuns making summer pictures based on novel ideas'.[17] That such productions are often co-financed in this way is itself a notable strategy through which the studios seek to hedge against the perceived risks of higher-budget or less obviously commercial films more generally, as suggested in the previous chapter and as will be seen in other examples below. Another feature in the same newspaper reported 'early studio anxieties that the film might be too complex or surreal to connect with a mass audience'.[18] From the perspective of the trade press, *The Hollywood Reporter* expressed concern about the difficulty the film appeared to pose for marketers. Pre-release 'buzz' had been stimulated by the presence of the A-list names of DiCaprio and writer-director Christopher Nolan, which was fortunate 'as the pic's cerebral mix of brain-teasing plot points and effects-driven fantasy defies easy characterization in a one-sheet tagline or even a trailer, judging by materials released to date'.[19]

This, again, is a cautious judgement from an industry perspective that might encourage the film to be viewed more positively from a quality point of view, a perceived challenge to the marketing department being one of the stronger markers of potential distinction and departure from the most commercially oriented understanding of the mainstream. A similar dynamic is often found in discourses relating to quality TV, in which one marker of distinction is a perception of hostility from sources such as advertisers. That the film balances its complexity and difficulties of this kind with more familiar components might help to explain its commercial viability as a project but does not, on its own, account for exactly *how* it was able to come into being in this particular form. Does the film, then, fit into any broader trends in studio production of the time? Or should we seek more proximate explanations? It is with the latter that this section begins, with an examination of the immediate production context of *Inception*, particularly in relation to the status of Nolan.

The most simple answer to the question of how *Inception* was able to come into existence as a major summer blockbuster with its puzzling qualities intact is that Nolan appears to have been given the scope to shape the film more or less as he wanted. He enjoyed a degree of 'artistic' freedom that itself requires explanation, so much does it go against the dominant conception of Hollywood as an institution characterised by the interventions of executives and marketing departments expected to focus solely (and thus conservatively) on the commercial bottom-line, particularly in productions of this scale and expense. If the freedom gained by Nolan is a major explanation of how the film came into being in a particular shape, the widespread reporting of this dimension itself contributed to the element of quality associated with the feature. Press accounts of the production process repeatedly emphasised the 'personal' nature of the project – a key marker of quality in many cases – recounting the story of the film's own inception as a long-germinated idea that first came to Nolan some ten to 15 years before being brought to fruition.[20] In this respect the film is positioned in public discourse in contrast to the more familiar (and critically denigrated) Hollywood process of decision-by-committee or multiple rewriting. Far from all potential viewers might be likely to read such accounts, particularly those in the 'quality' press, but the auteur-artistic dimension they suggest might be expected to appeal precisely to the constituency reached by such materials, in much the same way as the DVD extras considered above.

Nolan's agent was reported to have negotiated a deal that gave him final cut and that left 'unprecedented control' in his hands and those of his established producer and partner, Emma Thomas.[21] Rather than being able to intervene in a manner common for studio productions, Warner executives, according to these accounts, were only permitted to read the screenplay in Nolan's office. The chairman of co-producer Legendary Pictures suggests that the company is usually 'very hands-on', in a manner that indicates the kind of close corporate control associated negatively with studio production. But on this occasion 'Nolan was left alone' to 'do his thing' during production.[22]

It is worth noting in some detail the manner in which his relationship with the studio is articulated by Nolan. During post-production, at what is described as his 'home studio' in Los Angeles, Nolan is asked in one interview whether Warner would prefer him to be working on its own premises (and, its is implied, under closer supervision). Nolan replies that his team have 'really nice offices on the lot'. But, he adds, 'for the pure creative stuff, they've always been quite happy for us to go off into a little corner'.[23] A distinction is implied here between the 'pure creative' and what Nolan goes on to describe as the 'bigger mechanism' represented by films of this scale and the industrial system they are designed to feed – the former seeming to require some space if not to be undermined by the latter. At the same time, in other accounts, Nolan appears keen not to claim total autonomy over the shaping of the project. An interviewer from *The Hollywood Reporter* asks if the studio provided 'notes' on the script during the period in which Nolan was undertaking revisions of his own. Notes of this kind would usually involve suggestions for possible changes and are the kinds of markers of executive intervention that are often viewed as a measure of the inhospitable nature of the studio environment for creative work. But this is not the impression given by Nolan. 'Absolutely', he replies, with what appears to be a clearly positive emphasis, naming in particular the two senior executives involved, Jeff Robinov and Alan Horn, with whom he says he had 'a good dialogue'.[24]

In another interview, Nolan refers to unnamed executives from the studio as having been 'extremely fair and consistent as collaborators. Supportive but challenging'. He adds: 'They're extremely hard in their scrutiny of the way we put a film together – as they should be, because it's their money.'[25] The impression created here (assuming that we can take it largely at face value) is not one of the Romantically embattled auteur having to fight studio executives to get his way in order to do something more innovative within the highly commercial context of blockbuster production, but of a mutually beneficial arrangement.

The ability of any filmmaker to gain the kind of freedom enjoyed by Nolan with *Inception* is strongly reliant on one overriding factor: a strong track record in delivering commercial success, preferably with material of a broadly similar kind, and in the recent past. If *Inception* was likely to be seen in some respects as a risky project – because of the relative complexity of aspects of its narrative structure and its lack of any relation to a pre-sold franchise property – the best explanation we have for its existence is the commercial clout possessed by Nolan at the time, clout that appears to have enabled him to shape it without any unwanted executive interference. The primary basis for this was the performance of *The Dark Knight* (2008), the global box office gross of which topped the $1 billion mark, making it the biggest success of its year and giving it a position near the top of the all-time money-earners list at the time. Probably the single most important causal factor for the appearance of *Inception* in its finished form, including some puzzle elements that go beyond the norms of the summer blockbuster, was the enormous success enjoyed by Nolan's previous feature. The kind of auteur-associated freedom that can contribute to quality associations in a case such as this should not be understood as existing essentially in opposition to the corporate franchise-generating studio machine, then, but as a function of successful participation within exactly that domain. In this case, the location is at the very heart of recent/contemporary franchise blockbuster strategy, of which the *Batman* series has been considered to be an exemplar since 1989.

For the most part, this is a matter of sheer commercial numbers. Another factor might be a degree of similarity between *Inception* and *The Dark Knight*, the latter also being darker and more sombre in tone than is normal for so big a blockbuster hit. If the success of *The Dark Knight* suggested the potential bankability/reliability of Nolan generally at this point in his career, the particular nature of the film might have encouraged executives about the more specific ability of Nolan to generate large revenues from somewhat less than conventional blockbuster material. The reputation of the filmmaker at this stage was also sufficient in itself to contribute to the credentials of *Inception*; it had, as Will Brooker suggests, 'evolved into a powerful, unambiguous stamp of quality and a guarantee of values'.[26]

It is notable that Nolan's name was used prominently in one version of the theatrical trailer, although equally so that it was absent from others. The opening image and voice in each case is that of DiCaprio, but the first written text to appear across the screen in one example is 'from Christopher Nolan', followed by 'the director of *The Dark Knight*'. Other trailers follow the more common Hollywood practice of only including the latter, studio marketing tending to make associations with other previously successful films ('from the director of ...', 'from the producers of ...') far more than with the names of individual filmmakers who are likely to be less familiar to viewers beyond a very small elite group. This more familiar approach is also found in the later trailer for the Blu-ray/DVD provided on the film's website. Nolan's name appears in the 'above the title' position on the main poster/cover artwork, although again much less prominently than that of DiCaprio, which again suggests both its implied significance and the extent to which this is only relative and limited as far as the marketing of the film is concerned. Some versions include 'From the director of *The Dark Knight*' spread more widely across the image, directly below the title, to emphasise the more broadly familiar point of reference, although this is absent from others.

The Dark Knight is likely to be a reference point much more familiar to the majority of actual or potential filmgoers, but Nolan's name appears to have been viewed as an additional selling point in its own right. The president of worldwide marketing for Warner, Sue Kroll, is quoted in one report as saying: 'Christopher Nolan as a brand is very powerful. You can only say that about a handful of directors.'[27] The resonances of the director's name might be expected to spread wider than his involvement in the *Batman* films for some viewers – and, importantly, for critics and other media commentators who supply discourses surrounding the film – including other points of reference that might be germane to the positioning of *Inception*. After his first feature, *Following* (1998), Nolan made his name with the indie hit *Memento* (2000) before breaking into larger budget films with *Insomnia* (2002), *Batman Begins* (2005), *The Prestige* (2006), *The Dark Knight, Inception* and *The Dark Knight Rises* (2012). His films are noted for dark, sombre qualities (particularly to the fore, for example, in *Insomnia*) and a penchant for narrative complexity, confusion or trickery (especially *Memento* and *The Prestige*). A key role in establishing any distinctive quality/auteur 'brand' was played by the high profile gained by *Memento*, noted for the reverse direction of its main narrative thread and for the relative box office success of a film that initially struggled to achieve theatrical release. As a filmmaker associated with such work, combined with the major blockbuster success of *The Dark Knight*, it is hard to imagine anyone better placed by such a conjunction of factors than Nolan was at this point to introduce some dimension of the puzzle film into a high-profile summer release.

That a number of different trailers were used suggests some uncertainty on the part of marketers about exactly how best to sell the film, although the presence of DiCaprio and the connection with the director of *The Dark Knight* (if not his name) are points of clear consensus. Trailers vary in how far they attempt to evoke the specifics of the inception plot device (which is not easily encapsulated within these confines), but a strong sense of Hollywood glossy action-thriller is conveyed in each case, to the accompaniment of urgent music and plenty of instances of the two kinds of spectacle examined above. The resonances differ to some extent from one trailer to another. One, for example, begins with a repeated invocation of the phrase 'an idea', which highlights at least partially the more 'intellectual' dimension of the film. Overall, however, they seem to position the film in a manner that reflects the blend of mainstream and relatively distinct characteristics exhibited by the text itself.

To a large extent, then, the puzzle that is posed not by the narrative of the film but by its existence as a relatively unconventional high-cost blockbuster, is most easily resolved by recourse to these proximate factors: the particular *balance* offered at a textual level between more and less usual components of the blockbuster, and the specific factors that resulted in a figure with the proclivities of Nolan being able to shape the work without any unwanted studio interference. What, though, of any broader contextual factors relating to Hollywood or the wider American film landscape? Should *Inception* best be seen as an exception explained by a particular conjunction of forces, or can it be seen as part of a wider pattern? Proximate explanations have the advantage of tending to be more concrete and specific, by definition, than attempts to explain the existence of such films in broader terms. One of the core arguments of this book is that we have to look at local industrial factors if we are fully to understand the nature and presence of films that make claims to quality from within the Hollywood system: to understand exactly why they might appear in a particular form in a particular time and place. This is not to rule out the possibility of broader grounds of explanation, although a consideration of how some of these might be applied to *Inception* suggests that they can be of somewhat questionable status, as was also seen in the case of some of the press accounts considered in the Introduction.

Genre and social context

One possible argument would be to suggest that the puzzle film, or other variants of relatively complex narrative, had gained broader currency in the years leading up to the production of *Inception*, making some of its qualities likely to be familiar to a larger constituency than might have been the case in the past. Some evidence for such a trend might be found in the presence of puzzle qualities in productions from the Indiewood realm, rather than their being restricted to the commercially more marginal parts of the indie and art-film sectors. Examples here might include *Eternal Sunshine of the Spotless Mind* (2004) and *21 Grams* (2003). Whether or not such a presence would be sufficient really to have an impact on the broader bounds of what is likely to be found in the most mainstream of Hollywood productions is open to question, however, and not easy to determine. The success of *Inception* might have been sufficient to prompt others to follow its example, although too little time would have elapsed for this to include two other relatively high profile films with reality-manipulation plots (*The Adjustment Bureau* [2011] and *Source Code*) that were released in the following year.

It is always easy to over-simplify the relations between individual films of broadly similar type that appear more or less together,
sometimes perhaps by chance. It might be that all these are better
seen as examples of longer-standing generic or sub-generic categories, including in the case of *Inception* that of the 'heist movie'. This is
certainly a category to which *Inception* seems to belong in some key
dimensions and is one that offers another quite firm point of orientation for viewers who might be confused by any of the particular
details: what remains clear throughout much of the action, along with
Cobb's quest to return home, is that there is a 'job' to pull off that
has the usual kinds of technical/logistical complications found in the
heist format.

A strain of science fiction that involves shifts between dimensions
of reality and its replication or falsification provides another generic
grounding for the film, particularly a version often associated more
or less directly with adaptations of the work of Philip K. Dick. Along
with its more immediate successors cited above, *Inception* might be
associated here with films such as *Blade Runner* (1982), *Total Recall*
(1990) and *The Matrix* (1999). The latter was highlighted by some
commentators in connection with the perceived risks associated with
Inception, as an example of an original/inventive predecessor (also a
Warner production) that proved highly successful in the blockbuster
arena and that might be seen as a model for Nolan's film on that
basis.[28] The success of *The Matrix*, and its ability to create its own new
three-film franchise from scratch, might have made *Inception* seem less
risky than would otherwise have been the case. Nolan himself associates the development of the film with the period of *The Matrix* and
its contemporaries *Dark City* (1998) and *The Thirteenth Floor* (1999)
rather than 'alternative-reality' films from closer to its period of production such as *Surrogates* (2009) and *Avatar* (2009).[29]

Genre can itself be a factor that motivates or can be seen to contain
certain departures from classical-type Hollywood norms. This might
be the case on some occasions with both this brand of science fiction
and the heist movie as far as particular kinds of narrative complication or trickery are concerned (for more on the role of genre in the
contemporary quality film, see Chapter 4). Narrative puzzle or complexity might be a marker of something closer to indie or art-film

status – and a greater challenge to the viewer – in the absence of motivation by generic factors.

Whether or not all these films have any broader shared basis at the socio-cultural level is, as is usually the case, more difficult to establish with any certainty. Readings of this kind are tempting and can be useful but often risk over-simplification and over-statement, as has been the case with some interpretations of the puzzle film or similar formats. Genre has often been seen as a dimension of Hollywood that lends itself particularly well to symptomatic socio-cultural readings, on the basis of the repeated attention to particular issues that can often be found within one genre or another.[30] In this case, Garrett Stewart reads what he terms 'Hollywood's recent ontological thrillers' – among which *Inception* might be included – as expressions of cultural anxiety about the integrity of reality and/or the self and, simultaneously, of 'cinema's own institutional fears' of the replacement of the indexical status of celluloid with the malleability of the digital.[31] It might be reasonable to speculate that part of the appeal of such work is its broader social resonance with discourses relating to the prevalence in some sectors of various virtual worlds or heavily mediated realities, online or elsewhere (the fear that might exist *within* the medium here – if not actually its own fear – has much in common with the basis on which physical effects are sometimes valorised in preference to the digital, as argued above). But in Stewart's account such conclusions tend to be asserted or assumed and, for those not convinced by it, somewhat mired in heavy doses of psychoanalytically grounded discourse. Warren Buckland risks a similar over-simplification in the statement that 'experiences are becoming increasingly ambiguous and fragmented; correspondingly, the stories that attempt to represent these experiences have become opaque and complex'.[32] I would want to add heavy qualification to these kinds of claims. *Some* experiences might be thus, and *some* stories might plausibly be seen as a response to this, but what evidence is there to suggest that this is the case in other than a minority of cases? To what extent are Stewart's cultural anxieties at all widely shared among the broader population, as opposed to a relatively small circle?

I find a similar problem in Thomas Elsaesser's account of what he terms 'the mind-game film'. Elsaesser suggests that such films often have cult status and uses this as a basis for arguing that they might be treated 'as symptomatic for wider changes in the culture's way with moving images and virtual worlds'.[33] Cult status implies an intense level of engagement with these films, but by a minority rather than the broader audience. This is a constituency on which it seems questionable to base a claim to wider symptomatic status (even for anyone who agrees with the specifics of Elsaesser's reading of these films, which shares with Stewart a sweeping, epochal, and, as a result, less than convincing approach). Films of this kind are often of greater than usual interest to critics and theorists because they offer particular kinds of grist to the critical or theoretical mill. They are good 'to think with', to quote Claude Levi-Strauss out of context, or useful to illustrate particular theories. A substantial gap exists between this, however, and claims that such texts are representative of broad cultural trends. The prevalence of certain narrative or other tropes in a particular period might provide some provisional evidence of the wider resonance of such material, or at least offer a starting point for such analysis, as might the spread of the puzzle film in some cases into more mainstream-commercial realms. But we should not forget the larger number of films that do not display these characteristics. If the puzzle film represents cultural change or 'crisis' of some kind, what do all the others that outweigh them in number – if not attention from such critics – represent? The answer might be that a variety of different currents can be identified, as suggested in Chapter 1, although this is not a qualification made in the accounts outlined above. Responses to the film from critics and a wider range of viewers offer little, if any, evidence of interpretation along the lines of the cultural readings considered in this section, although such a level of engagement would be unlikely to be expected from sources of this kind.

The reception of *Inception*

The response to *Inception* from professional critics was generally positive, often based on appreciation of what were considered to be the more challenging and original dimensions of the film. There were some significant exceptions, however, and an element of backlash followed an early wave of what some considered to be excessively over-hyped reviews, a phenomenon that gained press coverage in its own right. One central issue that emerges from a number of reviews in higher-profile US media sources (print and online) is that evaluative judgements often depend on the extent to which critics believe the film is successful in mixing its puzzling narrative dimensions with other qualities. Positive reviews suggest, in many cases, that *Inception* succeeds precisely by combining its mind-bending elements with what would usually be seen as more conventional mainstream ingredients. Negative judgements often identify a failure to achieve any such synthesis and an over-emphasis on the puzzle element. Dimensions such as the use of conventional action-movie sequences and the provision or otherwise of satisfying emotional material feature centrally in a number of these accounts. A limited sample of reviews is considered in more detail below, to draw out some of their implications in the relative positioning of the film, but these are broadly representative of trends in a larger number that have been consulted.

One of the nationally best known critics in the US, Roger Ebert, praised the film for being 'highly original, cut from new cloth', seeing this as a clear point of difference from the Hollywood norm of the time, when 'movies often seem to come from the recycling bin these days'.[34] This is a characteristic marking of quality, distinct from familiar suspects such as 'Sequels, remakes, franchises'. Ebert's initial praise is for the puzzle dimension in which 'Nolan tests us with his own dazzling maze', within which we are often 'lost and disoriented' – a quality here given positive connotations. At the same time, the action leads 'to a great many gunfights, chase scenes and explosions, which is the way movies depict conflict these days'. This latter point appears more negatively tinged (what movies do 'these days' being implied to be something worse than whatever they did at some point in the past), but Ebert proceeds to offer a more positive spin even on this point: 'So skilled is Nolan that he actually got me involved in one of his chases, when I thought I was relatively immune to scenes that have become so standard.' To have got Ebert involved through the use of such lower-quality material is a substantial achievement, it is implied, a clear positioning of the critic as of a discerning nature and not usually won over by such routine fare. The reason for this, he explains, is that he cared about who was chased or doing the chasing.

An in some ways similar appreciation of the balance of qualities offered by the film (between elements associated with the puzzle dimension and more familiar ingredients of Hollywood entertainment) is provided by Kenneth Turan, another critic of national repute, in the *Los Angeles Times*. In a highly positive account, Turan notes that specific aspects of the plot can be hard to pin down but that 'you always intuitively understand what is going on and why'.[35] A factor in this process, he suggests, and one of the most satisfying aspects of the film, is 'its roots in old-fashioned genre entertainment, albeit genre amped up to warp speed'. The result is 'a tremendously exciting science-fiction thriller' and 'popular entertainment with a knockout punch so intense and unnerving it'll have you worrying if it's safe to close your eyes at night'.

The focus on caring about the characters expressed by Ebert – which suggests a successful creation of emotional as well as intellectual engagement – is echoed by Ann Hornaday in *The Washington Post*, who also begins by emphasising the complexity of the film, one with 'a tightly coiled plot, cerebral conceits and formidable ambition'.[36] It was Hornaday who was quoted above on the fact that, for all its complexities, the film centres on the familiar desire of Cobb to return home, a dimension that 'gives what could easily have been a chilly, impenetrable exercise a surprisingly strong emotional core'. The fact that this is considered to be surprising seems significant, suggesting that such a quality would not usually be expected in this kind of material.

Other critics were less convinced on this point. A generally mixed review in the more popular *USA Today* finds the film to be 'so clever and intricately structured it may require repeat viewings' but adds that 'perhaps because we are so engaged in figuring out its plot, *Inception* doesn't fully connect emotionally'.[37] A similar sentiment is expressed by David Denby, another 'name' critic in the very differently positioned (more upmarket) *New Yorker*, who concludes that the scenes involving Cobb and Mal 'are the only humanly involving elements in the movie. The rest is strenuous process'.[38] This viewpoint reflects a more widely held opinion about Nolan: that his films tend to be cold and calculating in nature rather than emotionally involving.

It is worth stepping back here to consider the implications of such evaluations within the context of broader notions of what constitutes quality within Hollywood. It is notable that emotional connection is identified by some as a central issue, given the extent to which such a dimension might often be viewed as a form of melodrama, the associations of which are usually low in prevailing cultural hierarchies (an issue to which we return in relation to *Mystic River* in Chapter 4). A cold or more intellectual distance might be expected to be associated with works of higher culture (see, for example, the consideration of Kubrick in Chapter 6). The issue for critics here seems to relate to notions of what is appropriate to a mainstream Hollywood feature, in which the latter qualities alone would be considered unsuitable. Critics who responded negatively to the film also tend to question its intellectual pretensions – specifically, in some cases, to view the film as more limited in ambition than is suggested by its champions, and as thin and contrived rather than in any way challenging or profound. A number of such articulations are made by another prominent critic, A.O. Scott in *The New York Times*.

For Scott, *Inception* 'trades in' – significant terminology in itself, implying something defined primarily as commercial product – 'crafty puzzles rather than profound mysteries'.[39] It is 'more like a diverting reverie than a primal nightmare, something to be mused over rather than analyzed'. There is 'a lot to see' in the film but 'nothing that counts as genuine vision'. The film might offer some striking imagery but what is involved, this reading implies, is the playing of a game rather than any serious artistic exploration of issues such as the nature of the boundaries between the worlds of real life and dreams. The context of these comments, distinctly rhetorical in their articulation of such binary oppositions, is not just the film itself but what Scott describes as 'some of the feverish early notices hailing "Inception" as a masterpiece'. According to this account – which forms part of the backlash against such responses – the film is too lightweight ('crafty puzzles rather than profound mysteries') and not sufficiently dark (no 'primal nightmare') to qualify for such status, defined here in terms that seem typical of one of the strains of quality identified in the Introduction, particularly in relation to the postwar period. Nolan is praised for his 'virtuosity as a conjurer of brilliant scenes and stunning set pieces', but only faintly; this, and 'his ability to invest grandeur and novelty into conventional themes' having 'fostered the illusion that he is some kind of visionary'.

Clear distinctions are made here between what we might expect of more 'artistic' cinema (from the kind of filmmaker who might be considered a visionary) and what is deemed merely to be a certain level of technical facility; virtuoso conjuring, but still conjuring, a cinematic equivalent of pulling rabbits out of hats rather than any more substantial exploration of the issues potentially raised by the film. This is a familiar manifestation of the discursive separation of the realms of art and craft – a relative denigration of the latter as part of the basis of the elevation of the former – attributed by commentators such as Raymond Williams and Larry Shiner to a conjunction of social, cultural and economic changes dating back to the eighteenth century.[40] If the notion of what is figured as a more traditional variety of craft is valorised when compared with the negative qualities often associated with CGI, as suggested above, it still has to be put in its (lower) place, such criticism implies, when compared with any higher notion of the artistic.

A key issue in this review, and some others, is Nolan's treatment of the world of dreams and the unconscious. For Scott, Nolan's approach is 'too literal, too rule-bound to allow the full measure of madness – the risk of real confusion, of delirium, of ineffable ambiguity – that this subject requires', and as might be expected in more ambitious work. As Stephanie Zacharek puts it in a highly negative review on the Movieline website:

> This may be a movie about dreams, but there's nothing dreamlike or evocative about it: Nolan doesn't build or sustain a mood; all he does is twist the plot, under, over, and back upon itself, relying on Hans Zimmer's sonic boom of a score to remind us when we should be excited or anxious or moved.[41]

Andrew O'Hehir, another prominent online critic, makes a similar point on the Salon website, salon.com, going on, significantly, to link this dimension of the film to its reliance on the material of action films. Nolan's images 'don't look or feel anything like dreams [...].

Figure 2.4. Lower cultural associations? From the snowscape fortress action sequences in *Inception* © Warner Bros. Entertainment Inc. and Legendary Pictures

They look instead like mediocre action films from the '90s, or in the case of the supremely boring ski-patrol vs. Arctic fortress shoot-out found on Level Three, like the Alistair MacLean adaptation "Ice Station Zebra" from 1968' – the latter clearly not meant to be a compliment (see Figure 2.4).[42] The film may have been directed by Nolan, O'Hehir concludes, 'but Nolan's dreams are apparently directed by Michael Bay' (a figure often taken to represent the worst excesses of low-esteem, heavy-handed blockbuster production). Along similar lines, Denby also accuses Nolan of being literal-minded and adds: 'Cobb's intercranial adventures aren't like dreams at all – they're like different kinds of action movies jammed together. Buildings explode or collapse, anonymous goons shoot at the dreammakers.'[43]

On the one hand, then, for such critics, Nolan's vision fails to match the potential for more complex representations of dreams or the world of the unconscious (Scott mentions as positive comparators the work of Alfred Hitchcock and 'a lot of other great filmmakers' he does not name; Denby's point of contrast is the venerated art-house surrealist, Luis Buñuel). On the other, it not only fails to strive for something with more serious or lofty association, but goes to the opposite extreme in finding embodiment in something as lowly regarded as the material of the routine action film – and not even the action movie or any other popular genre in its more admirable form. The implication is that the film is neither fish nor fowl, a common verdict for some critics on products in the quality tradition that are seen as taking a middle position that possesses none of the virtues of either 'serious' art or 'unpretentious' popular culture, as in the tradition of attacks on 'middlebrow' culture considered above.

A sense of distinction-marking between media sources that themselves might be considered to be of higher or lower quality was also in play in some of the commentary prompted by the backlash against the initial wave of mostly highly positive reviews. It is notable that this phenomenon itself received coverage at some length in the two most prominent US newspapers, *The New York Times* and the *Los Angeles Times*.[44] *Inception* ended with an overall rating of 86 per cent positive on the review aggregation website Rotten Tomatoes (based on a total of 278 reviews), a very high rating for a blockbuster production, although at one early point this had been a perfect 100 per cent. It is not uncommon for films that gain highly positive initial coverage to be subject to more critical reservations in a second wave of reviews, the latter sometimes seeking to offer a corrective to what might be perceived to be initially excessive flights of enthusiasm. This is also a territory in which claims to higher cultural status can be staked out, however, some critics seeking to position themselves as more discerning than others and less easily fooled by what might be characterised as the surface gloss or superficial cleverness of a film such as *Inception*, or by its marketing campaign and/or pre-release 'buzz'. *The New York Times* and the *Los Angeles Times* articles about the critical coverage each suggest at least a partial distinction between the realms of online and print coverage, the latter tending to be viewed in general (although not in all cases) as more nuanced than the former. Critics interviewed in the *Los Angeles Times* suggest that a tendency exists in web culture to go to extremes in either praise or criticism. Both articles also argue that the process that affected *Inception* was at least to some extent the product of a particular strategy adopted by Warner in an effort to maximise positive word-of-mouth discourse ahead of the film's release.

As Steven Zeitchik reports in the *Los Angeles Times*: 'The constituencies for which a studio advance screens a movie, and at what intervals, are as calibrated a part of a movie's release strategy as on which

television program to buy advertising time.'[45] In this case, in a series
of tiered screenings,

> the studio showed it first to many of the online columnists who
> rightly or not [and, despite this disclaimer, he seems to imply the
> former more than the latter] are often characterized as not bringing
> the same level of scrutiny to a film as more veteran critics, judging
> it instead by the standard of whether it's smarter than many of its
> summer-movie counterparts.

One of the few notable print critics to see the film at this stage,
Zeitchik suggests, was Peter Travers of *Rolling Stone* magazine, 'known
for being one of the more generous of print reviewers', an admiring
quotation from whose review was subsequently used in TV advertising for the film. That the division between those who responded
most positively or negatively does not map simply onto an online/
print opposition is demonstrated by several other cases, including the
positive print response by Roger Ebert and the negative reviews on
Salon and Movieline. The suggestion that such a distinction can be
made in many instances, however, might be seen as part of a broader
concern about the threat to 'serious' review coverage often perceived
to have been created by the opening up of large numbers of new
fora online – a question relating to issues of quality in the sphere of
criticism that in some respects parallels those applying to the films
themselves.[46]

An implicit part of the message of some prominent critics who
respond negatively to the film – and often at the same time to the
most positive early critics – is that certain lines of quality need to be
defended; that a film such as this, even if in some cases admired at one
level as a piece of Hollywood entertainment, should not be discussed
in the same terms as those of higher art, in language such as that of
the 'visionary' filmmaker criticised by Scott. Whatever one's individual opinion of the film, the act of boundary-marking involved here
is very familiar from the history of articulations of cultural distinction in film or elsewhere. The views cited above (positive or negative) are in many cases those of a small coterie of reviewers who had
long careers as dominant critical voices – a privileged position seen as
being threatened by an upsurge of new online sources, more or less

professional in status, the credentials of which are often challenged. As with most such discourses, the issue here is not whether or not such an argument is justified (online critics range widely in type and level of engagement) but what it might contribute to our understanding of the various processes through which notions of quality are articulated, defended or challenged. The approach manifested by such critics fits into the category of the 'connoisseurial' review, the definition of which provided by Grant Blank underlines what might be considered to be at stake for those with investments in the protection of this kind of criticism from perceived attack.

In Blank's terms, such reviews 'rest on the unique skills, sensitivity, training, and experience of a single reviewer, a connoisseur' (as opposed to 'procedural' reviews based on the results of the testing of products such as computer software).[47] What is valorised in such cases is a cultural location in some ways similar to that typically ascribed to the creative artist or producer, and subject to similarly perceived threat (from below) from those deemed to be lacking in such qualities. In this case, the threat might be imagined to come from a wave of online reviewers without the requisite skills, sensitivity or training; or from sources lacking any guarantors of the kind of credibility – itself a hierarchical quantity – possessed by established and 'venerable' publications. The opening up of the critical sphere to an uncontrolled and potentially 'rowdy mob' of untrained online voices might be seen here as in some ways parallel to the democratisation of literary culture that occurred from the eighteenth century and the perceived threat to the cultural status quo posed by the early growth of cinema in the 1910s, the context of the Vitagraph quality productions considered in the Introduction.

It is notable that one of the targets of eighteenth-century commentators on literary-artistic 'decline' identified by Leo Lowenthal is a multiplication in the number of critics or would-be critics, especially amateurs newly empowered to challenge the basis of standards that had previously been the exclusive preserve of the existing literary establishment.[48] This is another respect in which contemporary discourse appears to retain some of the key parameters established in the earlier period. The characteristic response of dominant cultural forces, in many such cases, is a defensive attempt to restore existing boundaries. This was in some respects the case in the eighteenth century, as it seems also to be in the writing of some critics of contemporary Hollywood, including their attitudes towards online newcomers to the field.

Those who describe *Inception* in admiring terms, in both critical reviews and some of the many feature articles that accompanied its release, cite a number of more or less 'artistic' reference points as part of the process of effectively establishing its quality credentials (and, by implication, those of the writer possessed of sufficient cultural capital to make such references). This is another familiar dimension of the articulation of cultural distinctions, a process of validation-through-association that can lead, in Bourdieu's terms, to the 'consecration' of the position of the creator as legitimate artist.[49] Reference points employed by the press in relation to *Inception* include those of both 'higher culture' – separate from film – and those from already-consecrated filmmakers from the sphere of art cinema and a limited number of Hollywood titles or figures to whom such status has been conferred. In addition to Escher, non-cinematic names evoked to positive effect include those of the artists Rene Magritte and Salvador Dali and the architects Mies van der Rohe and Le Corbusier, along with the writers Haruki Murakami and Jorge Luis Borges.[50] Art-cinema reference points include the modernist icon *Last Year at Marienbad* (*L'Année dernière à Marienbad*, 1961) and Michael Haneke's *The White Ribbon* (*Das Weisse Band*, 2009). The two most often cited high-status American filmmakers are Alfred Hitchcock and Stanley Kubrick (alongside the earlier work of Nolan himself), while at least one critic also mentions films scripted by Charlie Kaufman such as the Indiewood productions *Adaptation* (2002) and *Eternal Sunshine of the Spotless Mind*. More mainstream film titles cited as markers of a particular kind of quality within Hollywood genre production include *Blade Runner* and *The Matrix*. In the most favourable responses, the impression is that, at its best, the film embraces something of the whole of this range, from more to less culturally exclusive markers of quality.

If this constitutes an ongoing process of consecration in relation to Nolan and his latest film at the time, others, as we have seen – notably Scott and Denby – seek to de-consecrate, to remove the critical 'blessing' offered by the enthusiasts. This is a practice that entails both the refusal of associations with those of higher standing and an emphasis on connections with the lower-status world of action cinema, as considered above, in an attempt to bring the filmmaker (or some other critics) back down to what is considered to be his proper place (from Buñuel to Bay).

Reviews are not generally believed to play an important role in the success or otherwise of blockbuster-scale films, negative responses to many of which are widely assumed to make little difference to their box office returns. Such films are often considered to be 'critic-proof', or at least considerably more so than work from the lower-budget art and indie sectors for which favourable reviews can provide key sources of publicity in cases where funds are not available for the kind of mass marketing and tie-in promotions associated with the largest of the franchised blockbusters. Empirical studies of the role of reviews distinguish between their ability to *influence* or merely to *predict* box office performance, the former being associated with films from the art-house sector, the latter with those of the mainstream.[51] An industry sense of lesser dependence on traditional reviews might help to explain the general favouring of online sources in the first tier of media screenings of *Inception* as potential sources for the promulgation of generally positive word-of-mouth about the film. Whatever their significance in relation to box office performance, however, reviews offer significant evidence of how individual titles or types of film are understood in relation to prevailing cultural hierarchies. They contribute actively to the maintenance or construction of distinctions, as seen in some of the responses examined above. They can also serve, as Blank suggests, to make visible the bases on which such distinctions are made, which is what makes them a valuable resource for this kind of work.

The position of print and online critics is to some extent mirrored in more general viewer responses to the film as measured here by an examination of a sample of 900 'customer reviews' posted on the amazon.com website.[52] Such opinion is generally positive, Amazon's own breakdown suggesting an average of 3.9 out of 5 stars, with more than half awarding the maximum 5 stars, although also combative in some cases in a manner similar to the more formally published critical debate. Reactions range from wild praise to more qualified positive responses and a substantial minority who either reject the film in general or argue against what they declare to be the hype offered by its greatest admirers. According to my interpretation, 98 respondents write in terms that explicitly mark the film out as a quality production in one way or another (many making rhetorical distinctions between *Inception* and usual summer blockbuster fare characterised by sequels, remakes and the like). Another 103 appear to make such value judgements in more implicit terms, making a total of 201 who express such a position in some way. At 22.3 per cent of the total, this might seem a relatively small proportion, but its significance might be greater than the numbers alone suggest given the varied nature of such responses, which range from many that are brief and fragmentary to more considered accounts that seek to offer something closer in tone and content to that of a professional review. This view certainly has a prominence among the more fully expressed responses that is striking enough to be unusual for the reception of a summer blockbuster-type production, offering confirmation of the potential the film offered for consumption in such terms.

   That the complexity of the film is such that it requires greater than average attention from the viewer is suggested by 75 respondents (8.3 per cent), although this is subject to contest from others, some of whom reject any such suggestion. Claims about the 'originality' of the film are common among those who respond positively and are usually expressed in a manner that marks distinction from the norms of the mainstream. But this is also contested by a smaller number who seek to point out, more or less critically, a number of films upon which *Inception* is said to have drawn (one of the most frequently cited here is *Dreamscape* [1984]). Other reservations expressed by critics cited above are also shared by limited numbers of Amazon reviewers, including the suggestion that the film is lacking in depth of character and/or in emotional appeal (an issue raised by 31) or that its representation of dream worlds is disappointingly pedestrian (12). A total of 32 reject the film more or less out of hand as 'boring'. Twenty-five find it confused or confusing, in negative terms. Another 32 suggest that it is confusing at times, not necessarily as a negative judgement. Nolan's name is a frequent point of reference, suggesting that he has gained quite substantial recognition as a 'name' filmmaker and marker of quality, cited approvingly by 123 respondents of whom 27 write in terms that label him as 'genius', 'visionary' or 'master' of his art. Such claims are, again, contested to various degrees by a smaller number, another respect in which the Amazon responses broadly tend to cover a range of ground similar to that found in the work of established critics in both arguing for (the majority) or against (a sometimes vocal minority) the kinds of quality claims made by or on behalf of the film.

Notes

1   Warren Buckland, ed., *Puzzle Films: Complex Storytelling in Contemporary Cinema*, Oxford: Blackwell, 2009; David Bordwell, *The Way Hollywood Tells It: Story and Style in Modern Movies*; Berkeley: University of California Press, 2006, pp. 72–103; Geoff King, *American Independent Cinema*, London: I.B.Tauris, 2005, pp. 84–101

2   On classical narrative, see David Bordwell, *Narration in the Fiction Film*, London: Routledge, 1986

3   Roland Barthes, *S/Z*, New York: Hill and Wang, 1974, p. 75

4   Justin Chang, 'Inception: A fiendishly intricate yarn set in the labyrinth of the subconscious', *Variety*, 5 July 2010, http://www.variety.com/review/VE1117943114?refcatid=31&printerfriendly=true

5   Kenneth Turan, 'Movie review: "Inception"', *Los Angeles Times*, 16 July 2010, http://articles.latimes.com/2010/jul/16/entertainment/la-et-inception-20100716

6   Claudia Puig, 'You definitely won't sleep through complex thriller "Inception"', *USA Today*, 16 July 2010, http://www.usatoday.com/life/movies/reviews/2010-07-15-inception15_ST_N.htm

7   See, for example, Sam Adams, 'Everything you wanted to know about "Inception"', salon.com, 19 July 2010, http://www.salon.com/2010/07/19/inception_explainer/

8   Ann Hornaday, '"Inception's" dream team weaves a mesmerizing tale', *The Washington Post*, 15 July 2010, http://www.washingtonpost.com/gog/movies/inception,1158861/critic-review.html#reviewNum1

9   King, *Spectacular Narratives: Hollywood in the Age of the Blockbuster*, London: I.B.Tauris, 2000, Chapter 4

10   Geoff Boucher, 'Christopher Nolan: All his altered states', *Los Angeles Times*, 9 December 2010, http://articles.latimes.com/2010/dec/09/news/la-en-chris-nolan-20101209

11   For more on this, see Stephen Prince, *Digital Visual Effects in Cinema*, New Brunswick: Rutgers University Press, 2012

12   Terrence Russell, 'How *Inception*'s astonishing visuals came to life', wired. com, 20 July 2010, http://www.wired.com/underwire/2010/07/ inception-visual-effects/

13   Jonathan Gray, *Show Sold Separately: Promos, Spoilers, and Other Media Paratexts*, New York: New York University Press, 2010, pp. 96–9

14   Gray, *Show Sold Separately*, p. 103

15   King, *Spectacular Narratives*; Geoff King, *New Hollywood Cinema: An Introduction*, London: I.B.Tauris, 2002, Chapter 6

16   See Bordwell, *The Way Hollywood Tells It*

17   Ben Fritz and Claudia Eller, 'Warner gambles on an unproven commodity', *Los Angeles Times*, 13 July 2010, http://articles.latimes. com/2010/jul/13/business/la-fi-ct-inception-20100713

18   Boucher, 'Christopher Nolan: All his altered states'

19   Carl DiOrio, '"Inception" is no dream for marketers', *The Hollywood Reporter*, 14 October 2010, http://www.hollywoodreporter.com/ news/inception-no-dream-marketers-25352

20   See, for example, Boucher, 'Christopher Nolan: All his altered states', and Taylor Antrim, 'Anatomy of a contender: Making of "Inception"', *The Hollywood Reporter*, 24 November, 2010, http://www.hollywoo-dreporter.com/news/anatomy-contender-making-inception-47634

21   Tatiana Siegel, 'Being nominated is the best revenge', *Variety*, 15 February 2011, http://www.variety.com/article/VR1118031878/

22   Fritz and Eller, 'Warner gambles'

23   Dave Itzkoff, 'A man and his dream: Christopher Nolan and *Inception*', *The New York Times*, 30 June 2010, http://artsbeat.blogs.nytimes.com /2010/06/30/a-man-and-his-dream-christopher-nolan-and-incep-tion/

24   THR staff, 'Christopher Nolan, "Inception"', *The Hollywood Reporter*, 4 February 2011, http://www.hollywoodreporter.com/news/ christopher-nolan-inception-96528

25   Steve Weintraub, 'Christopher Nolan and Emma Thomas interview', collider.com, 25 March 2010, http://collider.com/director-christopher-nolan-and-producer-emma-thomas-interview-inception-they-talk-3d-what-kind-of-cameras-they-used-pre-viz-wb-and-a-lot-more/20567/

26   Will Brooker, *Hunting the Dark Knight: Twenty-First Century Batman*, London: I.B.Tauris, 2012, p. 34.

27   Fritz and Eller, 'Warner gambles'

28   See, for example, Fritz and Eller, 'Warner gambles'; and Carl DiOrio, '"Inception" is no dream for marketers'

29   Geoff Boucher, '"Inception" breaks into dreams', *Los Angeles Times*, 4 April 2010, http://articles.latimes.com/print/2010/apr/04/entertainment/la-ca-inception4-2010apr04

30   For a classic example of such an approach, see Thomas Schatz, *Hollywood Genres*, Austin: University of Texas Press, 1981.

31   Garrett Stewart, *Framed Time: Toward a Postfilmic Cinema*, Chicago: Chicago University Press, 2007, pp. 70, 156, 162

32   Warren Buckland, 'Introduction: Puzzle plots' in Buckland, ed., *Puzzle Films*, p. 1

33   Thomas Elsaesser, 'The mind game film' in Buckland, ed., *Puzzle Films*, p. 39.

34   Robert Ebert, 'Inception: Dreams on top of dreams inside dreams', *Chicago Sun-Times*, 14 July 2010, http://rogerebert.suntimes.com/apps/pbcs.dll/article?AID=/20100714/REVIEWS/100719997/1001

35   Kenneth Turan 'Movie review: "Inception"', 16 July 2010, http://articles.latimes.com/2010/jul/16/entertainment/la-et-inception-20100716

36   Hornaday, '"Inception's" dream team weaves a mesmerizing tale'

37   Puig, 'You definitely won't sleep through complex thriller "Inception"'

38   David Denby, 'Dream factory: "Inception"', 26 July 2010, http://www.newyorker.com/arts/critics/cinema/2010/07/26/100726crci_cinema_denby?currentPage=all

39   A. O. Scott, 'This time the dream's on me', 15 July 2010, http://www.nytimes.com/2010/07/16/movies/16inception.html

40   Raymond Williams, *Culture and Society* 1780-1950, Harmondsworth: Penguin, 1961; Larry Shiner, *The Invention of Art: A Cultural History*, Chicago: University of Chicago Press, 2001

41   Stephanie Zacharek, 'Review: Is *Inception* this year's masterpiece? Dream on', 14 July 2010, http://movieline.com/2010/07/14/review-is-inception-this-years-masterpiece-dream-on/

42   Andrew O'Hehir, '"Inception": A clunky, overblown disappointment', 14 July 2010, http://www.salon.com/2010/07/15/inception/

43   David Denby, 'Dream factory: "Inception"', 26 July 2010, http://www.newyorker.com/arts/critics/cinema/2010/07/26/100726crci_cinema_denby?currentPage=all

44   Steven Zeitchik, 'The rise and reassessment of "Inception"', *Los Angeles Times*, 19 July 2010, http://articles.latimes.com/2010/jul/19/entertainment/la-et-inception-backlash-20100719, and A.O. Scott, 'Everybody's a critic of the critics' rabid critics', *The New York Times*,

21 July 2010, http://www.nytimes.com/2010/07/25/movies/25scott.html

45   Zeitchik, 'The rise and reassessment of "Inception"'

46   See, for example, Thomas Doherty, 'The death of film criticism', *The Chronicle of Higher Education*, 28 February 2010, http://chronicle.com/article/The-Death-of-Film-Criticism/64352/

47   Grant Blank, *Critics, Ratings, and Society: The Sociology of Reviews*, Lanham, Md.: Rowman and Littlefield, 2007, p. 7

48   Leo Lowenthal, 'Eighteenth century England: A case study' in Lowenthal, *Literature and Mass Culture*, p. 129

49   Pierre Bourdieu, 'The field of cultural production' in Bourdieu, *The Field of Cultural Production*, Cambridge: Polity, 1993, p. 78

50   These and the following references are from a sample including the reviews and feature articles cited above along with: Richard Corliss, '*Inception*: Whose mind is it, anyway?', *Time*, 14 July 2010, http://www.time.com/time/magazine/article/0,9171,2004109,00.html; and Michael Phillips, 'In "Inception," Nolan conjures up a fever dream', *Chicago Tribune*, 15 July 2010, http://articles.chicagotribune.com/2010-07-15/entertainment/sc-mov-0713-inception-20100715_1_dream-christopher-nolan-idea

51   See Gerda Gemser, Martine Van Oostrum and Mark Leenders, 'The impact of film reviews on the box office performance of art house versus mainstream motion pictures', *Journal of Cultural Economy*, vol. 31, no. 1, 2007

52   Sample accessed initially on 18 April 2012, http://www.amazon.com/Inception-Blu-ray/dp/B004FVHBXY/ref=sr_1_3?ie=UTF8&qid=1336669651&sr=8-3. Some qualifications are required in the use of such samples as a basis for analysis. They are self-selected and therefore cannot in any strict terms be taken to be representative of all viewers. They have the merit, however, of including large numbers and having been taken from a source that can be expected to include a fairly wide constituency.

3

The Social Network

'Smart' contemporary narrative meets the heritage film

Prevailing cultural hierarchies can at times appear fixed and unbending, but they are also subject to changes and reorientations. Television has sometimes sought, or gained, quality resonances through associations with film and/or the cinematic, either at the level of style and content or through literally marginal phenomena such as the growing tendency from the 1990s to adopt some degree of 'letterbox' format through the creation of noticeable black bands at the top and bottom of the screen to mimic a more cinematic shape.[1] It is a familiar procedure for media in one position in a prevailing hierarchy, or their associated institutions, to ape aspects of those perceived in general to occupy a higher location, in this way, in those parts of the medium that seek to increase their standing. Such has been the subsequent success of some forms of television in claiming higher-than-usual status, however, that by the early decades of the twenty-first century it was a common rhetorical trope for journalistic commentators to make claims such as that TV had become 'the place to go for adult storytelling', that cable in particular had 'replaced movies and networks as the destination for complicated, well-acted, well-shot dramas' or that 'If you're looking for great storytelling, the real action is on your TV set, not at the multiplex'.[2] It comes as no surprise, then, although it would have seemed unlikely a few decades earlier, that one of the grounds on which quality has been ascribed to *The Social Network* (2010) is in relation not just to its 'smart' and biting dialogue but to the fact that this was the work of Aaron Sorkin, creator in particular of *The West Wing* (1999–2006), one of the key quality network TV series of its time. The early involvement of Sorkin in the project gave it an imprimateur of quality from the start, providing a point of orientation for discourses surrounding the film which rivalled that provided by the 'name' director, David Fincher.

Like that of *Inception*, the quality dimension of *The Social Network* is established in large part through its narrative characteristics, both in the nature of the dialogue provided by Sorkin and a relative complexity and density of narrative structure. The film also makes claims to a certain seriousness and relevance – each characteristic of strands in the history of quality outlined in the Introduction and Chapter 1 – through its basis in contemporary events that had some substantial impact in the external world: namely, the development of the Facebook social networking site (and its use as a location in which to raise broader issues such as the nature of ambition and its impact on personal relationships). The claims to pressing contemporaneity made in this dimension are balanced, however, by the resonances *The Social Network* offers with what might seem a very different realm, that of the 'heritage' film, a format usually associated more strongly with British cinema and/or productions handled by the studio speciality divisions and with more traditional 'uplifting' varieties of quality. It thus combines a sense of immediacy and presence, and the youthful, college-age world of its protagonists, with a range of contrasting associations that seem to cement its quality claims and that might have opened its appeal to a wider range of audience constituencies. A similar mixture of points of reference can be found in the status of the film as a biopic: one that is highly contemporary in its subject but also a traditional quality format. Like its predecessor, this chapter begins with a close examination of the textual features through which such dimensions of quality are established, starting with narrative, before a consideration of the origins of the production and the manner in which its status was articulated through critical and associated discourses in relation to the film.

Distance, immediacy and an unsympathetic protagonist

A key aspect of the structure of *The Social Network* is a series of shifts between more or less immediate and distanced forms of narrative strategy. The process of narration is organised around two sets of legal depositions in which a fictionalised version of the founder of Facebook, Mark Zuckerberg (Jesse Eisenberg), is confronted by former partners or would-be employers who are suing him for what they consider to be their share of its riches. These are Zuckerberg's former friend and early financier Eduardo Saverin (Andrew Garfield) and the wealthy Winklevoss twins, Cameron and Tyler (both played facially by Armie Hammer, with Josh Pence providing the stand-in body of Tyler), who claim that the enterprise was based on their original idea. The legal sessions occupy the epistemological central ground of the film, as the points from which the rest of the action is being narrated. The existence of sources of active narration of this kind has a potentially distancing effect, creating the impression that the story is being told at one remove rather than that we are simply watching events unfold in a primary staging. This is particularly the case because of the regular basis on which the film returns to these points, to emphasise their presence. This approach seems itself, therefore, to have the status of a marker of quality, in a manner that might not be the case in a more routine instance in which, for example, the presence of a narrator might be acknowledged just at the start of a film, after which we slip into the more immediate story-being-told and perhaps return to the figure of the narrator occasionally or just at the end, a device not unfamiliar in Hollywood history (examples including Fincher's previous film, *The Curious Case of Benjamin Button* [2008]). To the regular return to the site of narration as a marker of quality, we can add the fact that there are two such sites and that the material generated from each is itself articulated, contested and combined in a manner that is considerably more complex

Figure 3.1. Ground of narration: one of the early legal deposition sequences in *The Social Network* © Columbia Pictures Industries, Inc. and Beverly Blvd LLC

than the Hollywood norm. This structure is entirely the work of Sorkin, nothing of the depositions existing in the original source material, the book *The Accidental Billionaires* by Ben Mezrich, which tells its version of the story in linear form.

It is far from the case, however, that the scenes of legal deposition, in which the narrative process is to some extent foregrounded, are the dominant experience offered by the film (see Figure 3.1). It would be possible to imagine a version of the story in which this were so, in which none of the other action were fully to be acted out separately and dramatised. The result would probably be something much more dry and austere, however dramatically staged in itself, perhaps more likely to be found in a theatrical treatment but also conceivably the stuff of a lower-budget indie film. Such an alternative is worth imagining, if only to underline how far that is from the nature of *The Social Network*, as what remains a largely conventional Hollywood feature in many respects. If the film offers a certain kind of distancing of narration, through reference back to the deposition sequences, much of the fabric of the narrative is presented in a more conventionally immediate manner, giving the viewer a familiar Hollywood/mainstream impression of something closer to direct immersion in the action. It is notable – and entirely unsurprising – that this is the case from the start of the film, with which the closer textual analysis offered by this chapter begins below. A central question is then to examine exactly what kind of balance is offered between the more immediate and distanced dimensions, along with the nature and degree of the relative complexity of narrative structure provided by the film. This section also includes consideration of some of the traits of the 'smart' dialogue provided by Sorkin as key markers of quality.

The Social Network opens very much *in media res*, in the middle of the action, in a noisy Harvard pub, rather than at one of the legal conference-room tables where the depositions are made. The viewer is given a rapid sketch of the character of Zuckerberg, through a dialogue-heavy sequence (another part of the script that has no equivalent in the Mezrich book) in which he is left by his girlfriend, Erica (Rooney Mara). The dialogue begins even before the images of the film-proper, Zuckerberg's first mile-a-minute line being foregrounded by starting just before the Columbia logo fades to black and the scene in the pub fades in. A subsequent sequence proceeds equally quickly to dramatise what is presented as a key creative moment in Zuckerberg's career, his response to rejection seeming to provide part of the initial spur for the creation of a crudely sexist 'Facemash' game that is situated here as one of the sources of inspiration for what he will eventually develop into the Facebook social network. Zuckerberg's motivation for this is also more substantial, however: he is seeking to do something eye-catching to gain the attention of the socially exclusive Harvard 'final' clubs to which he is seeking admittance as a way to favour his chances in the world, an endeavour in which he succeeds when demand for Facemash results in the crashing of the university network.

The opening directly establishes key aspects of character and central plot, and a characteristically Hollywood-style mutual articulation of the two. A continued narrative and thematic thread traces the extent to which Zuckerberg's activities are the result of his general lack of consideration for the feelings of others and his jealousy of the social status of figures such as the Winklevoss twins. The initial pub sequence also establishes concepts such as intelligence and sharp-witted dialogue, qualities attributed to Zuckerberg that might also seem to make claims on behalf of the film itself. Zuckerberg, talking at rapid pace, makes opening reference to high IQ levels in

China and to his own SAT scores, the script shifting speedily from one point of focus to the other. Erica struggles at times to follow his points, functioning in this sense as a likely surrogate for viewers (akin to the role of Ariadne in *Inception*) who might be similarly confused by some of his mid-stream changes of tack and by the abruptness with which they are plunged into such a density of words. Keeping up with him, Erica suggests, is exhausting. A conscious aim of the filmmakers appears to have been to create a similar impact on viewers, to require them to pay extra attention from the start in order to catch up,[3] a clear marker of quality status – although how exactly viewers might position themselves in relation to some of this is open to debate.

On one level the film seems to invite some reasonably substantial degree of allegiance with Zuckerberg, in his smartness, so closely does it seem to be aligned with the qualities being displayed by the film itself (we would also generally expect such a relationship with the central protagonist of a Hollywood feature). The opening sequence seems markedly to be making quality claims of this nature in the relative density of its discourse (by Hollywood standards) and what amounts to an almost spectacular display of smart dialogue. This is a smartness that suggests a broad relationship with what Jeffrey Sconce terms 'the American smart film', although, as noted in the Introduction, it does not involve the particular kind of ironic distancing strategy identified by Sconce as a key marker of his usage of the term (a variety in which an implicit distinction is made between viewers who might or might not 'get' the dark humour involved in the instances he examines).[4] At the same time as offering a parallel between the smartness of Zuckerberg and the film itself, however, another element of distance might also be created for the viewer in the rather dislikeable nature of the character that is so presented, and in the position of sympathy the opening exchanges construct for Erica. The less-than-likeable dimension of Zuckerberg, as characterised in the film, is another significant claim to the status of quality that might be identified in *The Social Network*, largely because of its potential to create this kind of distance and the difference it represents from the Hollywood norm, according to which we would usually expect a more unambiguously sympathetic central protagonist.

An emphasis on Zuckerberg's combined smartness and personal insensitivity is continued through the sequences in which he creates Facemash, in which his own rapid-fire discourse provides another source of overt narration; in this case a voiced-over version of the commentary he gives on his blog. The structure of this part of the film offers a mixture typical of the work as a whole, in the fore-grounding of one aspect of narration (in this case, via the device of the blog) and its blending with other qualities. What we see and hear of Zuckerberg's creation of Facemash suggests a fairly standard ver-sion of brilliant-hacker-at-work (the fast-paced arrogance of his com-ments and a speedy montage of various stages in the process). This is intercut with a separate sequence depicting the arrival of a coach-load of young women at a party being staged by one of the clubs to which Zuckerberg seeks entry: the Phoenix. The effect is to balance the 'dry but brilliant' world of the nerd/hacker with the more glamorous/ seductive resonances of the party, the images of which – some in slow motion – include those of women in various states of relative undress (imagery that gives this sequence something in common with the exploitation film tradition). If this can be read as a mixing of qualities of the kind that is characteristic of the contemporary quality film more generally, it is also a juxtaposition that serves particular narra-tive ends in this case. The 'exclusive' glamour signified by the Phoenix party is part of the realm that provides motivation for Zuckerberg's enterprise, while both this event and the creation of Facemash appear to share a similar basis in the exploitative objectification of women.

The immediate presentation of initial narrative events constitutes the opening 16 minutes of the film. The first shift forward in time to the scene of one of the depositions comes when Facemash crashes the Harvard network. We are taken here into one of the sessions relating to the legal action being pursued by Eduardo and exchanges between Zuckerberg and a lawyer about a statement provided by Erica. It becomes apparent that the content of the pub scene was based on a sworn deposition already provided by the latter, a fact that might have potential to encourage the viewer to treat the previous material somewhat differently in retrospect. Zuckerberg challenges the validity of her account. It is notable that the first words of this initial depos-ition scene are his: 'That's not what happened', followed by: 'She just made a lot of that up.' Such comments might, in themselves, increase the potential for viewers to question the veracity of some of what they have previously witnessed, a move that would be quite substantially unusual for a Hollywood feature. To pull the rug out from under the viewer in such a manner is rare in the mainstream and would usually require much stronger motivation – the kind that might be found, for example, in some kind of overt 'trick' or a mendacious source of narration provided by a figure who might more conventionally be suspected of such behaviour (a killer in some kind of thriller or horror film, perhaps, a now-classic instance being *The Usual Suspects* [1995]), or in a case in which the whole film revolved around a prominent ontological reversal such as those found in the generic territory occupied by the puzzle film considered in the previous chapter.

Generally, without strong indication to the contrary, the viewer is encouraged to believe the version of events that is acted out at length on screen rather than a verbal denial of its veracity, a broad tendency being to ascribe ontological priority to that which we appear to have witnessed ourselves in some way – if only on screen and in a fiction – rather than that which is recounted to us in a more obviously second-hand manner (showing rather than telling). It seems unlikely that viewers will seriously question the accuracy of Erica's account in its fundamentals, as dramatised, both because it has been portrayed in full before being questioned and also because we might already have been given more reason to doubt the reliability of Zuckerberg than Erica in relation to personal material of this kind. The balance of probabilities seems again to be characteristic of what might be expected in the Hollywood quality film. Some basis is provided, in literal terms, for a questioning of elements of material narrated by the film itself, but it seems unlikely to have the effect for most viewers of seriously undermining a central part of the fabric of the narrative or providing the kind of non-generic radical textual uncertainty more likely to be found in certain kinds of art cinema. Plenty of disputes remain between the various participants in the legal actions, but few of these appear to relate to solid matters of fact or to involve such direct diegetic challenges to the veracity of the dramatised material.

Individual sequences from within the deposition scenes are generally quite brief but closely integrated and intercut with the footage that presents the various events to which they refer. The first deposition sequence lasts barely a minute. It is followed by an introduction to the Winklevoss twins, leading to their discovery of Zuckerberg, and a shift to the first view of the legal session relating to their case against him. This deposition scene lasts a mere 15 seconds, before a cut back to the original events and Zuckerberg's appearance before a Harvard disciplinary hearing. We are shown the first meeting between Zuckerberg and the twins, their proposal to him and his reply 'I'm in', after which a cut is made to the Winklevoss deposition and Zuckerberg being asked if that was what he had said. He replies that it was three or four years ago: 'I don't know what I said.' Again, some ground is provided here for doubt about the exact veracity of the re-enacted material, but it appears relatively slight and to relate to matters of detail – and perhaps Zuckerberg's truculence as a witness – more than anything else.

A series of shifts then occurs between the two deposition scenes themselves, adding to the complexity of the texture, although the film employs a standard device to seek to reduce any potential confusion. As is the case with the different levels of dream-reality in *Inception*, distinct cues involving setting and visual quality are provided for the two sets of deposition sequences in *The Social Network*, to help to maintain the orientation of the viewer. Those involving Eduardo are in a clean-cut 'modern' space, in its décor and furniture; those relating to the twins occupy a more 'traditional' boardroom setting, characterised by warm wood tones and background detail such as bookcases and oil paintings, in keeping with their association with 'old-world' exclusivity and privilege.

The general strategy of the film is to knit together very closely the various threads provided by different moments in the original events and references to these in the deposition scenes. The movement back and forth often occurs speedily, within periods of less than a minute, sometimes for only a few seconds in briefly interjected lines of dialogue. Integration often occurs at the level of a line in one dimension being answered directly in another. Dialogue is also in some cases overlapped from one location onto another, a familiarly classical way of creating continuity across filmic shifts of time and/or place. The effect is to create a dynamic impression, one of pace and verve, even if highly 'talky' in nature, rather than anything more dour or down-beat in style. Some quite lengthy passages are articulated through close cutting from represented event to its discussion within one of the depositions, for example the sequence in which Zuckerberg first pitches his idea to Eduardo and in which this is discussed with the lawyers. The relative complexity of what is being narrated in some of this, largely the effect of the rapid-fire manner in which various elements are articulated through Sorkin's dialogue, is increased by the regular interweaving into such Facebook-plot related material of the ongoing theme of what appears to be Zuckerberg's jealousy at Eduardo's progress in his attempt to join the Phoenix club.

The viewer might at times gain a sense of narrative overload akin to the cognitive demands posed by *Inception*, although little of the material is very challenging in itself. One way this can be understood is as an attempt by the makers of the film to embody within its structure something like the mental acuity attributed to Zuckerberg (as also conveyed in some of his own dialogue). The potential corollary of this is that viewers who take pleasure from such material might gain a sense of sharing vicariously in such a capacity, in a manner characteristic of this dimension of the consumption of work at the quality end of the spectrum. Some of the extended intercut sequences also take on the characteristics of a more conventional montage approach, however, in which music is provided. This is the case in a sequence dealing with a series of emails between Zuckerberg and the Winklevoss twins and a later one revolving around a restaurant meeting between the former, Eduardo and Napster founder Sean Parker (Justin Timberlake). There is a relaxation of the demands placed on the viewer on these occa-sions, in both the more familiar nature of such a form of articulation and the degree of licence it offers to be experienced as a more expres-sive form of shorthand. The latter reduces any sense that it is expected to be followed closely in all its component detail.

Despite the occasional contradictory response found in the move from one thread to another, or within any particular part (the challen-ging or doubting of some specific points), the general tendency is to build an integrated narrative fabric through the close interweaving of the various strands. A fact or detail presented at one level is usually rein-forced or further explained at the other. The effect is one more of clarifi-cation and very careful explication than it is of generating any sustained confusion or really challenging viewers, even if they might at times feel a little stretched if they attempt to keep up with every single detail on every front. This is particularly the case as far as the explanation of key plot detail is concerned, and it seems entirely Hollywood-conventional for this to emerge as the priority and for some redundancy to exist in the shape of the reiteration of essential elements. The viewer need not entirely follow a sense of exactly what the source is of some specific details, or exactly what comes from where, in terms of dramatised events or shifts from these to depositions or from one of the latter to another. But the net effect is a reasonably clear exposition of the central narrative threads relating to both the creation of Facebook and its legal ramifications and what are presented as the underlying personal dynamics in relation to Zuckerberg himself. Overall, this has something in common with the verdict from the last chapter on the relative narrative demands created by *Inception*: the viewer is confronted with more cognitive work than is the norm in Hollywood, but is not required to engage exhaustively in every last detail in order satisfactorily to comprehend and enjoy the core narrative issues.

It is also important to note that the film generally obeys a quite strict chronological order in its exploration of the events preceding the depositions. There are no shifts back and forth within these segments of the film, which would have added considerably to the complexity of the structure overall, too much so for that to have been likely in a studio feature that is already more intricately structured than most. As suggested above, the deposition material is also fitted closely into this linear progression, most of the content relating specifically to the issues or events at hand in the main narration at the time of its placement. These sequences also have an immediacy of presentation themselves, despite the departure they involve from our experience of the narration of the original main events. Some important material is dramatically revealed around the deposition tables, not least the damning details of exactly how Eduardo is eventually tricked out of his share in the company. Much, then, remains broadly conventional and within the parameters of classical/canonical Hollywood narrative style, as was the case with *Inception* and as is typical of the studio quality film in general. *The Social Network* revolves around some of the most basic components of the classical style, including its focus on a strongly goal-directed central protagonist whose main subject-specific aims are paralleled and reinforced by more personal-emotional dynamics. At this fundamental level, however, the film continues to depart from the norm in some other elements.

There is little in the way of any sustained romantic sub-plot, usually a staple of the classical form. Zuckerberg's break-up with Erica might constitute a part of his motivation for the particular burst of activity that leads to the creation of Facemash, and it hangs over the film to a certain extent. He attempts a rapprochement at one point, but seems to fail to grasp the fact that the first thing he needs to do is to apologise, and is left at the end of the film seeking to restore contact. A pathetic irony ensures that the latter process is via a repeated updating of his own Facebook status in the hope that Erica will respond positively to his 'friend' request. But there is no real sense throughout the film that any renewal of the union is likely or is really in play as an active component in the mix, or that Zuckerberg is likely to form such a relationship with anyone else, despite a sympathetic approach during a lunch break from a young lawyer, Marylin (Rashida Jones), who is sitting in on the Eduardo deposition sessions. He seems, throughout, far too focused on the development of Facebook for anything else of this kind to significantly intrude.

The protagonist/antagonist relationship is also more complex than would usually be expected. The Winklevi, as Zuckerberg terms them, are established as antagonists, even if nothing is presented specifically to counter their claim that Zuckerberg had deliberately strung them along. They are portrayed, rather one-dimensionally, as unsympathetic and/or largely comic characters in their arrogance, sense of entitlement and their position as members of an old-fashioned elite. More complex is the status of Eduardo. He ends up formally as another antagonist to Zuckerberg but is without much doubt the most sympathetic character in the piece. This returns us to the largely unsympathetic manner in which Zuckerberg is portrayed and the role this plays in the relatively less Hollywood-conventional dimensions of the film.

A number of factors contribute to the extent to which the Zuckerberg of *The Social Network* is figured as someone less likeable than is the norm for the hero/protagonist. A key element is his insistence always on the rightness of his position, in literal terms, even when to do so might seem to involve gratuitous insult to others. He is generally presented as lacking social niceties or appreciation for the feelings of others, fitting in large part into a familiar stereotype of the under-socialised techno-computer 'nerd'. This is manifested not just in what we see of his relationship with Erica and others in the main narrative, but also on numerous occasions in the exchanges during the deposition sessions. A characteristic example is when one of the lawyers asks if he has Zuckerberg's full attention, or if he thinks he deserves it. Zuckerberg's response is to insist that he must be bluntly honest, as he is on oath, and to say:

> You have *part* of my attention – you have the minimal amount. The rest of my attention is back at the offices of Facebook where my colleagues and I are doing things that no one in this room, including and especially your clients, are intellectually or creatively capable of doing. [pause] Did I adequately answer your condescending question?

Such outbursts tend to receive a pained facial response even from his own lawyer.

A decisive moment in how the viewer might be encouraged to judge Zuckerberg in moral terms – a key factor in his status as hero/protagonist – comes at the point where we are told exactly how far he went in traducing Eduardo, whose share ownership is reduced to a tiny fraction while those of others suffer no such devaluation. The move is presented as a clear betrayal – even if it is made apparent that Eduardo should have taken independent legal advice at the time – and Eduardo's accusation that Zuckerberg has done this out of jealousy over his admission to the Phoenix club does not seem to lack plausibility. Exactly how this and some related material is articulated seems to complicate the picture, however, and to suggest some effort on the part of the filmmakers to blur the extent to which Zuckerberg is presented as nakedly culpable. Parker is an important component of the process, the film shifting some of the burden of blame onto his character in order to paint Zuckerberg in a slightly, but significantly, less negative light.

To what extent, then, might Zuckerberg's characterisation remain within the parameters of the conventional central protagonist, a figure who is quite usually capable of exhibiting significant flaws? The question here, as with many that relate to positionings within the quality versus mainstream-convention spectrum, is one of relative degrees rather than absolutes. A familiar mantra of Hollywood screenwriting advice is that protagonists should have some kind of flaw, as we saw in the previous chapter, to make them interesting and to provide some degree of apparent character depth, but that this should substantially be overcome during the course of the action. If Zuckerberg's central flaw is his lack of ability to feel or express much in the way of empathy towards others, it seems doubtful that this is overcome by the end. This can stand implicitly as a claim to quality status on the basis of 'honest' critical realism: implying that individuals do not, generally, change in any fundamentals or according to the kinds of 'arcs' beloved of some screenwriters, a marker of distinction often found in indie films. There is a politics to this position, a denial of deeply ideologically rooted notions of transcendent individualism, even if such implications are not drawn out in any explicit manner. At the same time, however, the film also appears to want to offer some further alleviation of this critical portrait, to draw its rendition of Zuckerberg a little closer to the norm that offers a more comfortable position of conventional allegiance. A small but significant role is played here by the figure of Marylin, the legal junior who sits through the Eduardo deposition sequences and acts as a kind of surrogate for the viewer in what is presented as her judgement of Zuckerberg.

Marylin's is prominent among the series of uncomfortable looks we are shown when the extent to which Eduardo's shares were diluted is revealed. She is subsequently given the role of providing a final verdict that seems designed to be more important, in its emotional impact, than that which will result from the deposition itself. At the end of the film she and Zuckerberg are the only ones left in the room. She tells him the lawyers will come back to start working on a settlement to which he should agree, as he will have no chance of winning a case in front of a jury. She then introduces the 'likeability' agenda explicitly, commenting on her own specialism in the process of jury selection and the bases on which potential jurors determine the likeability of the defendant. Zuckerberg's response to the term is a characteristically

Figure 3.2. Not an asshole, just trying so hard to be one: Mark Zuckerberg (Jesse Eisenberg) reacts to the personal verdict at the end of *The Social Network* © Columbia Pictures Industries, Inc. and Beverly Blvd LLC

quizzical 'Likeability?', underlining how little such qualities figure in his reckoning.

A series of titles subsequently informs us of the payment he made to the Winklevi ($65 million) and the undisclosed settlement with Eduardo. But what seems to count for most in these exchanges is Marylin's opinion of him as a person, the equivocal but still quite substantially sympathetic: 'You're not an asshole, Mark; you're just trying so hard to be (see Figure 3.2). From this we move to his attempt to 'friend' Erica. The fact that this is left as the final action of the film seems again to offer a greater sense of humanity on his part than is characterised by some of his earlier actions or their absence. There is nothing to suggest that this will be successful, but he is at least making an attempt, at some level, and this might be interpreted as leading to some degree of change on the basis of remorse that might have been created through the events he has been forced to re-experience via the depositions. Such a possibility is at least kept open and seems important to the overall impression left by the film.

If the Zuckerberg portrayed on screen remains an arrogant figure in many respects, particularly in his preparedness to communicate his own sense of intellectual superiority at various moments in the film, a balance might be established between this and his emotional inarticulacy. The viewer who does not feel likely to be the protagonist's intellectual equal might be encouraged to feel a sense of superiority at the moral/emotional level. Any such feeling might provide a broader source of compensation for anyone who feels challenged by the manner in which the narrative of the film is articulated, particularly if the latter is taken as a corollary of Zuckerberg's mental capacity. That the film seems open to be experienced in either way – as offering potential for viewers to make their own acts of distinction-marking through their ability to follow the relative complexities and to revel in the sharpness of dialogue, or to find other levels on which to balance any shortcomings on that ground – seems another typical characteristic of the studio quality film that seeks to mark distinctions while at the same time being open to appeal to a relatively broad rather than smaller-niche audience.

From headlines to heritage film: audio-visual quality in *The Social Network*

The dominant look of *The Social Network* is perhaps not what might be expected of a production that tells such a contemporary and technology-related story, with its broad basis in the creation of a real-world social media institution and directed by a filmmaker sometimes associated with a tendency towards the showy flourish. No attempt is made to give the film a texture related specifically to the world of computer-technological mediation. There is no sign of anything akin to the approach termed the 'desktop aesthetic' employed in some lower-budget features shot and overtly manipulated digitally, in some cases to mimic the world of social media (for example, the indie production *Four Eyed Monsters* [2005]).[5] *The Social Network* is presented in a broadly classical Hollywood style, employing neither the intensified continuity associated with many contemporary studio productions – as discussed along with its wider cultural associations in the previous chapters – nor an overtly slow style of the kind often found in the art or indie film sectors. The strongest resonances the film offers with any more particular style are those which seem reminiscent of the qualities associated with the heritage film, a well-established quality format. These involve a combination of visual style, some use of music, and the settings within which much of the film unfolds.

The audio-visual qualities of the opening scenes put the predominant emphasis on the creation of what are marked as 'subtle' and 'classy' impressions, of the kind often associated with the quality tradition. The opening image in the pub is lit in low-key style, the faces and tops of the heads of Zuckerberg and Erica being caught in golden tones set against a darkened foreground and behind which a number of other drinkers are lit in broadly similar fashion. We start with a longish two-shot of the pair before a cut to a very conventional over-Zuckerberg's-shoulder shot of Erica, her face again warmly lit from one side against a largely dark background. A reverse-shot follows to a similar image of Zuckerberg, after which these are repeated before the sequence moves in closer, to alternative head-and-shoulders shots of each character in turn, as the conversation develops. We are then taken back out to the over-the-shoulder shot/reverse-shot arrangement and then to a two-shot from the side, closer than that with which the sequence began. The same general – and very conventional – orchestration of shots continues through the rest of the exchange. The pace of the editing is sometimes reasonably brisk but in no way seems to attempt to match the rhythm of some of the faster-paced dialogue, while the framing remains classically static throughout, with no sign of the 'prowling camera' identified by David Bordwell in dialogue scenes of this kind in some examples of intensified continuity. The emphasis remains firmly on the content of the exchanges and the responses of the two characters, with no effort made to heighten this through expressive means beyond the local emphasis created by the lighting.

The quality resonance is reinforced as the opening sequence comes to an end. As Zuckerberg rises and a cut is made to the exterior of the pub – another dark brown-toned image with a few bright highlights – a slow and plaintive piano-led piece comes up on the soundtrack, itself a clear marker of subtlety and aspirations towards the creation of a classy impression. We are then given a slow pan across part of the local skyline, complete with elements of what appears to be colonial, or otherwise 'historical', architecture, and down towards the streets through which Zuckerberg makes his way home – all of this as the background to the opening credits. The next shot, at street level, has him hurrying past a brick wall that is, again, glowing in a golden light against a general background of dark tones. The camera pans to follow his figure, as he continues to move away towards buildings and trees that maintain generally similar qualities of golden light and shadow. The next cut takes us into a downwardly panning camera movement that, again, picks up Zuckerberg, repeating a similar lateral pan to follow as he passes and once more jogs away, along a street of elegantly tall brick buildings lit by lamps that have the appearance of old-fashioned gas lights. The shot after this is another in which the protagonist is seen moving away from the camera, which this time starts low and then lifts slightly upwards. Next we have a shot in which he jogs up towards the camera, into a scene that includes a figure playing violin in the foreground and with a building that includes a columnated structure to one side in the background. The camera pivots to follow Zuckerberg, who moves past a column close to the camera, before a final shot sees his arrival at the substantial building that stands in for his Harvard hall of residence.

Cinematic quality is signified here by a combination of factors, both general and those which lean in the more specific direction of the kinds of features associated with the heritage film. The music is both rich and sparse, creating a distanced and contemplative mood that, although somewhat mournful, perhaps runs counter to that of Zuckerberg's apparent state of excitement (and the fact that he is running) in the aftermath of his break-up. The lighting continues to embody the kind of 'elegant' chiaroscuro exhibited in the opening sequence. The movement of the camera adds to the impression of controlled and nuanced elegance in its smooth, unhurried and relatively modest pans and pivots, and its subtle and unexaggerated movements up and down. It creates an impression of assured, well-oiled professional Hollywood mastery, without being extended to the point at which it might be considered 'slick', a term the negative connotations of which suggests a context in which a more overt deftness of execution might be considered to be shallow, glib or a substitute for any real content. The final ingredient, of course, is the setting itself, the film employing a number of stand-ins at various stages to represent

Figure 3.3. Heritage resonances: one of the buildings standing in for Harvard in *The Social Network* © Columbia Pictures Industries, Inc. and Beverly Blvd LLC

parts of the Harvard campus and its surroundings, with its old-world ambience of history and exclusivity (see Figure 3.3).

What we have here establishes a location very much in line with the notion of quality examined in Chapter 1. This is created through a combination of positive associations with aspects of higher culture and more implicit negative markers of difference from the qualities conventionally associated with forms to which lower status is attributed. The music is of a broadly (if loosely) classical variety and further marked as being subtle and nuanced within that realm. The lighting, and the associated combination of muted dark backgrounds and golden highlights, also creates a broadly, if rather vaguely, 'artistic' impression, marked as subtle in quality (the more specific artistic associations of such imagery are considered further in the next chapter, in relation to a heightened usage of chiaroscuro in *The Assassination of Jesse James by the Coward Robert Ford*). The notion of the subtle, here and elsewhere, is one that tends conventionally to be associated with the kinds of cultural products designed for those of greater than average 'cultivation', a reasonably fine-grained sense of discernment appearing to be required for its appreciation – as opposed to that which might be characterised as more crude, clumsy, obvious or broad-brush in nature (and thereby available to anyone, without a requirement for any particular powers of discrimination).

The movements of the camera enacted in the credit sequence can be characterised in much the same way, again as might be contrasted with the variously faster, more unsteady or more showy treatments associated with intensified continuity or other such approaches (including some instances of attention-drawing or seemingly 'impossible' heightened camera movement in Fincher-directed films such as *Fight Club* and *Panic Room* [2002]). The overall impression created under the titles is an evocation of something of the broader cultural ground occupied by the milieu in which much of the film is located, through its Harvard and related settings, as a place of learning, elevation, culture (with violinists likely to turn up on any corner), and associated dimensions of which the film is in some ways more critical (while also luxuriating in some of their textures) such as a form of tradition based on inherited privilege.

The combination of dark brownish backgrounds and golden or ochre highlights creates something of an old-world resonance, implying a richly warm, burnished quality. This is the dominant palate for much of the film, including scenes set in the college rooms shared by Zuckerberg and those of the Winklevi and many others, interior and exterior. The world of *The Social Network* often seems to be a rather dark one, in which flat overhead lighting is hardly ever in evidence (similar tones are also favoured in Fincher's other films, but with fewer of the particular quality associations created here by the milieu in which they are located). In some cases the chiaroscuro effect is more pronounced than others, heightened examples including a sequence outside a party during which Zuckerberg sells Eduardo on the merits of the Facebook project (see Figure 3.4). The lighting in the deposition scenes is brighter than that of most other interiors, as seems required to maintain the plausibility of the working environment setting, but some of the same resonances remain. These are most obvious in the sessions involving the Winklevoss case, in the earthier tones of the more traditional boardroom, but some of the imagery from the Eduardo sessions also includes a similar appearance.

Heritage movie associations also run through considerable portions of *The Social Network*. These can be identified in much general footage of what stands in for the Harvard campus (on which filming was not permitted), in exteriors and interiors. More specific points

Figure 3.4. Pronounced chiaroscuro in the sequence outside the party in *The Social Network* © Columbia Pictures Industries, Inc. and Beverly Blvd LLC

of resonance with such qualities include the sequences involving the Winklevi rowing on the Charles River, the sport having generally elitist associations. These are heightened in scenes at the Henley regatta in England, a classic example of upper-class British culture (a world of straw boaters and blazers and a champagne reception graced by the presence of minor European royalty). Similar associations exist with other elements in the background of the principal diegetic events, including the Phoenix club initiation rites undergone by Eduardo and an *a capella* recital in a Harvard dining room. The world of upper-class privilege and the sense of 'old-world' tradition evoked in such material is much the same as that identified in Andrew Higson's analysis of the British heritage film or costume drama, a format in which the quality associations of the production are borrowed largely from the resonances of the milieux in which it unfolds.[6]

There are some instances, however, in which the distinction-marking resonances of quality and/or heritage are combined with others that might be expected to appeal on a rather different basis and in relation to the more contemporary aspects of the diegesis. The use of music, for example, suggests a greater mixing of cultural resonances. If a classically leaning piano-led piece sets the tone under the credits, the dominant presence in the remainder of the film is the distinctly more contemporary tenor of most of the soundtrack, composed by Trent Reznor, founder of Nine Inch Nails, and his collaborator, Atticus Ross.

The associations brought by Reznor, in particular, are very different from those of the established quality tradition or the opening theme. Thumping bass synthesiser pieces are employed to add a driving pace and dynamism to parts of the film, including the sequence that inter-cuts Zuckerberg's creation of Facemash with the party at the Phoenix club. The resonances here are more youth-oriented than those of the older-world more 'official' culture embraced by most of the formal qualities examined above. In one sequence – the montage-like passage relating to a series of emails exchanged between Zuckerberg and the Winklevi – the music combines both this kind of synthesiser-led material and a quiet piano theme of the type featured in the opening titles, a piece that seems to offer an appeal to both cultural constituencies at the same time.

How far the resonances of the music contribute to the broader positioning of the film is a factor that has been discussed by those involved in the project, particularly in the case of the title sequence. The composition used here was one of a number submitted by Reznor and Ross, without being designed in advance to suit any particular footage.[7] Both Reznor and supervising sound editor Ren Klyce say they expected one of the bolder and more strongly dramatic pieces to have been used at the start. An earlier rough cut used a temporary source from an Elvis Costello song which, Reznor suggests, had created a lighter and more casual effect – 'kids at college doing college kids stuff', 'feel-good', 'John Hughes-ish almost' – that would have situated the film rather differently.[8] Sorkin's screenplay had similarly envisaged the use of a 'high energy' song recorded by Paul Young, to create an impression of Zuckerberg's anger after the break-up, the writer also suggesting that the change of tack marked a distinction from the more conventional 'college movie'.[9] This point is germane to other aspects of the way the film positions itself at the level of narrative content and background to the principal events.

The Social Network contains relatively little in the way of typically Hollywood evocation of a student/youth/college milieu. There are some references to the use of initiatives such as Facebook by young men to attract girls for sexual purposes, but this features only peripherally in the depicted events. There are also some scenes of high-jinks of the kind that might be expected in a more typical college movie, such as the Facemash sequence, the shot-drinking that accompanies a contest staged by Zuckerberg to choose two new interns, and the setting up of a zip-wire into the swimming pool of the house at Palo Alto. Material of this kind is no more than occasional and pushed into the background, however. The dominant focus of the film is more akin to the manner in which Zuckerberg is characterised, concentrating on the primary material of the founding of Facebook and the personal and legal battles that result. There is plenty of humour, but it is generally situated as sharp wit, as suggested above, rather than the broader physical, sexual and/or gross-out variety more usually associated with cinematic incarnations of the college milieu that would conventionally be situated at the lower end of the cultural spectrum.

Production history: a 'for love' project?

How, then, did *The Social Network* come into being as an example of Hollywood quality, and to what extent did this represent studio business-as-usual or any special circumstances? The project began with a proposal for the Mezrich book, which entered circulation early in 2009 and initiated two strands of development that appear quickly to have come together.[10] An option on the rights to the book was bought by Dana Brunetti, president of Trigger Street Productions, a company created by the actor Kevin Spacey in 1997. Brunetti and Spacey had produced an earlier film based on a Mezrich book set in somewhat similar territory, *21* (2008), the story of a group of MIT students who employ their talents to earn a fortune playing blackjack. *The Accidental Billionaires* proposal was also picked up by rival producer Michael De Luca. Brunetti and De Luca agreed to cooperate on the project, which was pitched by the latter to Doug Belgrad, co-president of Sony's main film division, Columbia Pictures. According to one report in *Variety*, it was then the decision of the studio co-chair, Amy Pascal, to bring the producer Scott Rudin onto the project on the basis that he would be able to 'deliver' Aaron Sorkin as screenwriter. This, it is suggested, was a key step in making the project more attractive than would otherwise have been the case: 'Suddenly, the Sony brass could envision a pic with nonstop witticisms and fewer keystrokes.'[11] If a film is to be dominated by talk of a kind marked as 'smart', best that it be written by a figure with one of the strongest reputations in the business for delivering such talk. Sorkin's name could also be expected to draw additional attention to the film and to ensure its likely association with the quality end of the Hollywood spectrum.

Sorkin is reported to have read no more than four pages into the 14-page proposal by Mezrich before calling his agent and signing on.[12] The script was written quickly, drawing on the book and on the writer's own research, and completed before *The Accidental Billionaires* was published. A draft was sent to David Fincher (with whom Columbia's other co-president, Matt Tolmach, had an existing relationship), whose established name would add considerable additional weight and recognition to the project.[13] Fincher was reported to have been looking for his next film at the time and to have agreed to direct, on condition that there would not be a lengthy development process of the kind that often characterises studio operations. That is, that 'they didn't wait for eight rounds of development and nine drafts', as the director is said to have put it.[14] A key factor at this point was that Fincher was given the right of approval on the final cut of the film. Somewhat surprisingly, perhaps, this is reported by several sources to have been the first time Sony had given such a right to any director.[15] It was also said to have been a substantial concession for the studio because Rudin was a powerful producer who usually enjoyed final-cut status himself.

The agreement was understood to be contingent on Fincher remaining within the $40 million budget set for the film, a modest figure by contemporary studio standards and a fraction of the $150 million cost of his previous title, *The Curious Case of Benjamin Button*. According to one trade press account, Sony wanted to restrict the budget further, to $25 million, but agreed to come up to the minimum required by the director.[16] The 'final hurdle' to be jumped, according to another report, was 'to persuade Sony of its cast, whose biggest name was music star Justin Timberlake, one hardly synonymous with weighty dramas'.[17] The studio was reported to have accommodated Fincher's desire to have a free hand in casting, in contrast to the situation with his earlier film, *Zodiac* (2007), which had been in development at Sony before disagreement over the same issue led to the director taking the project elsewhere.[18] Another potentially complicating factor, from a legal perspective, was presenting an unflattering portrait of the central character without owning any rights to his story, the producers having been rebuffed in all efforts to gain any cooperation from Zuckerberg. The production appears to have been able to go ahead without such rights because it was able to use material that existed on record from the lawsuits.

That the film was co-financed by the outside investor Relativity Media, one of several such operations mentioned in Chapter 1 as supporters of some examples of quality studio production, suggests a desire to hedge any perceived risk, as was also seen in the larger-scale case of *Inception. Variety* included *The Social Network* among a number of films that were profiled through quotations about the production process by their producers, offering the following characterisation of the way the studio regarded the project (one of several passages collectively attributed to Brunetti, De Luca, Rudin and Fincher's regular producing partner, Cean Chaffin):

> They loved the script from the first draft and wanted to make it in a sane and responsible way, in the same kind of way we did. So once it was agreed we'd do it with David and everyone, we came up with a financial structure that worked for everyone and pulled it together. But it meant everyone taking huge cuts. No one got paid to do it. It was a 'for love' project.[19]

A 'sane' way is, presumably, one in which none of the participants seeks to maximise their own financial rewards to the point at which such a film is pushed in the direction of a budget the material seems unlikely to warrant, or that undermines any realistic chance of success (an example of 'insane' Hollywood, by this measure, would be a situation in which all or some of the principals – star(s), director, etc. – insist on deals so generous to themselves that a project has little potential to profit anyone else). That no one 'got paid' to do the film seems unlikely and to be a hyperbolic claim, even if it might be the case that some of the principals earned less than they might have done elsewhere. By not getting paid, they mean 'not getting paid vast sums' or not receiving their full rates. If it was a 'for love' project, that would appear to apply to the primary filmmakers more than to anyone else. Whether or not that includes the producers quoted here remains open to speculation.

It certainly seems unlikely that *The Social Network* was produced entirely 'for love' on the part of the studio itself; more that a certain 'sane and responsible' mode of production made it seem a reasonably safe prospect for a project that lacked many of the staples of studio output. The latter would include its status as a one-off rather than part of any franchise or as a film without any strong generic hook; its lack of any potential for the provision of spectacle or physical action, in favour of an emphasis on talk; the absence of any big-name star of the kind conventionally seen as being able to 'open' a film or one who seemed a natural fit with the material (i.e. Timberlake not really counting here); its general lack of any sustained romantic dimension; and the presence at its heart of a less than entirely likeable central character. For giving the go-ahead to such a project, Rudin credits the Sony leadership with 'some of the nerviest work on the behalf of a movie by studio heads that I can remember in many years'.[20] What the production did have in its favour was, as *The New York Times* put it, 'all the makings of a prestige project', largely on the basis of the combination of Sorkin and Fincher at the creative core of the picture.[21]

Whether or not, or to what extent, prestige itself might have been a factor for the studio or the executives involved is not the kind of topic that tends to be raised by such figures in discussions of this kind, and so remains subject to more generally informed speculation of the kind attempted in the Introduction to this book. One other possible factor in this case was that Columbia had not enjoyed a Best Picture Oscar success since 1988 (the year before it was bought by Sony), a fact to which attention was drawn by a number of press articles in the run-up to the 2011 awards. *The Social Network* was highly fancied, having picked up several other prizes seen as status markers and indicators of likely success. One commentator referred to the studio as having undergone 'a bothersome Oscar drought', in a context described as one in which 'although focused heavily on broadly commercial movies like Columbia's *Spider-Man* series or *The Karate Kid*, they [the major studios] still love the cachet of a best picture Oscar, not to mention the attendant revenue' and the 'intangible' benefits of awards in attracting desirable top talent in the future.[22] This seems to confirm the argument in the Introduction to this book that such awards do matter to the studios, for reasons both commercial and related to prestige, and potential combinations of the two, and thus that an absence of such prizes for any individual studio might contribute to the motivation behind the production of work at the quality end of the scale.

The Social Network eventually lost the major prize of Best Picture to The Weinstein Company's *The King's Speech* (2010), but the studio was again viewed as offering strong prospects in the following year with 'grown-up' dramas such as *Moneyball, The Ides of March* and the Shakespearean period piece, *Anonymous* (all 2011).The impression was created in some reports of something like a concerted presence of Oscar-hopeful material, although it is notable that one of these begins by quoting Michael Lynton, the chairman of Sony Pictures Entertainment, saying: 'This was not by design', which suggests the absence of any deliberate strategy to this effect, or on this scale. The reference here is to what is described as an 'eruption' of 11 films – the three cited above and eight releases from the speciality division, Sony Pictures Classics – that gave the company a dominant presence at the 2011 Toronto film festival, an event that can play a key role in establishing quality contenders through to the main awards season.[23]

Lynton suggests that the company had never stopped producing what the article describes as 'popular yet sophisticated films'. But it had 'stumbled into a bounty of them this year', with a number of projects that had come together all at once. This might more accurately reflect a reality in which the studios maintain a minority commitment to such work – when what are perceived to be the right combinations of ingredients fall into place – than the kinds of press reports cited earlier in this book that give a more hyperbolic impression of dramatic shifts between the abandonment and support of productions with quality resonances. Fincher himself offers a blunt assessment of the situation, attributing the existence of his film simply to the modest scale of the budget. Asked in one interview if part of the appeal of the project was working on a smaller scale than that of his previous film, he replies: 'No, it's just the reality of making a talky movie about people who aren't wearing spandex or capes.' Hollywood, he suggests, 'has a hard time marketing semi-adult dramas and has no faith that people want to see them, so you have to make them for a price'.[24]

The above sketch of the production history of the film does not suggest anything very far out of the Hollywood norm. But it indicates some nuances that help to create space for such work to appear at the heart of the studio system. As with all the case studies examined in detail in this book, it confirms that more room than usual can occur for certain degrees of departure from the norm when sufficiently powerful individual figures are involved and committed to a particular project. In this case, somewhat unusually, the screenwriter was the first key name to be recruited and to give the project a significant boost and quality imprimatur in its chances of reaching the state of being given the studio green light. The involvement of Sorkin would also appear to have played a strong role in the subsequent recruitment of Fincher, either on the basis of his name, the quality of his screenplay, or a combination of the two. The strength of this team, plus a number of producers with successful studio track records and relationships with those at the top of the executive hierarchy, especially Rudin, also ensured that the project could move ahead more swiftly than was usual for a studio production.

The speed at which the film was developed seems significant on a number of counts. For one thing, it made the film more likely to happen than is often the case in more extended periods of development, during which key talent or supporters can sometimes be lost through reasons including commitments to other upcoming projects or changes of senior studio personnel – factors probably more than usually likely to affect less commercially central quality productions of this kind. It also provided some protection to what might be seen as the integrity of the production, guarding it against the process of multiple rewrites into which many films are forced, as suggested by the terms in which this was put by Fincher in the quotation above about successive rounds of development. In addition, the skirting of such a process also provided another implicit marker of quality in relation to wider discourses surrounding the film – akin to some of those seen in the case of *Inception* – in seeming to separate it from any notion of the 'writing by committee' characterisation of what are seen as more standard Hollywood films. *The Social Network* was viewed from the start as a film written by a clearly marked and distinctively talented individual author/auteur (Sorkin), working with a director who also came with a reputation for being 'his own man' and less likely than usual to be compromised by the sort of commercial-operational dimensions of Hollywood that contribute centrally to its lower cultural associations. The sense of some guarantee of a strong degree of 'artistic' integrity was sealed by Fincher's status as having final cut. This was, as we have seen, conditional on the acceptance of a relatively low budget, by studio standards; but the lower budget itself, and the impression that those involved were making the film 'for love' rather than money, contribute further to the discursive positioning of the film as to some extent beyond the standard studio norm.

At the same time, there was plenty in the development process that was more typically Hollywood in character. The fact remains that *The Social Network* was a project initiated as a film by *producers* rather than by the creative figures who would become associated with its authorship: Sorkin and Fincher. Its starting point was very much in keeping with industrial norms. It is significant here that it did not develop even from a completed book by Mezrich, but from a proposal document that reached a number of Hollywood producers. The phenomenon of producers being on the lookout for upcoming projects of this kind and buying options, many of which are not eventually taken up, is a central part of the business end of studio activity. This stands in contrast to the notion of the more 'organic' development of a work, an issue considered in relation to various historical or contemporary notions of quality in the Introduction and in Chapters 1 and 2. Someone positioning themselves as a defender of the potential for quality within the studios might point to this situation, however, to demonstrate what can still be achieved from within the corporate Hollywood context: that even if not an originating source in this case, a figure such as Sorkin can create distinctive material inspired by a stimulus external to himself and using material brought to him by someone at the more commercial end of the business.

How *The Social Network* might reflect wider Hollywood trends of the time in any of the dimensions of its production considered above was subject to a number of questions raised in the trade press. One article that highlighted the final cut given to Fincher did so in the context of a suggestion that this was a phenomenon that was under threat, in a manner that was situated in relation to a standard opposition between the creative and a focus more solely on the commercial bottom line. For decades, the writer suggested, 'studios have acquiesced to agent demands by allowing high-profile directors the creative freedom to deliver their films as they see it'. In recent years, however, 'studio corporate overlords have become less amenable to risk of any kind and the list of final-cut directors has received a snip of its own'.[25] One unnamed 'studio chief' is quoted as saying that 'in the current climate' directors and stars who might previously have been able to gain such power were now taking a more back-seat position: 'Now, as the financials of the deals have become so much more challenging, creative rights are an afterthought.'[26] Even with those who still were able to get final cut – a list here that includes Peter Jackson, James Cameron, Steven Spielberg, Tim Burton, Clint Eastwood, David Fincher, Michael Bay, Martin Scorsese, Ridley Scott and Ron Howard – it is suggested that certain limitations were enforced, such as pre-negotiated running time, rating and budget limits. The fact that Sony had only recently offered final cut for the first time in the case of *The Social Network* is not viewed as contrary to the wider pattern because of the relatively low budget involved in this case.

Whether or not the business end of studio operation was really tightened up in any significant manner in this period is perhaps open to question. Such accounts have a tendency to exaggerate, similar to those examined in the Introduction that tend to over-state the degree to which Hollywood either does or does not invest in quality productions at any particular moment. This, too, was part of the discursive context in which *The Social Network* was located in the trade press. Peter Bart, in *Variety*, included the film in a round-up of what he termed 'art pictures' that had succeeded at the box office as well as achieving nominations for the Academy Awards of 2011, others including the speciality division releases *The King's Speech* and *Black Swan*. 'When many of the so-called "speciality" film units were shut down by the major studios a few years ago, we were told that the future belonged to the tentpoles, not to art movies,' he suggests.[27] 'But then how does that explain the box office results of several of this year's Oscar nominees', one of which, *The Social Network*, had at this stage achieved a worldwide gross of $200 million? Five examples between them represented a potential $1 billion at the box office, even before taking into account any boost achieved through the publicity that would come with any Oscar wins. If such a market exists, Bart concludes, 'that might provide a good reason to reassess the audience and realign studio spending'.

Another *Variety* feature from the same period speculated that the qualities of some of the films contending for the Academy Awards, including *The Social Network*, might be a product of the impact of 'the kind of intimately filmed, sophisticated storytelling' characterised by the type of contemporary cable TV series cited at the start of this chapter.[28] It also quoted the suggestion by one critic that

> It's notable that a film like 'The Social Network' is being made not by the studio (speciality) divisions that used to exist, but by Sony. Maybe the studios are revising the old calculation that they can't make films that cost in the $20 million–$30 million range.

What seems more likely, again, is that the studios have continued to support such films in certain circumstances of the kind examined above and in the rest of this book. Bart's is a good example of the rhetorical style that often dominates such commentary. A verdict that 'the future belongs to tentpoles', as the core and most important part of Hollywood business, does not seem at all to undermine the potential for *some* more quality-leaning films still to be produced within the same system and on occasion to enjoy more than usual success. The latter might encourage the continued support of such work, or occasional upsurges in its volume – but it would be unrealistic ever to expect this to represent a challenge to the centrality of the franchised tentpole. As suggested in the Introduction, Hollywood is not capable only of pursuing one kind of film, even if certain varieties clearly remain of higher priority than others and if the exact balance might shift as a result of particular strategic or local factors affecting one studio or another.

Another Hollywood trend with which *The Social Network* was more straightforwardly associated was the increasing use of digital cameras, a factor of considerable relevance to its budget, particularly in relation to the shooting preferences of Fincher. Digital was often associated with lower-quality resonances at this period in Hollywood history, as was seen in the previous chapter, in what it was conventionally taken to signify – including excessive malleability in post-production, cost-cutting and/or lesser quality of image – in contrast with production on celluloid or the use of physical rather than digital special effects. In the case of *The Social Network*, however, the fact that the film was shot with digital cameras – albeit high-end, modified versions of the then state-of-the-art RED One camera – was associated to a greater extent with its quality dimensions. It was the fact that the film was shot digitally that enabled Fincher to commit to the film on so relatively low a budget, given his preference for the use of large numbers of takes of every shot. The opening dialogue sequence was staged with two cameras running simultaneously to capture pairs of shots and their reverse counterparts, in an effort to maintain an integrity of performance, itself a marker of quality (of a kind related to a theatrical notion of sustained performance, rather than the fragmented form more typical of film). It was also said to have been staged a total of 99 times, a figure frequently cited in accounts of the production as testament to the meticulous (or, for some, obsessive) nature of Fincher's working methods.

Many other scenes were performed in 20, 30, 40 or more takes, something that would be impossible to achieve on celluloid without a larger budget. As the actors describe it, digital capture permitted large numbers of takes to be performed in quick succession, a process that, although exhausting, gave them an unusual freedom from pressure on any individual take and space for experimentation with different approaches. The associations here are, again, closer to those of working in the legitimate theatre, in which space is available to build a role across multiple performances, if in a somewhat different manner, or in forms of cinema less subject to the pressures created by the presence of large and expensive Hollywood-scale crews. The motivation for this approach on the part of the filmmakers was, they say, partly to tire the performers to the point at which less overt 'acting' was involved and a more casual performance style would result (the kind of approach more often associated, although somewhat differently, with 'heavyweight' art filmmakers such as Robert Bresson or Michael Haneke).[29] No improvisation was permitted at the level of the dialogue itself, however, which was considered to be inviolate, an additional marker of quality distinction in a studio system within which the status of the scripted word is usually low.

The digital medium is also cited positively in relation to the visual style of the film, rather than being seen as a lower-grade factor resulting from budgetary limitations, as is often the case in the indie sector or in the discourses that mourn the passing of celluloid.[30] It is the use of digital that permitted Fincher and cinematographer Jeff Cronenweth to shoot much of the film with the low light levels considered above, and again at relatively low cost (some similar use of digital is found in Fincher's preceding features, *Zodiac* and *The Curious Case of Benjamin Button*). As the director suggests in one of the extras provided with the Blu-ray release, shooting digitally enabled small sources, such as the table and wall units that appear to light sequences such as those set in Zuckerberg's college rooms, really to contribute significantly to the levels required, rather than just to act as dressing. The result was that none of these scenes took more than 20 to 25 minutes to set up, a substantial saving of production time that helped to create scope for the shooting of multiple takes.[31] The footage retains much of the glossily expensive texture associated with the Hollywood mainstream, however, rather than displaying the pixillation or other limitations characteristic of some lower-budget digital work.

A further impression of quality related to coverage of the production process can be found in the emphasis put in some accounts on the three-week period of rehearsal that took place in advance of shooting, and the fact that this took the form primarily of the principals sitting around a table and discussing the script, line by line, rather than involving activities such as the physical blocking-out of performance. Another Blu-ray extra contains substantial footage of this process, in which Fincher is shown closely quizzing Sorkin on various issues, in the presence of the lead performers, as further evidence of what is presented as his commitment to a personal inhabitation of the work.[32] What emerges from such scenes is an impression of intense collaboration between high-status writer and high-status director, something very different from the Hollywood norm in which the writer is treated as second-class citizen and not always even allowed on set. The effect of such paratexts, again, for those who consume them, is to highlight the more-than-usually literary – and therefore quality – status of the film that results.

Release, awards and critical responses

The theatrical release of *The Social Network* was much closer to studio norms, taking advantage of a great deal of advance publicity created by the nature of the subject matter, and its potential for controversy relating to issues of veracity, along with coverage tied to the presence of Sorkin and Fincher. It opened in a substantial 2,771 locations (on an estimated 3,800 screens), a large-scale release, if not quite on the scale of the largest of blockbusters, and was reported to have enjoyed 'vibrant pre-sales' that contributed to an initial weekend gross of $22,445,653, which put it at the number one spot in the charts. The date of the opening (4 October) is significant to our understanding of how the studio decided to position the film, after the end of the summer blockbuster season and in an early-autumn slot, giving it the ability, with full studio resources behind it, potentially to dominate a period usually seen as prime-time for speciality or indie releases, rather than directly taking on Sony's or any other company's summer tentpoles. The total domestic gross was put at $96,962,694. This was considerably less than half of the eventual worldwide total of $224,920,315, suggesting that it was not only action- or star-centred films that could succeed overseas as well as at home.[33]

The Social Network was certainly positioned as a quality production in key aspects of its main marketing materials, even if the scale of release might have suggested otherwise. The trailer begins with a relatively lengthy sequence of images from Facebook itself, before coming to anything from the film, this set to the tones of unusually low-key, piano-accompanied small-choir voices (akin to some of the music from the film) that extend across the whole of the piece. The emphasis of the remainder of the trailer is on establishing the basic narrative framework, a process during which it foregrounds some of the heritage-related texture of the film. The overall effect is distinctly different from the more assertive Hollywood norm, despite the selection of a number of moments of dramatically heightened dialogue. The original poster assumes pre-sold foreknowledge of the subject matter – which forms the main basis of appeal – large text stating the otherwise somewhat oblique 'You don't get to 500 million friends without making a few enemies' appearing across the length of the image, over a head-and-shoulders portrait of Eisenberg-as-Zuckerberg (a blue shade akin to that associated with the social network appears subtly in the right-hand margin). Subsequent US DVD cover artwork adopts a more conventional quality approach, images of Eisenberg in front of other members of the cast being dominated by admiring review quotations that seek to establish the distinctive credentials of the production by labelling it as 'a brilliant film', 'an American landmark', 'revolutionary', 'sensational', 'mammoth and exhilarating' and 'a remarkable rarity in contemporary filmmaking'.

The film was established from ahead of its release as a contender for the 2011 Academy Awards, a key target for most Hollywood quality productions, achieving eight nominations and three wins, the latter unsurprisingly including Sorkin for best adapted screenplay (along with awards for best editing and score). Among the nominees was Eisenberg for best actor, another dimension of the film's quality credentials being critical praise for his performance along with those of Garfield and Timberlake. The timing of the release was such that this was able to contribute little to the theatrical box office, figures cited by Box Office Mojo suggesting that only 1.5 per cent of its takings occurred after the nominations and none after the awards ceremony itself, because these occurred at the very end of the domestic run.[34] Release on DVD was timed to take advantage of any boost from the awards, however, the film going on sale just over a week before the nominations and selling more than half a million in its first seven days.[35]

It is no surprise that the great majority of critics responded positively to the film on the basis of the textual features highlighted above, qualities that gave it a distinctly critic-friendly appeal on various grounds, particularly the display of verbal pyrotechnics that would be expected to be approved by those writing for sources at the more serious end of the market. The review aggregation site Rotten Tomatoes gave a very high score of 96 per cent approval on the basis of a total of 277 notices, with an average rating of nine out of ten, a score that reached a perfect 100 per cent when only what the site considered to be the 18 'top critics' were included.[36] Metacritic came up with similarly high marks (a rating of 95 out of 100), which it termed 'universal acclaim' on the basis of 42 critics.[37] On both sites the scores for ratings by users were also high, if a little less so, at 89 per cent from 131,773 ratings on Rotten Tomatoes and 8.2 out of ten on the basis of 919 responses on Metacritic. Reviews tended to give pride of place to the roles of both Fincher and Sorkin, as would be expected, but it is noticeable that many highlight factors that make the film accessible as much as those that might mark it out as distinctive or of particular appeal to the kind of niche audience that might be attracted to films of an art, indie or Indiewood location.

For *Variety* this latter group, what it terms 'savvy moviegoers' will need 'no persuading' of the merits of the film, while 'critical enthusiasm and sustained media attention should upgrade "Network" to major-player status among the year's fall releases'.[38] The contemporary currency of the subject matter is such, this critic predicts, just ahead of the release, that 'Sony can rely on strong word of mouth to stimulate general interest'. This appears to have been the case, on the basis of the box office performance that followed, and seems to be an assumption around which the initial marketing was designed. While on its own merits it might appeal primarily to the 'savvy moviegoer', however, the film is declared here to be 'terrifically entertaining', a verdict shared by many others who also point out its more distinctive qualities. For Kenneth Turan, in the *Los Angeles Times*, for example, the film is both 'smartly written' by Sorkin and also 'a barn-burner of a tale that unfolds at a splendid clip', 'presenting a story about conflicts over intellectual property as if it were a fast-paced James Bond thriller' (Bond serving in this context as a more positive marker than it does in some of the reviews of *Inception* cited in the previous chapter).[39] Roger Ebert, in the *Chicago Sun-Times*, similarly finds the film to have 'the rare quality of being not only as smart as its brilliant hero' and to be so in the same way ('cocksure, impatient, cold, exciting and instinctively perceptive') and to offer 'spellbinding dialogue', but also to 'make an untellable story clear and fascinating' in a manner that 'we can immediately understand', rather than in a form likely to appeal only to a more restricted audience.[40]

For Manohla Dargis, in *The New York Times*: 'Despite its insistently unsexy moving parts (software, algorithms), the movie is paced like a thriller, if one in which ideas, words and bank books blow up rather than cars.'[41] These are combinations of qualities similar to those identified in the positive responses to *Inception*, examined in the previous chapter, and markers of the particular kind of balance often found in studio quality productions. Dargis also joins other leading critics in emphasising the mixture the film offers of 'a resonant contemporary story' and 'an older, familiar narrative of ambition'. For Turan, 'while nothing is more au courant than the Facebook phenomenon', the film succeeds 'because its story is the stuff of archetypal movie drama'. The latter is also emphasised in reported comments by the filmmakers themselves that seem designed to highlight a wider appeal rather than one limited to those more specifically interested in the timeliness of the Facebook story.[42]

Customer reviews on amazon.com are also mostly positive, with an average score of four out of five stars in a sample of 427 responses.[43] Those who comment positively on the film in relation to its subject matter tend to split between some who focus on what it offers in the particular realm of Facebook, social media or business more generally, and those who emphasise broader issues such as ambition and personal rivalry. It is evident from some of these that the film included plenty to appeal to those *without* any specific interest in the world of social networks and/or computing, as was the declared intention of the filmmakers. The number of positive responses that signify appreciation in distinction-marking terms in relation to quality is a smaller proportion than was the case in relation to *Inception* (only 13 make explicit articulations of this nature; another 20 seem to do so in an implicit manner, a total of 33 that represents just 7.7 per cent of the sample), although many more give high praise to the film without putting it in terms that specifically articulate a notion of superiority to the Hollywood norm. The merits of the film are strongly attributed to Sorkin and Fincher by a larger proportion, the two gaining broadly equal credit (57 positive mentions for Sorkin, 64 for Fincher).

This is an unusual degree of presence for a screenwriter, but unsurprising given the lead set by professional critics and the prominence given to dialogue and/or narrative more generally (but mostly dialogue) among the qualities of the film singled out for praise.

It is also useful to consider the terms in which the film is rejected by its detractors, as these can help to shed light on the limitations of the appeal of films of this kind. A significant minority of 77 reviewers award only one or two stars, of whom 24 (5.6 per cent of the total number of respondents) declare the film to be 'boring' either generally or only in part (mostly the former). Some of these, and some others, suggest that the film is confusing or that the dialogue is unclear and/or hard to follow (in negative terms, rather than as a marker of appreciated quality). A small number (five) complain that the visuals are too dark and indistinct. An interesting split can also be identified among those who comment on the unlikeable manner in which Zuckerberg is characterised. For 21, this is one of the positive attributes of the film, an acknowledgement of what is identified above as one of its markers of quality. For another 15, however, it is a shortcoming and a ground for lack of appreciation that appears to be the result of the difference between this and what might more conventionally be expected of a Hollywood central protagonist. Even if the numbers here are rather small, it seems notable that those who focus on this issue are divided in this way.

Even a brief sketch of these responses offers some evidence for the manner in which a film such as *The Social Network* might be both embraced or rejected on the basis of the dimensions that for some might establish its quality credentials, even if only a small number actually put it in those terms. Less than fulsome responses are far from always this polarised, however. More reviewers give a middling three stars (52) than are found in either the one- or two-star categories. A repeated complaint by many whose responses are neither fully positive nor entirely negative is less about the film itself than the perceived 'hype' with which it became associated, particularly in relation to the Academy Awards and its place at the head of the 'films of the year' lists compiled by many critics. For some of these, the film is merely 'average' or 'ordinary' in quality, rather than an object of either the highest praise or annoyed dismissal.

Notes

1   Michael Z. Newman and Elana Levine, *Legitimating Television: Media Convergence and Cultural Status*, New York and London: Routledge, 2012

2   Three of many examples, two from the *Guardian* newspaper in the UK – Malcolm MacKenzie, 'Kitchen confidential', 21 June 2011, G2 section, p. 20; Emma Keller, 'Dallas is back', 14 June 2012 – the third from the *Los Angeles Times*: Patrick Goldstein, 'The big picture: Hollywood's creative talent wants to be on cable', 26 June 2012, via latimes.com

3   A point made by Sorkin and others in commentary on the Sony Blu-ray release

4   Jeffrey Sconce, 'Irony, nihilism and the new American "smart" film', *Screen*, vol. 43, no. 4, winter 2002

5   For more on this, see King, *Indie 2.0*, Chapters 2 and 5

6   Andrew Higson, *English Heritage, English Cinema: Costume Drama Since 1980*, Oxford: Oxford University Press, 2003

7   This and the following is from a discussion involving Reznor, Ross and Ren Klyce, at http://soundworkscollection.com/socialnetworkpanel

8   Reznor, as above

9   Sorkin, Blu-ray commentary

10   Details that follow are from trade and wider press accounts including: David Carr, 'A zillion friends, and a few enemies', *The New York Times*, 17 September 2010, via nytimes.com; Dave McNary, 'Brunetti finds his Trigger points', *Variety*, 29 November 2010, via variety.com; Tatiana Siegel, 'Being nominated is the best revenge', *Variety*, 15 February 2011, via variety.com; Ian Blair and Anthony Kaufman, 'Producers: In their own words', *Variety* 10 December 2010, via variety.com

11   Siegel, 'Being nominated'

12   Carr, 'A zillion friends'

13   Connection between Tolmach and Fincher is from Andrew Stewart, 'Tolmach leaves Sony on a high note', *Variety*, 1 November 2010, via variety.com

14   Carr, 'A zillion friends'

15   For example, Tatiana Siegel, 'Fade-out on final-cut privileges?', *Variety*, 22 January 2010, via variety.com; and Siegel 'Being nominated'

16   Stephen Galloway, 'David Fincher: The complex mind of "Social Network's" anti-social director', *The Hollywood Reporter*, 2 February 2011, via hollywoodreporter.com

17   Siegel, 'Being nominated'
18   Galloway, 'David Fincher'
19   Blair and Kaufman, 'Producers: In their own words'
20   Quoted in Michael Cieply, 'Columbia Picture hopes to end Oscar drought', *The New York Times*, 2 January 2011, via nytimes.com
21   Carr, 'A zillion friends'
22   Cieply, 'Columbia Pictures hopes to end Oscar drought'
23   See, for example, Michael Cieply, 'Sony slate a big bet on dramas', *The New York Times*, 11 September 2011, via nytimes.com
24   Quoted in Ryan Dombal, 'Interviews: Trent Reznor and David Fincher', Pitchfork website, 27 September 2010, via pitchfork.com
25   Siegel, 'Fade-out on final-cut privileges?'
26   Ibid.
27   Peter Bart, 'Arty hits force rethink', 12 February 2011, via variety.com
28   Robert Koehler, 'Prime time for character', 9 January 2011, via variety.com
29   A point emphasised by Sorkin in Blu-ray commentary
30   See, for example, Manohla Dargis, 'The revolution is being shot on digital video', *The New York Times*, 17 December 2010, via nytimes.com
31   'Jeff Cronenweth, David Fincher on the visuals', special features on Sony Pictures Home Entertainment 'two-disc collector's edition' Blu-ray
32   'How did they ever make a movie of Facebook?' special feature
33   Figures from Internet Movie DataBase (imdb.com) and Box Office Mojo (boxofficemojo.com). On pre-release buzz and advance ticket sales, see Andrew Stewart, 'Will "Social Network" click with audiences?', *Variety*, 30 September 2010, via variety.com. Estimated number of screens involved in the release from Brandon Gray, 'Weekend Report: "Social Network" no wallflower in its debut', Box Office Mojo, 4 October 2010, via boxofficemojo.com. Detail about advance tracking and the association of drama with audiences of 25 and over is from Carl DiOrio, 'Moviegoers will friend "The Social Network"', *The Hollywood Reporter*, 30 September 2010, via thehollywoodreporter.com
34   Figures at http://boxofficemojo.com/oscar/movies/?id=socialnetwork.htm
35   DVD sales information from The Numbers website, accessed via the-numbers.com

36   Entry at http://www.rottentomatoes.com/m/the-social-network/

37   http://www.metacritic.com/movie/the-social-network

38   Justin Chang, 'The Social Network', 21 September 2010, via variety.com

39   Kenneth Turan, 'Movie Review: "The Social Network"', 1 October 2010, via latimes.com

40   Roger Ebert, 'The Social Network', 29 September 2010, rogerebert.suntimes.com

41   Manohla Dargis, 'The Social Network', 23 September 2010, via nytimes.com

42   See, for example, Carr, 'A zillion friends'

43   Sample accessed 10 July 2012, starting at http://www.amazon.com/Social-Network-Two-Disc-Collectors-Edition/product-reviews/B0034G4P7G/ref=cm_cr_dp_see_all_summary?ie=UTF8&showViewpoints=1&sortBy=bySubmissionDateDescending

4

The darkening of genre

The Assassination of Jesse James by the Coward Robert Ford and *Mystic River*

Genre frameworks offer useful points of departure for films that seek to mix the familiar and conventional with various degrees of distinction from the norms of the mainstream. Numerous examples of this approach can be found in the realms of art and indie cinema, along with a variable balance between the employment of convention and ways in which it might be undermined or rendered more complex. The same can be said of the studio quality film, both historically and in some of its contemporary incarnations, including the two main examples considered in this chapter. Although very clearly located within the familiar generic terrain of the western, *The Assassination of Jesse James by the Coward Robert Ford* (2007) is the film that leans furthest in the direction of art or indie cinema of all the case studies examined in this book. It is a production that might have been expected to be a release from a speciality division rather than the main arm of the studio concerned, Warner Bros., an issue considered further below. This is less likely to have been the case with *Mystic River* (2003), for reasons elaborated in this chapter, the generic location of which is within what might be termed the crime melodrama.

Both films offer a dark and sombre approach to their material that marks a significant point of distinction from the dominant associations of studio output. From an industrial perspective, however, a number of differences can be identified between the status of the two Warner productions, which contributes to our understanding of the position occupied by such work within the studio environment. *The Assassination of Jesse James* is an example of some of the troubles that can accompany the emergence of the quality film, including disputes about the nature of its final form and the verdict that it was a commercial failure. *Mystic River* demonstrates a more stable and regularised relationship between the filmmaker, in this case the iconic figure of Clint Eastwood, and his studio base, although even here initial difficulties were experienced in getting the production off the ground. This chapter follows much the same structure as the previous two, initially examining the quality markers offered by each film in turn – including aspects of narrative, visual style and differentiation from more conventional generic traits – before turning to an examination of the production history that might account for their existence as studio features. The analysis of *The Assassination of Jesse James* also includes a more extended discussion of a number of issues relating to notions of the classical and the post-classical, and their association or otherwise with particular forms of cultural value.

The Assassination of Jesse James: narrative distance, denial of generic staples and aestheticisation

If one of the potential markers of quality in *The Social Network* is a degree of distancing from the main diegetic material created through the use of the deposition sequences as sources of narrative organisation, *The Assassination of Jesse James* employs a form of overt narration that is in some respects more familiar as a cinematic device (if not in common usage at the time). It is used, however, in a manner that increases the impression of periodic withdrawal from the events dramatised on screen. Explicit narration is provided in the tones of a clearly marked external narrator, unidentified, who provides a storytelling voice at various intervals during the film. This mode of expression – particularly given the somewhat archaic writing style and the cadences of the voice-over – creates a distinctly literary impression as well as one of elegiac distance from the material, each of which contributes centrally to the quality resonances of the piece. As with *The Social Network*, however, this remains distinct from the ironic form of distance diagnosed in the Sconce variety of the smart film. A notable point of difference from *The Social Network* is that it is in the more distanced mode that the film begins, rather than plunging the viewer into any of its directly represented events, one of a number of markers of the greater claims the film makes to a position closer to the art-film end of the spectrum.

The opening voice-over strikes a markedly literary note in its third-person evocation of Jesse James in the latter part of his life, 'growing into middle age and living then in a bungalow on Woodland Avenue', the first line of the film and of the source novel of the same title by Ron Hansen, from which *The Assassination of Jesse James* is closely adapted. Something akin to a poetic impression is created in some of these lines; for example the slight obliqueness in 'His children knew his leg, the sting of his mustache against their cheeks', a line taken from much later in the book. Jesse had a condition of the eyelids that caused him to blink more than usual, we are told, prosaically enough, but with the additional and more lofty-sounding interpretation that this were 'as if he found creation slightly more than he could accept'. 'Rooms seemed hotter when he was in them', the narrator adds, in more expressive mode, far from the literal evocation of character: 'Rains fell straighter. Clocks slowed. Sounds were amplified.' The words are accompanied here by similarly expressive visual devices, considered in more detail below, such as time-lapse images and a blurring of the edges of the frame. The combination makes a clear pitch for the status of something closer to art cinema than is

the Hollywood norm (including the norms of the historical quality
tradition), an approach sustained in various ways throughout the film.

The voice-over recurs at regular intervals (five times, for example,
in the first 32 minutes), its existence and the particular manner in
which it is employed contributing to the sense of distance created
from the events dramatised on screen. The second instance comes
about 13 minutes in, offering an elegiac note characteristic of much
of the film's mode of expression, in its observation that the train robbery about to be committed by the James gang was to be its last
hold-up, and that all the original members other than Jesse (Brad
Pitt) and Frank (Sam Shepard) were by this time already dead or
imprisoned. A subsequent commentary, accompanied by images of
the departure of Frank, notes that 'Alexander Franklin James' (a formal manner of reference that adds to the sense of distance) would be
in Baltimore when he read about the assassination of Jesse. Even if
the fate of Jesse might already be known to the viewer – and it is, of
course, telegraphed very clearly in the title of the film – it is unusual
in mainstream cinema for so major a plot point to be spelled out so
clearly in advance within the body of the narrative. The overt manner
in which this is enacted adds significantly to the general impression of
distance from the immediate action created by the film. The emphasis
is put on exactly why, how and when Robert Ford (Casey Affleck)
will carry out the deed – and particularly on aspects of character
and attitude as much as events – rather than on whether or not any
such key action will happen. This effect is sustained across the length
of the film and emphasised again in the latter stages as the climactic
event comes closer. A later voice-over tells us that 'the day before he
died was Palm Sunday', before going on to inform us about some of
Robert's actions on that day, heavily foreshadowing how soon the
killing is to follow and underlining the sense of inevitability that over-
hangs the film.

Another marked quality dimension is the general slowness of narrative development, a familiar characteristic of work from the art and
indie film sectors. The first material to be dramatised, for example, is a
sequence on the eve of the train robbery, but one in which the focus
is not on the preparation for action but on dialogue-based character
development. We are introduced to Robert Ford (known generally

in the film as Bob) in the camp of the James gang and as he seeks to ingratiate himself with the brothers. An exchange with Frank is awkward and uncomfortable, as is the characterisation of Bob in general. Frank dismisses the ambition the latter expresses to become a 'sidekick', eventually being sufficiently annoyed to chase him away at gunpoint. Jesse seems more open to Bob's approach. Such exchanges are interwoven with other material including extended sexual banter among other members of the gang: Bob's brother Charley (Sam Rockwell), Jesse's cousin Wood (Jeremy Renner) and Dick Liddil (Paul Schneider). The exchanges between Bob and the James brothers establish a central theme of the film – the desire of the former to align himself with such figures, and a suggestion of some of the personal qualities that might not suit him for such a role – but the development of narrative momentum seems to take second place in such scenes to a more leisurely evocation of character and milieu. This remains the case throughout the lengthy, 160-minute running time of the film, during which a number of tensions are elaborated – sometimes somewhat obliquely, sometimes more directly – between Jesse, Bob and figures such as Charley, Dick and Wood.

The downplaying of major narrative action is a familiar ingredient of films from the art or indie sectors that adopt conventional genre formats as points of departure for their markers of distinction. *The Assassination of Jesse James* takes its place in a tradition of revisionist approaches to the western that stretches from some work of the 1950s to the Hollywood Renaissance of the 1960s and 1970s, and examples from the more recent indie sector such as Jim Jarmusch's *Dead Man* (1995) and Kelly Reichardt's *Meek's Cutoff* (2010). All of these entail some critique of the underlying ideological implications of the genre, although the extent of this varies from one example to another and typically remains implicit rather than overt in contemporary studio examples such as this. A key component of such work is an assertion of greater claims to realism and authenticity than is associated with classic examples of the genre, a claim often rooted in large part in the denial of more conventional and/or heroic forms of action. Only one instance of robbery by the James gang is depicted in *The Assassination of Jesse James*, for example, and one that, although given some mythological dimensions in the manner in which it is shot – particularly the evocation of the approaching train through patterns of light and shadow – appears largely to be unsuccessful in the modest amount of cash found in the mail car safe and unheroic in the brutal pistol-whipping meted out to the chief clerk. Likewise, only one 'shootout' sequence is provided, another instance in which the action is distinctly unheroic and some distance from the classical six-gun play of mythology (the norm for other Hollywood renditions of the Jesse James story is to include a regular supply of both robbery and gunplay, even in Renaissance-era versions such as *The Great Northfield Minnesota Raid* [1972] and *The Long Riders* [1980]). This is an exchange between Dick and Wood, who fire repeatedly at each other in a clumsy, sustained close-range encounter in a bedroom that results in Bob shooting Wood in the head.

Although various motivations are provided for actions such as this – a gradually thickening web of mistrust and suspicion, increasingly but not exclusively directed towards the Ford brothers – the overall impression is one of implacable drift in such directions, rather than a more classical/conventional brand of narrative momentum. The film dwells at length on relationships usually found only as minor sub-plots, if at all, in more conventional Hollywood iterations of the James mythology. The development of events is generally slow and ponderous, and often interrupted by shifts from one element to another. A particularly teasing example of this comes on another occasion that offers the prospect of action closer to the conventional generic scale, in which Jesse takes Ed Miller (Garret Dillahunt) out 'for a ride' – the murderous purpose of which seems clear but the outcome of which is both delayed for some 30 minutes and intertwined, potentially confusingly, with another sequence involving what appears to be a similar threat to Dick.

The downplaying, or in some cases more complex treatment, of what might otherwise be more straightforward generic action is accompanied by mockery of conventional forms of western heroic mythmaking, another familiar ingredient of more or less critically revisionist texts.[1] Hidden away in a shoebox under his bed, Bob has a collection of pulp volumes about the James gang that becomes the subject of a sustained bout of laughter from Charley and Wood, to which Bob reacts with typically childish petulance. Later, Bob himself appears disillusioned, having made a deal with the authorities to seek to bring about the capture of Jesse and feeling increasingly under suspicion. 'You think it's all yarns and newspaper stories', suggests Charley, to which Bob replies: 'He's just a human being.'

How exactly the two central figures of Bob and Jesse are characterised by the film is another clear marker of distinction. If it includes much that puts the viewer at a distance from the action, the opposite pole to this would be the establishment of emotional proximity to the central character, one of the key characteristics of mainstream studio production. Relatively little of this is provided in either case. Jesse is presented in a manner that keeps him at much the same distance as that established in the opening voice-over, with little direct access provided to a sense of his interior emotional experience. In some respects, he is presented as something less than the figure of attractive myth, particularly in occasional moments of brutality, one of which is inflicted on a youth, and in some of his rather doom-laden musings. In others, he remains a larger-than-life figure – implacable in his pursuit of those by whom he feels betrayed and given a presence within the diegesis that generates fear among many of those who come into his orbit; but not really a figure whose feelings the viewer is invited to share.

Bob occupies the position closest to that of the conventional protagonist and with which the viewer is encouraged most closely to become engaged. He is the outsider who works his way into the confidences of Jesse, up to a point at least, structurally located as our *entre* into the same. But, even more so than the Zuckerberg of *The Social Network*, he offers an uncomfortable point of allegiance. From the start, he is positioned as a difficult and awkward figure, a source of embarrassment in his combination of arrogance and ingratiating pusillamity. Frank James might speak for many in his early observation to Bob that 'the more you talk, the more you give me the willies'. We might be able to share some of his reactions at some points, including the increasing threat posed by Jesse in the latter stages of their relationship, but we might also feel much of this to be deserved. The characterisation, and the particular nature of the performance by Affleck – who captures strongly both the vulnerable and the dislikeable qualities of Bob – is such as to encourage a much greater distance

Figure 4.1. Uncomfortable protagonist: Bob Ford (Casey Affleck) giving Frank James (Sam Shepard) 'the willies' in *The Assassination of Jesse James by the Coward Robert Ford* © Warner Bros. Entertainment Inc. and Virtual Studios LLC

than would be the norm for a Hollywood protagonist, a clear and central contribution to the quality credentials of the film (see Figure 4.1).

Further adding to the quality associations, and slowing the sense of narrative momentum, are various digressions that contribute to the sombre and brooding nature of the film, including musings that are pitched at the kind of 'philosophical' level seen in some parts of the opening voice-over. What access we are given to the interior state of Jesse's mind comes partly from this distanced source and partly from his own comments. After the beating of the youth he breaks down in tears. The voice-over elaborates that he was sick, suffered from insomnia and read various omens of bad luck. Jesse refers to having out-of-body experiences and, while journeying with Charley across a frozen riverbed, he asks the latter if he ever considered suicide, adding that, 'You won't mind dying once you've peeked over the other side.' Such passages contribute to a generally doom-laden atmosphere that characterises much of the film, underpinned by a bleak and often mournful soundtrack, and to a growing impression that Jesse eventually seeks his own demise. In the characterisation of both figures, the film seems to invest in notions of psychological depth in a manner similar to some of the higher-prestige westerns of the 1950s, notably the moody performance of Paul Newman used to provide distance from the mythology surrounding another legendary figure, William 'Billy the Kid' Bonney, in *The Left Handed Gun* (1958).

Clear markers of quality/distinction are also provided in the visual style of the film, which operates in close conjunction with many of the aspects of narrative outlined above, including the creation of impressions of distance from the main unfolding of events. A number of stylised effects are used, often during the voice-over sequences, contributing in large degree to their generally 'arty' associations. The opening images, after which the initial voice-over begins, are time-lapse sequences of clouds in rapid movement against the sky, variations of which are used on other occasions during the film. Such images create a broadly other-worldly impression, a general sense of temporal dislocation perhaps, as well as being aesthetically pleasing in their own right and suggesting something beyond an immediately realistic rendition (time-lapse photography has been used to generally similar effect in numerous other instances, including examples from the American indie sector such as *Boys Don't Cry* [1999], *LIE* [2001] and some of the films of Gus Van Sant).

In some of the images that follow the opening time-lapse, of Jesse and his home and family, a noticeable blur or distortion is present in the lateral margins of the frame, another device employed regularly in such sequences during the film. The effect is again one of rather general stylisation, but it also contributes to the sense of distancing from the action, through the attention that might as a result be drawn to the frame, as if the images are being viewed through an additional lens of nostalgic removal (the effect was created through adaptations including the mounting of an extra lens in front of the camera).[2] A partial source of motivation for such an effect is introduced when some images are taken through the distorting lens provided by the imperfections in nineteenth-century window panes, a combination in this case of expressive touch and the making of claims to historical verisimilitude at the level of background detail and texture. Additional time-lapse sequences contribute something closer to an abstract impression, in images of patches of shadow and light moving and flickering in otherworldly fashion through the spaces of a Kansas City home abandoned by Jesse and his family, in this case seeming to

evoke something of the preternatural ability suggested by his decision to leave shortly before the capture of four members of the train
robbery gang.

Many of the interior sequences of the film share some of the visual qualities of *The Social Network* in their use of warm brown and
golden tones, with subtle, low-key lighting that gives the impression
of coming from small gaslight sources (elements that were augmented
through the use of stronger concealed bulbs). But the film also reaches
for more pronounced chiaroscuro effects in some sequences, particularly in night-time exteriors where lighting is motivated by lanterns.
This seems in keeping with the generally stronger claims to art-film
status made by the production. The early sequences in the woods
include much that is carefully back- or rim-lit, displaying 'magical
hour' qualities of cinematography that are within the bounds of regular convention. Such impressions are considerably heightened, however, once darkness falls. One shot here, the first in this sequence,
is illustrative of many in the film, employing an extreme version of
chiaroscuro (literally, 'light-dark') in which a small number of elements
are picked out in golden or golden-brown light against an impene-
trably dark background (see Figure 4.2). In this case the diegetic light
sources are two lanterns, one at mid-screen in the right foreground,
the other in the lower left, further back and less pronounced. The
brighter of the lanterns casts its strongest light onto the trunk of a
tree that is rendered gold on one side and that divides the right half
of the screen into two. To the left of the trunk the face of Frank James
is visible, a brown-toned mask appearing as if out of a black void,
cut off at the top by the darkness of his hat, his lined features etched
deeply by shadow lines. Part of his wrist and hand is visible below. To
the other side of the tree is another face, set a little further back and
less clearly lit. A third visage is faintly visible to the left side of centre
screen, apparently taking its light from the same source. A fourth, and
part of the accompanying bodily clothing, can just be discerned to the
extreme left, in the vicinity of the secondary light source.

The following shot captures two of the gang members from closer
range. A lantern source at the extreme left edge makes visible the faces
of Wood and Charley, along with the pale brown of the hoods they
wear around their necks in preparation for the robbery, and the hand

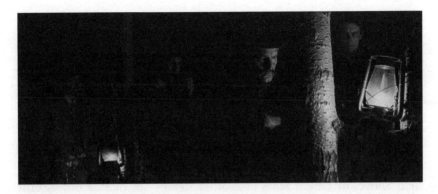

Figure 4.2. Expressive chiaroscuro: extreme contrast in the woods in *The Assassination of Jesse James by the Coward Robert Ford* © Warner Bros. Entertainment Inc. and Virtual Studios LLC

and a stick held by the former (see Figure 4.3). Neither of these shots is held for particularly long, but the effect here and in other examples is striking and seems quite overtly to make claims to the status of a form of quality production that carries broadly – and maybe also some more specific – artistic associations. How, then, might the effect of this be understood further? The resonances of the less heightened version – the use of muted dark backgrounds and golden highlights more generally – were considered in the previous chapter, as evoking a broad if rather vaguely artistic impression, as part of a definition of quality marked by characteristics such as subtlety and nuance, designed to meet what might be positioned, hierarchically, as a more 'cultivated' taste. Much the same might be said of this version as found in *The Assassination of Jesse James*, in interiors such as the dinner table sequence at Bob's sister Martha's house. A general impression of greater-than-usual care is suggested in the lighting tones of such material, which is also marked in its establishment of a 'period' impression – period drama itself, in many cases, being located closer than most studio production to the quality end of the scale. The film positions itself in many ways as a Victorian period piece as much as a genre production, buying into the higher cultural associations of the former and distinguishing itself from the conventionally lower status of the latter.

The quantity of darkness involved in the more heightened examples of chiaroscuro might be related to the thematic dimension of the film – the sense of impending doom that lingers over the entire affair. This is a key marker of quality, both generally and as reflected in some of the attitudes attributed to Jesse. A similar impression is created by the spare, cold and bleak nature of much of the music, in tones that echo the general mood but in a manner that seems to contribute to the overall effect of distancing from, rather than melodramatic heightening of, the events on screen. The most striking imagery might also draw on some more specifically artistic associations, particularly in the exaggerated use of dark and light. Images such as those examined above, in which faces and other details are picked out against very dark backgrounds, seem to invoke a distinctly painterly tradition, alongside the literary associations created by the distanced and sometimes slightly archaic language used in the voice-over. The associations here are those broadly of the 'Old Master' tradition, in general, or more particular sources in the work of artists such as Rembrandt or Caravaggio (see Figure 4.3). These are frequent reference points in claims made for higher status on the part of the art of the cinematographer, in Hollywood or beyond, Caravaggio being credited with having played the most prominent role in the spread of extreme chiaroscuro as a major artistic device. The resonances attached to the work of Caravaggio might seem particularly apt to the use of such an approach in a film of this kind, a defining characteristic of his painting being an association with a grittily realistic depiction of biblical or mythic figures, often situated in contrast to a rival tradition of classical idealisation. It might not be going too far to draw a parallel in some respects between this and the attitude towards a mythologised figure such as Jesse James taken by *The Assassination of Jesse James*, along with other revisionist versions of the western, although the broader 'artistic' or 'painterly' associations are more likely to be in play for most viewers than anything so specific.

A moderate use of this kind of lighting – the sculpting of figures through local and/or directional light sources – is more widespread in cinema. This includes plenty of examples of the Hollywood blockbuster (from *Inception* to what are positioned as lower-status productions, such as the films of Michael Bay) and others in which the connotations might not be anywhere near those of Old Master painting or the art film. Expressive lighting involving the use of high contrast

Figure 4.3. 'Old Master' resonances? A closer-shot example of strong chiaroscuro in *The Assassination of Jesse James by the Coward Robert Ford* © Warner Bros. Entertainment Inc. and Virtual Studios LLC

and dark shadows has a long history in American film, dating back to examples including crime melodrama from the nineteen-tens.[3] Such effects gained higher cultural resonances in some cases in Hollywood horror and film noir in the 1930s and 1940s, when associated with works of German Expressionism from the 1920s (the context of the release of *Sunrise*, considered in the Introduction). Some Hollywood productions of this kind were subsequently accorded higher status than their generic location might otherwise be expected to dictate. This remains the case despite the fact that their heritage was more mixed and less acknowledgement given to their domestic forerunners, texts that drew on a style widespread in popular cultural realms such as theatrical melodrama and graphic illustration.[4]

A number of different functional imperatives can be identified for the style of lighting employed in *The Assassination of Jesse James* (or any other example), as suggested by Patrick Keating in his study of Hollywood lighting in the studio era. Four key factors outlined by Keating are: the demands of storytelling; the making of various claims to the status of realism; the creation of an impression of glamour, particularly in relation to the figure-lighting of the star; and the provision of pictorial quality in its own right. These imperatives might overlap, permitting the same lighting to accommodate more than one, but can also come into conflict. A studio might want the emphasis to be put on selling the glamour of an in-house star, for example, while a cinematographer or director might want to create a more realistic or narrative-based effect. This might result in various forms of compromise or the innovation of new techniques, but one might ultimately be favoured over the other. As Keating suggests elsewhere, contemporary Hollywood cinematographers are generally likely to sacrifice the glamour lighting that was a major norm in the classical era in the name of realism, the work of Gordon Willis in the first two *Godfather* films (1972, 1974) often being cited as playing an important role in the transition from one approach to the other (further examples in which a higher cultural status was attributed to works of otherwise lower generic associations).[5]

In the era of silent Hollywood, Keating suggests, the cinematographers' trade body, the American Society of Cinematographers (ASC), promoted an eclectic set of aesthetic ideals that could embrace all four of the imperatives identified above. This was a period in which the body sought to construct a new and higher status for the role, one that included notions of artistic talent as well as technical skill – an early example of the making of higher quality claims on the basis of the medium/institution as a whole. After the coming of sound, its discourse became more closely allied to the notions of what became known as the classical Hollywood style, with an emphasis on the invisibility of technique and its role in the support of narrative. Cinematography became an art of balancing the various imperatives, as Keating puts it. In the late 1930s and 1940s, he suggests, developments including the use of Technicolor and deep-focus photography created new possibilities that were, in some cases, integrated into the classical style but in others led to a pushing of its limits through the intensification of one function or another, 'making the film more expressive, more realistic, or more pictorial'.[6] Cinematographers are divided by Keating into two broad groups: those who work at the centre of the classical style, seeking an optimal balance between different imperatives; and those who operate at the margins, 'favouring a mannered approach that sacrifices certain functions in order to intensify others'.[7]

The latter is a context in which we might usefully situate *The Assassination of Jesse James*. The visual style of the film appears to be driven by three of the imperatives identified by Keating. It makes claims to the status of realism, in the apparent replication of low-level diegetic light sources (akin to those found in *The Social Network*) and in the rendition of the general texture of the diegetic universe as that of a western-as-period-piece. The style also appears to reinforce key narrative attributes, including the establishment of mood – in a film in which this dimension is quite strongly to the fore – as well as at the more basic level of ensuring the clarity of key story events and the delineation of character. Little is found in the way of traditional glamour lighting, as might be expected in a feature of such downbeat qualities, although this would be less likely anyway in the contemporary era and particularly for a film whose star is male. As Keating suggests, even at the height of the studio era the norm was for male stars to be given harsher lighting of the kind generally found here (to emphasise facial lines and 'character'), rather than the softer and more frontal illumination provided for the idealisation of female stars. Some of the low-key directional lighting of figures or faces might create an element of glamour or prettifying of a somewhat different nature. But the film also reaches quite clearly to establish pictorial qualities ('painting with light', as the cliché goes) of the variety outlined above. Of the four imperatives, the latter appears to be the one given greatest prominence in some of the most heightened sequences. The more extreme examples of chiaroscuro are still motivated to some extent on the basis of verisimilitude, however, in relation to the presence of small diegetic light sources, which ensures that some balance is retained. They are also sequences in which narrative material is developed, without directly being hampered in any significant manner by the style. But the effect in these instances, and other examples such as the edge-blur effect and time-lapse photography, might be so pronounced as potentially to gain attention in its own right and to appear to be motivated artistically; that is to say, as material that seems to exist in order to create a striking effect for its own sake, drawing attention to the formal qualities of the work and/or the skills of its creator, rather than being (entirely) subordinated to any other rationale.

How far this mixture remains within the bounds of classical Hollywood balance is open to question. The precise point at which such constraints are exceeded, or how much can be contained within them, has been the subject of much academic debate and disagreement.[8] The prominence on some occasions of the pictorial, or that which might appear to be artistically motivated is sufficient to give the film something of the status of the *mannerist*, however, the term from art history employed by Keating to describe films that push the limits of the classical style through the intensification of the realist, the expressive or the pictorial. In its art historical usage, the term describes certain works produced between the periods of the High Renaissance and the Baroque, and is associated with heightened or ornamental forms that depart from notions of classical harmony and restraint.[9] It is also used more widely, as here, to suggest such qualities in a broader sense, not limited to any specific period or medium. Keating's key intervention into debates about the nature of the classical is to suggest that expressive lighting, in a more general sense, was central rather than marginal to the classical style of the studio era. Rather than being an exception, primarily limited to generically motivated realms such as horror and noir, he suggests that the expressive was a core component of the approach that became institutionalised within the industry via the services of the ASC.[10] Expressivity, in the sense in which it is used here – to mean the underlining of emotionally charged situations – is seen as an approach entirely compatible with the classical emphasis on both storytelling and general invisibility of style.

A distinction is made by Keating between this understanding of the expressive and more heightened and foregrounded forms such as are found in parts of *The Assassination of Jesse James* and in capitalised formulations of Expressionism.[11] Lighting can be expressive, in a manner that underpins the emotions of a sequence, without being drawn overtly to the attention of the viewer. This is the case in most of the instances considered so far in this book, and in the other example examined in this chapter, in which the visual impression of quality is likely to be subliminal rather than pronounced. Such an approach can be distinguished from more exaggerated forms including some of the usage of chiaroscuro in *The Assassination of Jesse James*, which would seem to qualify for Keating's notion of the mannerist. This remains a matter of degrees, however, as are all the markers of quality examined in this book, rather than any total departure from various options provided by the classical repertoire. The model employed by Keating provides a direct connection to the tradition of painting cited above, based as it is on a formulation from the art historian E.H. Gombrich. For Gombrich, a similar blend of difference *and* continuity characterises the distinction between the painting of the Renaissance and that of Mannerist or Baroque artists, the latter including Caravaggio.[12] This is a more subtle difference, Gombrich suggests, based on differing *degrees* of balance, than the clearer-cut distinction established by an art history tradition according to which one is labelled classical and the other anti-classical. The argument here is clearly resonant with those about the status of the classical and post-classical in film style.

In Keating's account, the mannerist heightening of certain imperatives entails some degree of sacrifice of others, including, potentially, some of the basic principles of cinematography such as the employment of lighting that creates an impression of depth in the image and the three-dimensional modelling of figures or objects. Some such sacrifice can be identified in the two instances of extreme chiaroscuro examined above. In the first shot, of faces and other details lit against large expanses of black, a flattening of background results, even if the light maintains a clear sense of dimensional modelling in the faces that are given the strongest illumination. The second, a closer two-shot, is flatter than its longer-shot predecessor, in the areas picked out by the light. But this, in itself, is in keeping with classical convention, according to which less depth of field is customarily employed in closer shots, to put the emphasis on more specific detail. Some sacrifice of narrative clarity is also involved in the former of these two examples, in which not all the figures are fully recognisable, although the images remain narratively located as part of the period of quiet that precedes the train robbery. More substantial narrative development is sustained entirely clearly in the sequence that follows, in which similar extremes of light and shadow offer heightened dramatisation (rather than detracting from the depiction) of the moments leading up to the arrival of the train and the expressive rendition of its progress via the light shining through the trees.

Other basic functions of classical lighting elaborated by Keating are also maintained through the entire passage: the clear establishment of temporal and spatial location (the passage from rim-lit evening to the darkness of night, along with an outdoor location in which sources of artificial lighting are limited). Such functions are easily overlooked, in what might appear to be their very obviousness. This demonstrates Keating's argument about the extent to which even effects at the mannerist end of the scale can also serve, or be at least partially motivated by, more conventional purposes. The same can be said of some of the other stylised imagery used in the film (as was suggested above), such as the time-lapse sequence in the Kansas City house that stands out quite prominently from the norms of classical style but also seems to be motivated thematically, through an invocation of a sense of otherworldliness.

Distinctions such as those made between the 'classical' and 'post-' or 'anti-classical' also tend to bring with them judgements about cultural value of the kind that are at the heart of the issues addressed by this book. 'Classical' implies a number of positively coded resonances, drawn in large part from associations with the classical antiquity of ancient Greece and Rome, a period to which some look back as a lost golden age and one that has had a huge influence on Western art as well as broader cultural and political discourse. The Latin term from which it is derived implies something of first-class quality, an attribute originally reserved for a limited corpus of work but subsequently more loosely ascribed to a wider range of material seen as representing an established and exemplary standard.[13] In David Bordwell's influential usage, in one of his contributions to *The Classical Hollywood Cinema: Film Style and Mode of Production to 1960*, 'classical' suggests 'decorum, proportion, formal harmony, respect for tradition, mimesis, self-effacing craftsmanship, and cool control of the perceiver's response'.[14] Against such a measurement, that which disrupts the positive sense of balance conveyed by these terms is liable to be judged negatively unless the grounds on which the judgement is based are overtly challenged. The notion of the classical carries considerable evaluative baggage, in other words, of the kind associated with claims to a particular social/class status, most obviously rooted in the possession of cultural capital gained from traditional elitist – 'classical' – forms of education, although also diffused more widely in prevailing hierarchies and institutionalised cultural assumptions.

It is for this reason that qualities identified with the classical can be viewed as markers of distinction, particularly in a contemporary

Hollywood context in which the classical is often viewed (with much exaggeration) as being under threat from sources such as some of those considered in Chapter 1, including a supposedly post-classical (i.e. unbalanced, indecorous, disproportioned) emphasis on spectacle or that which is embraced by the notion of intensified continuity. Other markers of quality distinction might also be challenged, however, if they are viewed as involving departure from classical notions of balance and are thus criticised for being 'showy' and drawing attention to themselves (not 'self-effacing craftsmanship'). Hence the often less positive associations of terms such as 'mannerist' and 'baroque', the connotations of which in general usage tend to imply qualities of excess and extravagance. While the latter might be valorised in their own right (as has certainly been the case in some strands of film theory, particularly that which claims a radical potentiality in the notion of 'excess'), such a position generally has to be asserted against the grain of prevailing Western cultural-value hierarchy, in which the classical tends to be situated in opposition to negatively valued notions such as the 'vulgar' or otherwise imbalanced, issues to which we return in Chapter 6.

A more positive characterisation of the 'post-classical' is offered by Eleftheria Thanouli, in reference to a more overtly expressive sample of films ranging from the mannerist end of the Hollywood spectrum to the more commercial regions of the art or indie spheres.[15] Characteristics identified by Thanouli include a strengthening of artistic motivation, in a usage of overt reflexive devices (a characteristic example is *Amélie* [2001]) that has implications such as a more fluid and expressive rendering of cinematic time and space (including some uses of intensified continuity). These are related to particular conjunctures of the commercial and the artistic – such as aspects of recent European, Brazilian, Hong Kong and American cinema – similar in some respects to those considered here, although generally leaning some way further towards the 'artistic' than is usually the case in studio quality production. The two principal Hollywood manifestations cited by Thanouli are *Natural Born Killers* (1994) and *Fight Club* (1999), films that opt for a more artistically intensified form of expression, especially the former, than is the norm even at the quality end of the mainstream spectrum. Whether or not the combination of textual characteristics she identifies is sufficient to constitute a distinctive narrative mode is open to question. Whether it is helpful to bracket off a particular portion of the cinematic spectrum and give it so grand a title seems highly debatable to me, even if the particular blend of characteristics identified by Thanouli, in a particular body of work, remains of interest and significance.

An in some ways similar argument in favour of the existence of the post-classical, attributed particularly in this case to the influence of music video, is made by Carol Vernallis in another account that draws on a range that includes certain highly stylised studio, indie, Indiewood and overseas productions.[16] It is again questionable, I would suggest, whether the examples of 'intensified audiovisual aesthetics' identified by Vernallis are sufficient to constitute a whole new stylistic regime. This might remain a question of balance and degree, which are likely to be variable from one instance to another. As far as quality designations and cultural hierarchies are concerned, however, the films identified as key examples by Thanouli and Vernallis include some that are of interest here because they were subjected to mixed critical responses, partly on the basis of their blending of characteristics associated with art cinema and what some considered to be more 'excessive', 'flashy' or overly commercial stylistic traits (for example, *Natural Born Killers*, *Amélie* and *Moulin Rouge!* [2001]).

More convincing than the use of the term post-classical for such films in the studio context is Adrian Martin's argument that qualities such as the classical and the mannerist co-exist, sometimes quite flexibly, in the Hollywood of recent decades, rather than being as radically opposed as is often implied. Martin identifies three tendencies: films that embody classical restraint and balance in the relationship between style and meaning, in which the former is closely related to the latter but in a manner that does not draw attention to itself; those in which a broader fit can be identified 'between elements of style and elements of subject', such that general strategies of style enhance or reinforce the general 'feel' or meaning of the subject matter; and mannerist films, 'in which style performs out on its own trajectories, no longer working unobtrusively at the behest of the fiction and its demands of meaningfulness'.[17] These practices are associated by Martin with particular filmmakers, but he suggests that many 'wander between these categories, and also mix them up in hybrid forms', a more balanced understanding than that which associates each with a particular era or epoch. It is far from necessarily the case that the most heightened uses of form will fall into the mannerist category as defined in these terms, given its potential still to be motivated by aspects of subject matter such as subjective character experience.

Where exactly a more sober example such as *The Assassination of Jesse James* might be located, within oppositions between the classical and the excessive or showy, remains open to interpretation given the extent to which some of its more pronounced visuals remain balanced by other functions. It would be unlikely to be located at the more extreme end of the cinematically excessive that has been celebrated by some scholars, particularly in relation to the transgressions of dominant norms manifested by some examples of cult film. A number of prominent journalistic critics responded negatively to some of its visual qualities, however, implicitly mobilising the kind of discourse outlined above as they situated it towards the end of the spectrum at which the artistic is judged to give way to the excessive or the indulgent. Manohla Dargis, in *The New York Times*, for example, suggests that the visuals 'often dazzle and enthrall' but counters this with criticism typical of such discourse, suggesting that the images

> also distract and, after a while, help weigh down the film, which sinks [i.e. being unbalanced] under the heaviness of images so painstakingly art directed, so fetishistically lighted and adorned, that there isn't a drop of life left in them.[18]

For the *Los Angeles Times*, Kenneth Turan finds director Andrew Dominik's 'self-consciously artistic style' hard to digest. While cinematographer Roger Deakins is credited for 'some remarkable images', Dominik is taken to task for a directing style considered to be 'unrelievedly languid and overblown', drama taking 'a back seat to artifice and indulgence'.[19] Stephanie Zacharek, on the Salon website, suggests, along similar lines, that the film 'is so finicky it feels more like a doily than a western'.[20] Anthony Lane, in *The New Yorker*, adopts more directly the category suggested by Keating, in reference to the use of the edge-blur 'period' effect. At first 'this glance at the photographic

Figure 4.4. 'Perfectly judged' or a 'lapse' into mannerism? An example of the stylised edge-blur effect in *The Assassination of Jesse James by the Coward Robert Ford* © Warner Bros. Entertainment Inc. and Virtual Studios LLC

manner of the period is perfectly judged'; 'after it has been used a dozen times, however, it lapses into a mannerism' (see Figure 4.4).[21]

Michael Cimino's epic western *Heaven's Gate* (1980) is among a number of works cited in relation to *The Assassination of Jesse James* by critics (not necessarily in positive terms), one of several sources identified by Dominik and Deakins themselves as direct influences on the look of the film.[22] These combine the resonances of two of the imperatives outlined by Keating: the realistic/historical and the expressive/pictorial (the filmmakers focus, as might be expected, on more immediate precedents, rather than the longer artistic tradition invoked in places above). Sources of a realistic/historical nature include a number of period photographs. Those of the expressive/ pictorial variety include *Heaven's Gate* and *Days of Heaven* (1978), two late Hollywood Renaissance productions that similarly combine western settings with leanings towards the art-cinema end of the spectrum, each of which received a combination of praise and criticism for its pictorial (or pictorially excessive) qualities. Echoes of both can be identified in Dominik's film, including some of the more expressive skyscapes and images of wind-blown wheat fields (*Days of Heaven*) and the use of warm local light sources in night-time interiors (*Heaven's Gate*).

The darkness of the imagery was deliberately enhanced in post-production, along with a desaturation of colour, through the use of a partial bleach-bypass during the treatment of the negative, a technique that involves a reduction of one of the normal stages of processing. This is another approach that contributes significantly to the quality associations of the film, at the level of visual texture, one that tends to be used by a limited number of more expressive filmmakers and that is often viewed as risky by studio executives when applied to the original negative, as was the case here. If the pronounced use of the chiaroscuro that results from this and other effects is not unique to films that position themselves in the quality arena, it seems to contribute significantly to such resonances in a case such as this in which similar associations are created by other dimensions of the work, in both narrative material, mode of narration and other visual qualities.

The Assassination of Jesse James also shares with *The Social Network* a less overtly evident reliance on broadly classical shot structure and editing regimes, the pace of which is in keeping with the narrative design and a considerable distance from the style of intensified continuity. The camera moves fluidly in some sequences, including a Steadicam that tracks Bob's initial movements into the James gang camp and the use of a crane for some higher perspectives. Much is also shot statically, however, or with just minor adjustments of framing, including conventional usages of medium- and close-range pairs of shots and reverse-shots to handle dialogue exchanges between characters. Sequences involving groups, such as those involving the musings of Charley, Dick and others before the train robbery, are laid out in classically careful compositions. No evidence of intensified continuity is found in the film's more dramatically/action-heightened sequences. A very slight hand-held unsteadiness is detectable on occasion during the train robbery, but not in any pronounced manner. The same is the case when the camera moves into carriage aisles, as members of the gang steal from passengers, but without any of the exaggerated rush that would characterise an intensified rendition. One quick pan is inserted into the shootout sequence that leads to the death of Wood, but this, again, is a passing moment in material that is handled in a relatively understated manner. The camera moves to capture the movements of Dick and Wood as they fire on one another, the former squirming in mid-shot along the floor, the latter at the same scale in answering shot, in neither case doing more than to follow the action in broadly classical fashion.

Emphatic cutting and movement to closer shots is used in a sequence in which Jesse holds a knife to Bob's throat (purportedly acting out how he intends to threaten a bank clerk in an upcoming robbery), but this also seems entirely within the bounds of classical norms. The assassination of Jesse itself is shot in a slightly stylised manner, the emphasis of which is on the creation of distance from the action rather than the heightened impression of mobile presence characteristic of the intensified style.

Mystic River: the darkening and thickening of a police procedural

Mystic River has some elements in common with *The Assassination of Jesse James*, in particular its dark, sombre tone and the creation of an impression of seemingly inevitable drift towards further tragedy, in this case partly as a result of the weight carried by events from the past. It obeys the usual conventions of the crime film to a greater extent than *The Assassination of Jesse James* does those of the western, in terms of familiar procedural elements, but with a thickness of gloom and character texture that marks it to some extent as beyond the regular Hollywood norm. The latter dimension also provides scope for emotive performances of the kind likely to attract major awards attention, as proved to be the case: a more traditional aspect of the quality dimensions of the film.

A crime is at the heart of the narrative dynamic of *Mystic River*: the murder of 19-year-old Katie Markhum (Emmy Rossum), daughter of one of the three main protagonists, the tough Boston former criminal Jimmy (Sean Penn). The other two main figures are Jimmy's childhood friends, now estranged: Sean (Kevin Bacon), a homicide detective put on the case, and Dave (Tim Robbins), who appears never fully to have recovered from the trauma of being kidnapped and sexually abused as a child. A key marker of distinction is the sympathetic space the film allows for the figuration of Dave, despite growing suspicion – both within the diegesis and that encouraged on the part of the viewer – that he might be the killer. This eventually proves not to be the case, but the revelation of the truth comes very late in the film and only after the viewer has been offered an uncomfortably uncertain relationship with the character, a factor that gives the film something in common with the use of less than conventionally appealing protagonists in both *The Social Network* and *The Assassination of Jesse James*.

The opening 35 minutes, in which the initial scenario is elaborated, is handled in a classically conventional narrative manner, more so than is the case in either *The Social Network* or *The Assassination of Jesse James*, even if with a tone that marks a location at what presents itself as the more seriously dramatic end of the crime movie spectrum. Like *The Assassination of Jesse James*, *Mystic River* makes quite clear claims to the status of a variety of realism at the level of its depiction of a specific milieu, in this case the markedly blue-collar landscape of an old Boston neighbourhood, the confines of which stand in contrast to the spacious suburban or glossy urban settings more typical of contemporarily set studio output. A prologue sequence establishes an historical background to the relationship between the three principals within this terrain: the childhood kidnapping of Dave, while playing with the other two; and the sense, developed later in the film, that any one of their lives could have been different had they been the unlucky victim on the day.

The articulation and foreshadowing of events leading up to the discovery of Katie's body is in keeping with classical convention, full of closely interwoven hints and intimations of things to come (that some of these seem deliberately designed to mislead also remains conventional within the genre territory). We learn that Katie is to go out that night with friends and that she is very close to her father, along with the fact that Jimmy does not approve of her secret boyfriend Brendan (Tom Guiry). We see Dave with a friend in a bar, at which Katie and her friends arrive, noisily dancing on the counter. Dave mentions that he has known her since she was a kid, at which point the camera moves in closer as his eyes, looking upward in Katie's direction, swivel down, up, and down again, creating a shifty and uncomfortable impression. The next scene has his arrival home at 3am, hands covered in blood, saying 'I fucked up' and seeming less than convincing in his story to his wife Celeste (Marcia Gay Harden) of having been attacked by (and subsequently having probably killed) a mugger. A strong seed is thus planted for the suspicion that he is the killer of Katie, even though any such fate is yet directly to be suggested on her part.

Hostility is subsequently confirmed between Jimmy and Brendan (and discomfort on the part of Jimmy towards the latter's mute younger brother, Silent Ray [Spencer Treat Clark]), for no clear reason, establishing a line of suspicion relating to Brendan but offering no basis for what will prove to be his lateral connection to the crime. Various other foreshadowings are offered, including a number of significant looks from Jimmy that contribute to the eventual confirmation of Katie's fate. Plenty of 'police procedural' material is also provided as the investigation develops. If Dave is positioned as one suspect, connections to Brendan establish an alternative line of inquiry.

Parallel narrative crosscutting is used in a manner that is, again, mainstream-conventional, both generally and in the generic territory, in the climactic scenes of the film. Dave is eventually killed by Jimmy, while intimations of the full story of Katie's murder begin to emerge through scenes involving Brendan, Silent Ray, a young friend of Ray's, and Sean. Jimmy insists repeatedly and menacingly that Dave confess to the murder, in which case he says he will let him live. Dave at first maintains his innocence, claiming instead to have killed a child molester (which proves to be the case). Jimmy is disbelieving and pressures Dave until he submits and says he killed Katie, because seeing her that night had reminded him of the youth he had lost. Jimmy then stabs Dave at close quarters before finishing him off with a gunshot. These exchanges are closely intercut with scenes at Brendan's home, in which it is made clear that something of great significance is about to be established. Sean locates Jimmy the following morning and tells him – too late, of course, to save Dave – that the killers have confessed. Silent Ray and his friend shot Katie, accidentally at first, it turns out, after an incident during which they were initially playing with the gun; they then chased and killed her, to prevent her from telling what had happened.

Much of this seems generically conventional enough, in the twin lines of suspicion and investigation, although the resolution is one in which the crime appears to have occurred for arbitrary reasons,

motivated neither by anything relating to the past experiences of Dave
nor the specific connections that are uncovered between Brendan and
Katie's family. The revelation – the material itself and the manner in
which successive parts of the puzzle are pieced together – is typical generic material, but less so is the oblique manner in which it is
related to the murder case. A logical process of unveiling occurs in
everything except the most important detail: the actual reason for the
killing of Katie. This represents a significant departure from the more
conventional variety of crime/detective thriller. The sense of arbi-
trariness is potentially unsettling, removing any sense of solid underlying motivation or explanation. It is notable, as a marker of how far
this is untypical of classical-mainstream narrative, that precisely such
an element of chance or accident in so crucial a detail is viewed by
András Bálint Kovács, elsewhere, as a component not just of art cinema but of the more radical variant he defines as modernist in character.[23] Like *The Assassination of Jesse James*, the film can be understood
to share such a dimension with predecessors of the kind associated
particularly with the period of the Hollywood Renaissance, examples
in this case such as *The Long Goodbye* (1973) and *Night Moves* (1975),
with a similarly implicit critique of the ideological underpinnings of
more conventionally affirmative varieties of the justice-restored crime
thriller.

The other major factor that distinguishes *Mystic River* from the
generic norm is the space given to the emotional responses of the
main protagonists, especially Jimmy and Dave. Sean performs the
most conventional role, as the more objective investigator of the
scenario, and thus provides the easiest point of entry for the viewer.
Jimmy and Dave are characterised in a manner that gives the film
more than a little in common with the prestige-level male melodrama
of the postwar period identified by Thomas Schatz, as cited in the
Introduction (some such space is also given to Sean, if less developed,
via the scenario regarding silent calls he receives from his absent wife).
The marker of distinction here, in relation to the genre, stands in contrast to that employed in *The Assassination of Jesse James*: an expansion
rather than a limiting of grounds for emotional proximity to central
character experience. If Jimmy is a tough guy, he is shown also to
be capable of displays of overt emotional suffering, one example of

Figure 4.5. Wracked with guilt and confusion: Dave (Tim Robbins) as another uncomfortable source of allegiance, in *Mystic River* © Village Roadshow Films and Warner Bros. Entertainment Inc.

which is witnessed in an uncomfortable sequence in which he opens up to Dave, at that stage unaware of anything to cast suspicion on his former friend.

Dave is granted, if anything, greater emotional depth, particularly because it is difficult clearly for the viewer to sound during most of the film. He is presented as a figure who has truly lost his way; who seems uncertain, at times, whether he is guilty or not (see Figure 4.5). That such a suspicion should eventually be undermined makes this appear a more conventional narrative strategy; that of the 'wrong man' accused, a staple of the crime format. That such a revelation comes too late to save him gives it a darker tone. But what really seems to have the greatest impact in the overall balance established in this dimension of the film is the fact that the viewer is left for so long with a combination of substantial sympathy for a figure darkly wracked in this way, and substantial grounds for thinking that he might indeed be guilty of a heinous crime (little such weight attaches to the offence he turns out to have committed, the killing of a paedophile figure who remains absent from the diegesis and of a kind more straightforwardly demonised in the prologue). His presence as an uncomfortable source of allegiance has something in common with those of the figures of Zuckerberg in *The Social Network* and Bob in *The Assassination of Jesse James*, although the effect is reduced in this case by the presence of Sean as a stronger source of more conventional allegiance.

The associations attached to terms such as 'melodrama' and 'drama' are worth some further consideration here, in the analysis of how films such as these are likely to be positioned within prevailing cultural hierarchies. The term 'melodrama' has often been associated with films targeted particularly at women, and featuring tales of strong female passion and/or suffering, particularly during the classical studio era from the 1920s to the 1950s. Within industry discourse it was also applied to male-oriented action-genre films of the studio era, as Steve Neale argues, although its later dominant association with a notion of the 'women's film' – and/or often with a crude variety of emotional manipulation – has tended to produce connotations of low cultural status.[24] The concept of the 'male melodrama' is, then, an interesting one, notwithstanding the extent to which very many Hollywood films can be understood to include melodrama in the more literal usage of the term (as a widespread variety of mainstream-commercial film practice in which music or other effects are used to heighten the expression of character-related emotion).

Within the broader patriarchal context of contemporary society, a film such as *Mystic River*, featuring moments of intense male emoting, is more likely to be accorded the conventionally higher status of 'drama', 'serious drama' or even the ultimate peak, in these terms, of 'tragedy', rather than melodrama. This might result from a combination of the status of male figures and the fact that the performed emoting involved tends to be one that is presented as only barely escaping its repression. It is 'brooding' and restrained, much of the time, with periodic outbursts of anguish such as those expressed by Jimmy, rather than more consistently outwardly expressive (which could lead into further analysis of the politically loaded connotations of a term such as the 'hysterical', traditionally associated with supposedly excessive displays of female emotion). It is notable that in the sequence in which Jimmy opens up, to some extent, to Dave, he bewails his inability to cry over his lost daughter, it being left for the latter to point out that he is actually shedding tears at the time.

The status of serious drama or tragedy rather than melodrama was widely accorded to the film by journalistic critics in their mediation of the film to potential viewers, the majority responding positively (an 87 per cent rating by critics on Rotten Tomatoes, 86 per cent for audience reviews). This is most unequivocally the case for A.O. Scott, in *The New York Times*, one of the most influential sources given the national status of the publication, who declared it to be 'the rare American movie that aspires to – and achieves – the full weight and darkness of tragedy'.[25] The 'conventions of pulp opera' are grounded 'in an unvarnished, thickly inhabited reality', a clear marker of quality for this critic, which elevates the otherwise lowly world of 'pulp opera'. Some scenes 'swell with an almost unbearable feeling [...] but the movie almost entirely avoids melodrama or grandiosity'. Stephanie Zacharek, of Salon, finds in the film a notion of fate 'straight out of Greek tragedy by way of film noir', the latter an apt mediating source for the understanding of how such qualities might be embodied within generic territory of this kind.[26]

Such a view is qualified by some other critics, but the general context remains one in which the film is measured quite positively against the highest of tragic standards. For the *Washington Post*, the film is 'tragic on a Shakespearean scale'.[27] It might be 'just a bit overplayed, a tad too highly pitched' – that is, risking some accusation of melodramatic excess – but 'it still resonates with grief and fury and feeling'. *The Boston Globe*, from the city in which the film is set, identifies a striving for lofty status on the part of both the film and the novel by Dennis Lehane of which it is a close adaptation. The book 'wanted very, very much to be a Shakespearean tragedy set on the mean streets of South Boston, and it ultimately succeeded almost in spite of those ambitions'.[28] The film is said to have retained both the strengths and weaknesses of the book: 'a pulp thriller that strains – sometimes pretentiously, at other times with gutter magnificence – to reach that level of basic human truths'. Reviews of this kind, like some of those of *Inception* examined in Chapter 2, give us a sense of the tensions involved in decisions about whether or not the terms of highest cultural status are considered to be applicable to works that mix elements usually associated with varied hierarchical standing.

The main climax of *Mystic River* has a bleakness unusual for Hollywood, in the death of Dave and the revelation that he was telling Jimmy the truth. Exactly why Dave confesses to a crime he did not commit is unclear, adding to the discomfort created by this sequence and the film overall. The bleak note is continued into the scene in which Jimmy finds out that he has killed the wrong man. Asked by Sean when he last saw Dave, he pauses before saying 'That was 25 years ago', in the back of the car in which he was abducted, after which Sean ponders that maybe all three of them got in the car that day and all the rest had been a dream of how their lives might have been had they escaped. This is another untypical note for a studio feature, in its emphasis on the potentially overwhelming weight of events of the past – and again of the contingent – and their ability to shape our perceptions. More usual, in the commercial mainstream and in keeping with dominant American ideologies, would be to emphasise the possibility of escape from any such confines.

It is notable, however, that in its final scenes the film relents somewhat, bending back some degrees closer to the mainstream norm in its offering of some more positive resonances. Immediately after this exchange, Sean receives another initially silent call from his wife. This time he offers an apology and she responds, telling him also the name of the baby he has not seen, the characteristically sombre music of the film shifting here into a lighter and more optimistic note. In closing sequences, to the background setting of a passing street parade, we see Sean and his family reunited, a glimpse of something like a more conventional happy ending in this strand of the narrative. Jimmy also seems to receive a kind of absolution from his wife, as he talks to her about having killed the wrong man. If he appears somehow to be excused for the killing of Dave, this seems to be another way in which the film avoids any too black-or-white characterisation of its main protagonists. A sense of ongoing trauma is added to the mix here in the figure of Celeste and an exchange of looks between herself – seemingly pained and disoriented – and the more assured features of Jimmy's wife. A certain sense of closure is imposed at the end, if only by the removal of the most obvious source of dis-comfort in the film – the agonised figure of Dave – but this remains some distance from a more broadly happy ending of the kind often associated with the Hollywood norm in anything other than Sean's family reunion.

The visual style of the film is another dimension in which it shares some features with *The Assassination of Jesse James*, but also where it appears to aspire considerably less to anything like the status of art cin-ema. Some instances of stark contrast between darkness and highlights are employed, a notable example being the sequence that climaxes in the killing of Dave, in which he is confronted by Jimmy at night. A thematic motivation can be suggested here, much the same as that available in the case of *The Assassination of Jesse James*, the darkness of some of the cinematography seeming to reflect and contribute to the generally dark and sombre nature of the material. The effect is quite striking in some cases, but the use here of black and white tones cre-ates a less specifically painterly impression than that employed in the previous example. In general, *Mystic River* is another instance of the employment of a variety of classical camerawork and *découpage* that suggests a 'restrained' approach, in contrast to those of intensified con-tinuity or heightened mannerism. An example of this can be seen in the earlier exchanges between Jimmy and Dave cited above, ending with the former's complaint about his inability to cry, a heavily charged sequence set on the porch of Jimmy's home after Katie's funeral, one over which hangs the pressure created by the suspicion that has been developed in the direction of his former childhood friend.

The main body of this sequence begins with alternating shot/reverse-shot pairs, the components of which are a variety of the over-the-shoulder perspective, in this case more like an over-the-legs position: each shot presents one figure in approximately mid-shot, part of the other appearing in the foreground (part of the legs of Dave, for example, in the shots of Jimmy). After a number of such pairs, the camera moves somewhat closer, as Jimmy's discourse lifts into a more emotive register. Now we have an alternation of sin-gle shots of each character, without the over-the-legs component, starting from a similar distance but with the camera pushing grad-ually in closer, eventually framing Jimmy's head and shoulders as he reaches the emotional peak of the sequence. The effect is a standard

Figure 4.6. Contained melodrama: the camera pulls away overhead from the agonised Jimmy in *Mystic River* © Village Roadshow Films and Warner Bros. Entertainment Inc.

and conventional one, a movement into closer physical proximity to the camera, and emphasis on the single figure, to mirror the shift to higher emotional tone. But it is also done in a manner that is subtle and restrained, rather than in any more overtly emphatic or heightened style. The result is something that seems to abide by the conventions of 'drama' – presenting itself as 'realistic' and restrained – rather than to carry the connotations of melodrama, in its negative usage.

A relatively more melodramatic heightening is used at one point, to underline the moment at which it becomes clear to Jimmy that his daughter's is the body that has been found, but this is also employed in a restrained manner for so key an emotive peak of the film. The camera pulls upwards away from Jimmy's contorted features, as he wails and struggles in the arms of a group of policemen, into a god-like overhead position, accompanied by a conventional welling of strings on the soundtrack (see Figure 4.6). A fade-to-black follows quite quickly, however, and the camera does not climb very high, rather than the initial effect being extended. A dissolve is then made, to an overhead view of the nearby site in which the body was found, after which the camera tilts upwards and pans across a view of tree-tops and sky. The music reaches a crescendo in the latter movement, but one that constitutes a relatively modest usage of the available melodramatic apparatus. More overtly expressive material is reserved for the evocation of aspects of Dave's kidnapping, including first-person and other unstable camerawork employed to signify his escape, running through a wooded landscape, but such flourishes are clearly motivated, and contained, through their association with a heightened/remembered experience of this kind.

Production history: from initial reluctance to disputes over final cut

The two films examined in this chapter were both produced by the same studio, Warner Bros., on broadly similar budgets ($30 million for *The Assassination of Jesse James* and $25 million for *Mystic River*) well below the level of the Hollywood norm. This alone suggests clearly, as in the case of *The Social Network*, some of the limitations put on this kind of production within the studio context. Once given the green light, the progress of each film was rather different. *The Assassination of Jesse James* ran into sustained difficulties, particularly in post-production, while the production and post-production of *Mystic River* appear to have been entirely untroubled, a factor attributable to the reputation and working methods of director Clint Eastwood. Even in this case, however, and with the unusually long-standing relationship he had with the studio at the time, dating back to 1975, along with a track record of producing films on budget and on time, Eastwood had to struggle to convince Warner to go ahead with the film.

Eastwood's relationship with Warner is an example of a key dimension of the operations of Hollywood in the recent/contemporary era, one in which major talent is usually semi-attached to individual studios via first-look or other such deals. Through such arrangements, stars, directors or producers are provided with space and other resources, usually on the studio lot, in return for a certain degree of loyalty towards the company involved – a relationship very different from the fixed long-term contracts of the earlier studio era. How strongly they are tied down varies from case to case, often on the basis of the clout of those involved. A first-look deal is one in which the studio is required to be given right of first refusal on any projects developed with the help of its resources. Many of those with such arrangements, or variations on the theme, also continue to work for rival studios as well. Eastwood's relationship with Warner at the time

of *Mystic River*, through his company Malpaso Productions, was a relatively open one, with nothing more than picture-by-picture commitment. But this had resulted in him producing, directing or starring in
something in the region of 30 Warner projects since his role in *Dirty
Harry* in 1971, before Malpaso's formal arrangement with the studio.[29]
Eastwood was clearly viewed by Warner as a desirable commodity in
his various roles, particularly as star and/or director, commentary on
his performance in the latter capacity almost invariably citing his status as a figure considered to be one of the most solid and reliable in
the business, even if his films were not of the highest-earning blockbuster variety. At the opposite end of the scale from David Fincher,
Eastwood's capacity to bring films in on time and on modest budget
was partly a function of his preference for shooting only single takes
of each shot, a practice continued with *Mystic River*.

For all this, when Malpaso developed the project, with a script by
Brian Helgeland (with whom Eastwood had previously collaborated
on *Blood Work* [2002]), the studio appears to have been distinctly cool
about its prospects. According to the trade press, Eastwood was told
he could offer the script to other studios, which he appears to have
done.[30] The film 'wasn't your basic greenlight speed job', he is quoted
saying in one report: 'Everybody didn't just queue up to produce this
film. I took it to one studio, and they told me they don't do dramas.'[31]
The reason for such reluctance appears at least in part to have been
the dark nature of the project. If the film had a vigilante dimension
that chimed with one of the major associations of Eastwood's screen
persona, from the figure of Dirty Harry onwards, it was one in which
such action was viewed at best equivocally. The fact that Eastwood
was not to appear in the cast might have been an additional factor,
although it is not clear that this was the case. His next film, *Million
Dollar Baby* (2004) – another work with a tragic dimension in which
he did appear, in a role that fitted his established star-persona – faced
similar reluctance before getting the go-ahead from the studio (subsequently making the company question its reticence, in this case,
by hitting the jackpot in the prestige stakes, winning Oscars for best
film, director and actress). When Warner eventually signed on for
Mystic River, it did so on a basis that included the presence of a 50
per cent funding partner, the Australian company Village Roadshow,

a regular participant in such deals with the studio. This is another example of the co-financing (shared risk) strategy seen in the previous chapters and often a condition of existence for films of this kind. *Million Dollar Baby*'s approval was subject to such a deal with another financier, Lakeshore Entertainment.[32] Eastwood was also required to forfeit any up-front salary on *Mystic River*, a further indication of the compromises often required for the pursuit of films with quality associations – particularly those of a downbeat variety – even when the budget is modest, a funding partner is involved and so established and reliable a figure as Eastwood is involved.

The Assassination of Jesse James came to Warner via the involvement of another talent-based company, in this case Brad Pitt's Plan B Films, the first lead role it developed for the star. An option on the book was bought jointly by Plan B and Scott Free Productions, run by the mainstream directors Tony and Ridley Scott, before the full rights were bought by Warner, with Pitt and Ridley Scott among the producers. This is another case in which an outside financial partner was involved in the production. *The Assassination of Jesse James* was one of six titles involved in a deal with the studio that saw the creation of Virtual Studios, a private equity fund (others among these with quality resonances were *Blood Diamond*, the subject of the next chapter, and Steven Soderbergh's *The Good German* [2006]).[33] The 'driving force' behind the project was the writer and director, Andrew Dominik, the connection to Pitt being reported to have come from the actor's admiration of his debut feature, *Chopper* (2000), an adaptation of the autobiography of a notorious but charismatic Australian criminal (not exactly a latter day Jesse James).[34] Dominik had written a number of other scripts he hoped to direct, but had been unable to get any of them off the ground without the presence of a star.[35] In the case of *The Assassination of Jesse James*, then, the filmmaker was a figure with very much less clout than that possessed by Eastwood, but this was balanced by the on- and off-screen presence of Pitt, a major A-list Hollywood player. The power of the star was to prove significant to the appearance of the film in its eventual shape, after a number of tensions between studio and writer-director.

The making of *The Assassination of Jesse James* was described by *Variety* as 'a long and arduous process' involving 'a well-publicized tug-of-war' between Dominik and Warner over the nature of the final cut, a struggle that led to its release being delayed by more than a year.[36] The studio was reported to have been unhappy about the length of the film, one initial cut of which ran to four hours. According to one report: 'Studio production executives were tearing their hair out, because they saw a potential B.O. winner in a downsized version.'[37] At one point, Pitt and Scott were said to have offered a cut of their own, alternative to that of Dominik, but it was said not to have tested very well, leading them to return to that of the director. Cuts of varying length, the shortest around two hours (described by the director as 'not good'), were reported to have been sent to a number of different critics for their opinion, a process said by Dominik to have added to the impression created by the delayed release that 'this was a movie in deep trouble'.[38] He was removed from the editing process on several occasions, the kind of move likely to be interpreted as a marker of studio hostility to less conventional work. The studio, unsurprisingly, was said to be concerned about the commercial prospects of the film, and to have wanted less contemplation and 'at least a bit more action', which would have bent it some degrees closer to the Hollywood norm.[39]

Dominik's inclinations were reported to be in the direction of the more artistic and distanced style of Terrence Malick, whose *Days of Heaven* was cited above as one of the reference points for the visuals. The studio wanted something closer to the approach of Eastwood (whatever their initial reservations had been about some of his recent work at the time).[40] Dominik's use of distinctive imagery such as that examined above might have been motivated at some level by a desire overtly to mark his own creative presence, as a newcomer to Hollywood, a not-uncommon feature of earlier-career work in general. A context similar in this respect, although obviously very different in others, is suggested by the art historian John Shearman for the appearance of mannerist art in the sixteenth century, a period in which a new patronage system emerged that stressed the character of the work as one of virtuoso performance by the creator. This presaged the subsequent development of contemporary notions of individual artistic creation – as opposed to the 'mechanical' market forces that developed from the eighteenth century – that underpin so many conceptions of quality of the kind considered in this book.[41]

The studio eventually agreed to go with Dominik's version, although he had, unsurprisingly, no contractual right to final cut. A major factor in the decision appears to have been the backing he received from Pitt, who can be assumed to have wielded considerable influence with studio executives, as a star with whom they would want to maintain a positive relationship.[42] Pitt was also reported to have exerted his clout to ensure the retention of the full and cumbersome title of the book, another factor that would not have been seen as adding to the commercial prospects of the production. How far a studio will go to maintain a relationship in this way is difficult to determine, however, when weighed against concern about the box office potential of a project such as this, and not a subject that tends to be discussed openly by those involved. That a figure as renowned as Eastwood initially found it difficult to get Warner to support projects such as *Mystic River* and *Million Dollar Baby* gives us some suggestion of the limits that exist, even in what might be expected to be the most established of such arrangements. It is notable, however, that one of the *Variety* reports on which the above account is based suggests that another major reason for Warner acceding to the Dominik cut was that it considered itself to be a 'filmmaker-friendly' studio and that this had been 'one of the hallmarks' of the tenure of Jeff Robinov, as president of production at the time (one of the figures cited positively by Christopher Nolan in relation to his later experience at the studio with *Inception*). The report then quotes one unnamed Warner executive saying: 'We're not a place that says, "It's my way or the highway."'[43]

How far this latter point should be taken at face value remains open to question, although the suggestion in this period that Warner was 'the studio most invested in filmmaker relationships' was also made elsewhere, in contexts including discussion of the production of *Inception*.[44] Some scepticism is required in relation to such comments, as was suggested in Chapter 1, but they reinforce the impression that, at the very least, studios often like to *present* themselves as something other than corporate machines within which any creative agenda is heavily outweighed by commercial concerns. This might be a matter of how they wish to appear in the wider society, or a more local concern with wanting to seem attractive – or, more so than rivals – to important sources of talent, especially for a studio such as Warner which had at the time a reputation for a greater-than-average reliance on very large-scale tentpole blockbusters. Robinov, in particular, was credited with investing in relationships with filmmakers, writers for the *Los Angeles Times* suggesting during his tenure, in 2010, that: 'It's no secret that Warners has the most top filmmakers in its fold because, unlike some studio bosses, Robinov actually recognizes that the true source of creativity on a film derives from the filmmaker, not meddling studio executives.'[45]

Whether or not such a recognition would have led to a filmmaker such as Dominik eventually being given his way against the preferences of the studio if it had not been for the strong support of an A-lister of the status of Pitt – as was the case in *The Assassination of Jesse James* – remains very much open to question, however. The phrasing chosen by Robinov to describe his strategy seems telling and to imply distinct limitations to the notion of being 'filmmaker-driven', a term he himself employs. Every movie needs a strong vision, he says, 'and the people that have the most exciting and interesting and accessible vision possible are the filmmakers. So they are the ones we want to build a long-term relationship with'.[46] 'Vision' might be valorised here but in a form that is strongly qualified, as might be expected, by more mainstream-sounding terms such as 'exciting', 'interesting' and 'accessible' (of which *The Assassination of Jesse James* might only qualify for the middle term, for the majority of cinemagoers). The emphasis on the building of long-term relationships is also significant in this case: clearly applicable to the career of Eastwood and others including Soderbergh but not (as of the time of writing, at least) to that of Dominik, whose next film, *Killing Them Softly* (2012), a similarly less-than-conventional genre (crime) film, was produced independently and distributed in the US by The Weinstein Company.

If one reason for the studio to have acceded to Dominik's wishes on *The Assassination of Jesse James* had been its desire to maintain relations with Pitt, such a strategy appears not to have been very successful. *Killing Them Softly* was co-produced by Plan B and starred Pitt, while in the years between the two films only one of his five major roles was in a film in which Warner was involved, as co-producer with Paramount of *The Curious Case of Benjamin Button*. The star showed a marked preference for films at the speciality or quality end of the spectrum in this period, primarily in films from established 'name' directors, as he had done previously in the case of the studio release *Fight Club* (David Fincher, Fox). His CV included *Burn After Reading* (Coen brothers, Focus Features, 2008), *Inglorious Basterds* (Quentin Tarantino, Universal and The Weinstein Company, 2009), *The Tree of Life* (Terrence Malick, Fox Searchlight, 2011) and *Moneyball* (Bennett Miller, Columbia, 2011).

This is a useful point at which to consider further the question of how we should understand the relationship between productions of the kind considered here, from the studios themselves, and those of their speciality divisions. Warner had a speciality division at the time of the production and release of both *The Assassination of Jesse James* and *Mystic River*. Warner Independent Pictures (WIP), subsequently closed as part of a more general studio reduction of such operations in 2008. As a genre production of polished appearance (however downbeat the material), with a cast of solidly established stars such as Penn, Bacon and Robbins in the main roles and involving a figure such as Eastwood with an established relationship with the main division, *Mystic River* is the kind of film that would not be expected to fall into the category of speciality release and so raises no particular issues here. *The Assassination of Jesse James* is also a work of polished – not noticeably low-budget – appearance and features numerous established performers and, of course, one major star. In other respects, however, in the more 'artistic' leanings detailed above, it is a film that might appear ideally suited to the speciality domain. It is with other films from this realm, along with the independently released *Killing Them Softly*, that it seems to have most in common, rather than with other studio quality films. One of numerous examples similar in some broad respects – in general cultural pitch – that could be cited from the Indiewood/speciality realm at the time would be Paul Thomas Anderson's *There Will Be Blood* (2007), a co-production by Paramount Vantage and Disney's Miramax. Another from the same partnership in the same year that might also be comparable, in some respects, is *No Country for Old Men*. So, how should we understand the presence of *The Assassination of Jesse James* in the operations of Warner's main film division?

The first point to make is that there is no necessarily complete match between individual films and exactly where they fit in the industrial spectrum. A close correlation exists in most cases – generally, the less mainstream in qualities a film is, the further it is likely to be found from the main studio operations – but this is always subject to possible exceptions, if limited in numbers, degree and dependent on particular circumstances. These might include the release by speciality divisions of some films of very low budget credentials, for example, that might usually be more likely to be associated with smaller, stand-alone indie distribution; or some blurring of the lines between what exactly might fall within the orbit of a speciality or a main studio arm at any particular moment. More specifically, though, uncertainty seems to have existed at some studios about the exact nature of the relationship between major and speciality divisions. This seems likely to have been an increased factor at the studios whose speciality operations were least well established or had enjoyed less consistent success. These latter would include both Warner and Paramount, two of the casualties of the speciality shakeout of 2008 and after (Warner was the last of the majors to create its own label, in 2003).

According to trade press reports, WIP was hampered from the start by conflict between Robinov, the main studio's president of production, and the head of the division, Mark Gill. It was said, as a result, to have 'never hit its full stride' and to have 'spent most of its young life in limbo'.[47] Gill was also reported to have been given less autonomy to pursue projects of his own choosing than was the case at most other speciality arms, which suggests that what was said to be a personality problem was also connected to the central question of how the function of such units was conceived by the studio.[48] Gill was effectively forced out in May 2006 – while *The Assassination of Jesse James* was in the works at Warner – and replaced by Polly Cohen, a figure described as offering 'a direct conduit to Robinov'. The latter at this point outlined a strategy according to which the division would be 'a place where favored studio directors can go to make smaller movies' and would also be expected 'to foster new directing talent that could then jump to big Warners'.[49] Either of these strands could, from this point, have embraced *The Assassination of Jesse James* as a product of the division, given the presence of an upcoming director to fit the latter, and of a major established star, likely to be included by the former. So might any strategy Gill had sought to pursue greater autonomy, however, given the extent to which the film would seem to fit the bill for speciality production more generally: that is, different enough from mainstream norms while with some features that might put it beyond the pocket of most stand-alone independents. Why the film did not come from WIP would appear in large part to be a function of the general hampering of the division's operations during Gill's tenure, the period when it came into the Warner orbit. The studio might also have been keen to keep a star of Pitt's magnitude closer to the heart of its operations.

The clarification of the function of WIP under Robinov's more direct control was not sufficient to save the unit from closure. The Warner move in 2008 involved the shutdown of both WIP and Picturehouse, the latter created in 2004 in a reconstruction of the speciality operations of the corporation's New Line Pictures division. The justification offered by the studio at the time was that this was a rationalisation of operations. New Line was folded into the main Warner pictures operation while Warner's president and chief operating officer Alan Horn – Robinov's immediate boss – said that maintaining the separate Picturehouse and WIP infrastructures was not 'the most economic use of our resources'. Horn added: 'We have the capacity to distribute and market anything.'[50] The latter was a departure from prevailing speciality practice in the preceding decade, in which the accepted wisdom had been that special expertise was required in the handling of such material, as was provided by separate divisions operating with varying degrees of autonomy from their parent companies and employing key figures from the indie sector (Gill himself having spent eight years at Miramax). Horn maintained that the move did not constitute an abandonment of indie or other speciality material, citing among other things the studio's established relationship with figures such as Eastwood, George Clooney and Soderbergh. In the reporting of these developments and the comments of Horn, however, *Variety* emphasised a lack of clarity that had already existed at Warner 'about which entity would release which film', *The Assassination of Jesse James* being cited here as an example that seemed to lend itself to speciality treatment, as suggested above, and that had underperformed when it went out through 'big Warner' (another example included here is the Eastwood-directed *Letters from Iwo Jima* [2006], which started out on the WIP side of the ledger and met a similar fate when released by the main division).[51]

How, then, were *The Assassination of Jesse James* and *Mystic River* handled by Warner, while WIP remained in existence, and how much did this have in common with the strategy that would be expected of a speciality division? Both were released in the prime indie/speciality autumn season – escaping the blockbuster-heavy summer and Christmas holiday competition and during the run-up to the major awards – the former in late September, the latter in mid-October. Both were also opened on numbers of screens that seem typical of the indie or Indiewood/speciality sectors, a source of quality associations in its own right: *The Assassination of Jesse James* on five, *Mystic River* on 13. These are numbers that might be employed for either an unattached indie or speciality division title, although not at the very lowest scale of the single or two-screen version of the platform release strategy (an approach designed to enable less obviously mainstream productions both to save money and to seek to build momentum through critical praise and word-of-mouth).

The marketing materials for both films were largely in keeping with the pitch of the texts themselves, each giving a sense of their relative darkness by Hollywood standards. The star presence is inevitably foregrounded in extract footage used in the trailers, although in each case the names are only spelled out on screen towards the end rather than being used as part of a more overtly up-front sales pitch. The trailer for *The Assassination of Jesse James* opens with some of the more stylised imagery and a voice-over commentary similar to that from the film itself, followed by music that establishes a broadly elegiac tone and footage and dialogue combinations that set out aspects of the relationship between the two principals, with little in the way of more overt action (this is not a case in which the limited amount of action in the film is exaggerated in the trailer, as is commonly the case in promotional materials that seek to bend less conventional films towards the norm by including disproportionate elements of action or comedy).

The main *Mystic River* promo employs a more conventional 'big trailer voice' to intone portentous lines such as 'There are places … that make us … who we are', but the impression created is one that combines dark melodrama with aspects of police procedural in much the same way as the film itself. The latter stages are accompanied by critical endorsements that seek to establish the quality status of the film in terms such as 'remarkable', 'powerful' and 'masterpiece'. DVD covers for each film feature the star names above the title and 'moody' images of the protagonists: three unidentifiable inverted silhouettes in the water in the case of *Mystic River*, with the film's Oscar awards highlighted below; a three-quarter figure of Pitt/James in *The Assassination of Jesse James*, set against an 'atmospheric' lowering cloudy sky and a field of wheat, the connotations of which are somewhat 'artistic' and 'contemplative' in accordance with the general tenor of the film.

Mystic River was considered to have opened strongly, grossing $591,390 on its first weekend after receiving very positive reviews. It took an average of just under $45,500 per venue, a figure described as 'mind-bending' by *Variety*.[52] The release was promptly expanded much more widely, to take advantage of critical momentum, to 1,467 screens. This is a number more in keeping with the scale of operations of which a studio or studio division is capable, on which its weekend gross was a very healthy $10 million plus. *The Assassination of Jesse James* performed more modestly on its opening weekend, $147,812 representing a per-screen average of $29,564, but expectations appeared already to have been lowered by the reservations of studio executives about the nature of the final cut, as appears to be reflected in its subsequent treatment.[53] The film remained on five screens for its second week (the weekend gross dropping to $92,351) before being expanded to 61 in week three and to its maximum of 301 in week five (when it grossed $531,282, an average of $1,765 per screen). Both also made pre-release appearances at major film festivals, another source of prestige associated in particular with speciality strategy. *Mystic River* premièred in competition at Cannes in May and received a further boost by opening the New York Film Festival a week ahead of its release, while *The Assassination of Jesse James* appeared at Venice, where Pitt picked up the best actor award. By the end of its run, *Mystic River* far out-performed its stable-mate, grossing $90 million domestically and $66 million overseas (a total of $156 million that represented a very healthy return on the budget). *The Assassination of Jesse James* grossed a mere $3.9 million in the US and $11 million overseas, a total of $15 million that was only half the cost of production.

Both films earned returns for the studio on the prestige front, as measured by critical responses and awards, particularly Academy Awards, although here again *Mystic River* came out clearly in front. Its status as a film with roles that highlighted strong performance (a traditional dimension of quality repute) was confirmed with glowing reviews for the principals and Oscar wins for best actor (Penn) and best supporting actor (Robbins). It was also nominated for the most high-profile award, best picture, which ensured a prominent place in pre-awards coverage, and best director. *The Assassination of Jesse James* received lower profile nominations, for supporting actor and cinematography. The latter was a recognition of the visual qualities highlighted above, but one that would translate less readily into the currency of the kind of media hype that surrounds the more prominent categories. *Mystic River* was, as a result, also more successful in translating this source of prestige and publicity into commercial returns, particularly during the period between the nominations and the awards. Its release had been scaled back to 133 screens the week before the Oscar nominations but was then expanded to 1,327, closer to the level of its opening weeks, to take advantage of the fresh wave of publicity, a level it maintained for the five weeks leading up to the ceremony (after which it dropped somewhat, but still remained at more than 1,000 for the next two weeks).[54] Slightly more than a third of the film's domestic gross ($31,368,817) was taken in the weeks after the announcement of the nominations, a substantial boost to its fortunes that would make it an ideal representative of the studio quality film strategy, seeking to gain some of its commercial success directly from its sources of prestige.

The theatrical release of *The Assassination of Jesse James* received a tiny expansion at the time of the nominations (from four to eight screens) but it was at that point pulled from theatres and released on DVD, the strategy in this case being to seek to use its more limited Oscar presence to kickstart its post-theatrical career.[55] Domestic

DVD sales amounted to an estimated $9.8 million, an improvement on the box office gross but a figure that still left the film's takings at this point below the level of its budget, even without considering publicity and other release costs.[56] Equivalent sales figures were not available for *Mystic River* (or figures for overseas DVD sales for either) but some idea of the comparative performance can be gained from its figures for DVD and VHS rentals, which at $66.9 million made it the second most successful film of 2004.[57]

The difference in commercial performance might come as little surprise, given the significantly less mainstream qualities of Dominik's film – even if it does posses the bigger star attraction of the two – although the extent of the divergence can also be attributed to studio choices made after the initial week or weeks of release. Titles that perform strongly at first are more likely to receive continued support and expansion, while those that do less well from the start are likely to be given less time or space to improve. Both such situations seem to apply to the examples examined here. This kind of approach might be more typical of studio main divisions, indie/speciality platform release being designed to allow more time for a slower building of an audience, as suggested above. But the level of competition in the speciality business has ensured that similar pressures are felt, if at different scales, at both ends of the market, including the middle territory represented by the operations of the studio divisions. *The Assassination of Jesse James* was clearly not abandoned after its first couple of weeks, expanding to a level of release that could have been widened further had its performance merited such a move. How far a lack of enthusiasm or expectations on the part of the studio, as a result of its dislike of the final cut, might have reduced such a possibility remains a matter of speculation, although it is hardly likely to have helped the film's prospects in this respect.

Overall, from the outside, there is little apparent evidence to suggest any clear difference between the manner in which either of these films was handled on release and what might have been the case if *The Assassination of Jesse James* had gone through the speciality division, WIP. It was accompanied by plenty of critical praise, the securing of which is one of the major goals of a speciality release. The key factor in its performance might reasonably be argued to remain at the textual level, in the various factors – including length, length of title, slowness, lack of action and general distancing from the material – that marked the film out as likely to appeal primarily to a limited speciality audience, the presence of Pitt notwithstanding. Such audiences can still be substantially larger than those attracted by this film, however, as plenty have demonstrated. It is possible that Warner could have done more to support the release, but a number of commentators suggested that the problem in the autumn 2007 season was a more general one, created by too crowded a schedule for such films, combined with what appeared to be a general lack of audience enthusiasm for titles including *The Assassination of Jesse James* and WIP's critically well-received Iraq-war related *In The Valley of Elah*.[58]

The number of films of this kind on release at the same time was seen as putting increased pressure on the traditional indie/speciality model, making it difficult for films to maintain their place long enough to build support if they did not do well from the start. This was a problem faced by indie films from the late 1990s onwards, one that was seen as being exacerbated in this period by the volume of speciality releases and the presence of films such as *The Assassination of Jesse James* in the schedules of the main studio arms.[59] The biggest difficulty in such circumstances is likely to be faced by unattached independent distributors, generally unable to afford the scale of marketing spending available to studios or their speciality divisions. Figures for the amount spent on the two films examined in this chapter are not available (it would be useful to be able to compare the two, to see if Warner spent more on *Mystic River* after losing faith in *The Assassination of Jesse James*, as might be expected), but *Variety* suggested in 2007 that a speciality unit might be expected to spend $10 million per title, a fraction of the $100 million lavished on a blockbuster such as *Inception* but far more than would usually be available to an independent.[60]

Even in the case of *Mystic River*, which performed so much more strongly than *The Assassination of Jesse James*, a distinct note of pessimism was struck in one *Variety* report about the potential size of the audience in the autumn season for what it termed 'grown-up' films of this kind. *Mystic River* was declared to be 'the real scary movie this Halloween' because, despite its cachet, cast and rave reviews, it and other such films were 'fighting for breathing room' in what was described as 'a dense thicket of genre titles' that offered more immediate appeal to many moviegoers.[61] Such reporting might be considered to be more than a little hyperbolic in nature – like some other instances of trade and general press coverage considered elsewhere in this book – given the box office success of *Mystic River* (a good deal more than the judgement of this piece that it would be 'lucky to eke out $50 million' in American theatres). Another of the titles included in this report also turned out to be a notable hit, the Universal division Focus Features' *Lost in Translation* (the worldwide gross of which was a very healthy $119.7 million on a budget of just $4 million). But it highlights industry perceptions of the difficulties often faced by films of this kind, the suggestion in this case being that the more 'adult' viewers to which such films are most likely to appeal were either increasingly hard to find or too thinly divided among competing films at the quality/speciality end of the scale. This, and the escalating marketing costs likely to result from such pressures to find an audience, was a substantial part of the wider industrial context for the shakeout among the studio divisions from 2008.

Notes

1   Other examples include the presence of a mythmaking writer in *Unforgiven* (1992)

2   Stephen Pizzello and Jean Oppenheimer, 'Western destinies', *American Cinematographer*, October 2007

3   See Patrick Keating, *Hollywood Lighting: From the Silent Era to Film Noir*, New York: Columbia University Press, 2010, pp. 73–4

4   Keating, *Hollywood Lighting*, pp. 76–7

5   'The art of cinematography', *Trinity: The Magazine of Trinity University*, January 2010, http://www.trinity.edu/departments/public_relations/magazine/issues/10_january/cinematography.htm

6   Keating, *Hollywood Lighting*, p. 11

7   Ibid., p. 189

8   Argument for the persistence of classical features has been led by David Bordwell in his contributions to David Bordwell, Janet Staiger and Kristen Thompson, *The Classical Hollywood: Film Style and Mode of Production to 1960*, London: Routledge, 1985; and elsewhere. For a list

of works that have questioned this approach, see Keating, *Hollywood Lighting*, p. 268, note 6

9   John Shearman, *Mannerism*, Harmondsworth: Penguin, 1967/1990

10   Keating, *Hollywood Lighting*, p. 72

11   Ibid. A source acknowledged here by Keating is Barry Salt, *Film Style and Technology: History and Analysis*, London: Starword, 1992

12   Ibid., p. 191; Gombrich, 'Norm and form' in *Gombrich on the Renaissance: Volume 1, Norm and Form*, London: Phaidon, 4th edition, 1985

13   See, for example, the definitions offered by Oxford Dictionaries online, at http://oxforddictionaries.com/definition/english/classical?q= classical

14   David Bordwell, 'The classical Hollywood style, 1917–60' in Bordwell, Janet Staiger and Kristin Thompson, *The Classical Hollywood Cinema: Film Style and Mode of Production to 1960*, London: Routledge, p. 4

15   Eleftheria Thanouli, *Post-Classical Cinema: An International Poetics of Film Narration*, London: Wallflower, 2009

16   Carol Vernallis, *Unruly Media: YouTube, Music Video, and the New Digital Cinema*, Oxford: Oxford University Press, 2013

17   Adrian Martin, '*Mise-en-scène* is dead, or the expressive, the excessive and the stylish', *Continuum*, vol. 6, no. 2, 1992, p. 3, manuscript copy kindly provided by Adrian Martin

18   Manohla Dargis, 'Good, bad, or ugly: a legend shrouded in gunsmoke remains hazy', 21 September 2007, via nytimes.com

19   Kenneth Turan, '"The Assassination of Jesse James by the Coward Robert Ford"', 21 September 2007, via latimes.com

20   Stephanie Zacharek, '"The Assassination of Jesse James by the Coward Robert Ford"', 21 September 2007, via salon.com

21   Anthony Lane, 'Outlaws', 1 October 2007, via newyorker.com

22   Details from sources including Pizzello and Oppenheimer, 'Western destinies', as cited above, and Steve Chagollan, 'Roger Deakins', *Variety*, 2 January 2008, via variety.com

23   András Bálint Kovács, *Screening Modernism: European Art Cinema, 1950–1980*, Chicago: University of Chicago Press, 2007, pp. 73–4

24   See Steve Neale, *Genre and Hollywood*, London: Routledge, 2000, pp. 179–202

25   A.O. Scott, 'Dark parable of violence avenged', 3 October 2003, via nytimes.com

26   Stephanie Zacharek, '"Mystic River"', 8 October 2003, via salon.com

27   Ann Hornaday, 'Bred in the bone', 8 October 2003, via washington-post.com

28   Ty Burr, 'Unfortunate sons', 8 October 2003, via boston.com
29   David Carr, 'Clint Eastwood, still fighting for the green light', *The New York Times*, 13 February 2005, via nytimes.com
30   Steve Chagollan, '"River" runs deep', *Variety*, 18 December 2003, via variety.com
31   *Variety* staff, 'Clint Eastwood', *Variety*, 5 February 2004, via variety.com
32   Carr, 'Clint Eastwood, still fighting for the green light'
33   Pamela McClintock, 'Sea change at H'wood newbie', *Variety*, 15 May 2006, via variety.com
34   Michael Fleming, 'WB aims for Pitt with "James"', *Variety*, 17 March 2004, via variety.com; see also Fleming, 'Brad motors to WB oater', *Variety*, 24 January 2005
35   Emanuel Levy, 'Interviews: Assassination of Jesse James: Andrew Dominik', undated, 'Emanuel Levy Cinema 24/7', http://www.emanuellevy.com/interview/assassination-of-jesse-james-andrew-dominik-7/
36   Pamela McClintock, 'Pitt's star power couldn't help "James"', 21 December 2007, via variety.com
37   Anne Thompson, 'Prestige pictures get super-sized', *Variety*, 4 October 2007, via variety.com
38   Levy, 'Interviews: Assassination of Jesse James: Andrew Dominik'
39   McClintock, 'Pitt's star power'; and John Horn, 'With both barrels', *Los Angeles Times*, 2 May 2007, via latimes.com
40   McClintock, 'Pitt's star power'; and Horn, 'With both barrels'; the reference to Eastwood is from the latter
41   Shearman, *Mannerism*, p. 44. For an account that supports Raymond Williams, in tracing the origins of the institutionalisation of contemporary notions of art and the artist to the eighteenth century, despite some earlier foreshadowing of such concepts in the Renaissance era, see Larry Shiner, *The Invention of Art: A Cultural History*, Chicago: University of Chicago Press, 2001
42   See, for example, McClintock, 'Pitt's star power', and Thompson, 'Prestige pictures get super-sized'
43   McClintock, 'Pitt's star power'
44   Patrick Goldstein and James Rainey, 'The big picture: Could Chris Nolan have convinced anyone but Warners to make "Inception"?', 'The envelope: The awards insider' blog, *Los Angeles Times*, 19 July 2010, http://latimesblogs.latimes.com/the_big_picture/2010/07/could-chris-nolan-have-convinced-anyone-but-warners-to-make-inception-.html

45   Goldstein and Rainey, 'The big picture'

46   Quoted in Goldstein and Rainey, 'The big picture'

47   Pamela McClintock, 'Warner Independent Pictures', *Variety*, 5 September 2008 and 'Warner Independent Pictures', 10 September 2006, via variety.com

48   Pamela McClintock, 'Warner bridges gap at indie arm', *Variety*, 8 May 2006, via variety.com

49   McClintock, 'Warner bridges gap'

50   Dave McNary and Dade Hayes, 'Picturehouse, WIP to close shop', *Variety*, 8 May 2008, via variety.com

51   McNary and Hayes, 'Picturehouse'

52   Carl DiOrio, '"Mystic River" rises rapidly in limited run', *Variety*, 12 October 2003, accessed via variety.com. Other details relating to box office and numbers of screens from Internet Movie Database, imdb.com

53   Warners had 'tempered its expectations', according to McClintock, 'Pitt's star power'

54   This and the subsequent similar data for both films is from Internet Movie Database, imdb.com

55   Diane Garrett, 'DVDs boost pre-kudos awareness', *Variety*, 11 January 2008, via variety.com

56   DVD figures from the film's entry on the-numbers.com

57   Marcy Magiera, 'Rental finishes flat in 2004', *Variety*, 29 December 2004, via variety.com. I was unable to find rental figures for *The Assassination of Jesse James*

58   On the level of competition, see for example Pamela McClintock, 'Prestige films compete for attention', *Variety*, 14 September 2007, via variety.com; on lack of audience enthusiasm generally and in relation to the titles cited, see Paul Dergarabedian, 'The fall movie season: Great films, not-so-great box office', *Boxoffice*, vol. 143, no. 12, December 2007, p. 8.

59   McClintock, 'Prestige films compete for attention'

60   Ibid.

61   Jonathan Bing, 'Where are all the grown-ups?', *Variety*, 2 November 2003, via variety.com

5

Making a difference and/or making a buck?

Blood Diamond and the contemporary social problem film

> Danny Archer: So, don't tell me, you're here to make a difference, huh?
> Maddy Bowen: And you're here to make a buck.

What kinds of strategies might we expect to find in a contemporary studio version of the social problem film, a category that often carries quality associations, some of the earlier history of which was considered in the Introduction? If industry perception is that the audience for more 'serious' or 'adult'-oriented films is limited – or where strong competition is faced from too many features from the more clearly specialised end of the market seeking to reach a similar constituency – this is another area in which a particular combination of more and less mainstream-leaning components is likely to exist. A mainstream feature that raises difficult or potentially challenging issues, even if primarily in the background, might be expected to mix any such dimension with the deployment of more familiarly comfortable Hollywood routines. If the contemporary social problem film is a format more often found in the indie or Indiewood sectors than in the output of the main studio divisions – as seems to be the case, at least in relation to the kind of subject matter considered in this chapter – this might also lead us to expect any studio version to be either toned down, in its treatment of any particular social issue, or to mix such material with a stronger dose of mainstream ingredients. The latter certainly appears to be true of the main case study example in this chapter, *Blood Diamond* (2006), a film that combines a treatment of more overtly socio-political issues than any of those considered in the previous chapters with some elements that lean more strongly towards the commercial mainstream than any of the other case studies included in this book other than the blockbuster-scale *Inception*. Compared with the features analysed in the previous two chapters, *Blood Diamond* is simultaneously more distinctive from the Hollywood norm, in addressing overt issues of pressing social concern, and closer to such norms in its deployment of core elements of melodramatic action-adventure.

The social problem film is defined primarily, as the term suggests, through its focus on some kind of social problem or issue, to which critical attention is drawn. The format involves a process of diagnosis that might or might not be followed by any clear prescription for change. For Peter Roffman and Jim Purdy, writers of the most sustained study of this phenomenon, the problem film 'combines social analysis and dramatic conflict within a coherent narrative structure. Social content is transformed into dramatic events and movie narrative adapted to accommodate social issues as story material through a particular set of movie conventions'.[1] For these writers – focusing on films from the 1930s, 1940s and 1950s – the conventions are sufficient to establish the format as a genre, the narrative focus of which is on the interaction of the individual with social institutions. Other studies have traced the form back to the earlier decades of cinema, including examples from the 'progressive' tradition considered as part of the history of quality examined in the Introduction.[2] Whether or not the social problem film is quite so clearly distinguished as a genre as Roffman and Purdy suggest remains open to debate, but it has remained a persistent, if usually minority and sometimes only occasional, strand in Hollywood output across the decades.

Classic Hollywood social problem films – prominent examples including those dealing with issues such as race and ethnicity in the immediate postwar years, some of which were cited in the Introduction – are usually located at the national level, addressing problems on the home front. A notable feature of some of their recent equivalents, in Hollywood and more frequently in the Indiewood sector, is a more international focus. R. Colin Tait and Andrew de Waard identify a distinct format they term the 'global social problem' film, instances of which include *Blood Diamond* among others such as *Traffic* (2000), *Syriana* (2005) and *Hotel Rwanda* (2004). 'If the original social problem film was concerned with the individual in conflict with a social institution,' they suggest, following Roffman and Purdy, these involve 'a multitude of interconnected individuals facing an array of problems; instead of a solitary institution, we get a network of immobilising social institutions.'[3]

This is largely the case with *Blood Diamond*, although the focus is less strongly on institutions as such than is the case with some other examples, the title of which refers to diamonds mined in African war zones, in this case the civil war in Sierra Leone in the late 1990s. The primary issue addressed by the film is the sale of diamonds to fund such conflicts, for which the blame is placed on unscrupulous traders and corporations as well as those (absent from the film itself) who might knowingly buy such luxuries in other parts of the world. This particular focus is mixed with a broader element of social concern about the problems faced by countries such as Sierra Leone and a diffuse notion of 'Africa' more generally. The significance of the specific difficulties faced by Sierra Leone can, to some extent, be seen as emblematic of a wider range of problems in numerous parts of Africa at the time, giving the one example more weight as a point of focus than might otherwise be the case, especially given the status of the 1990s as a period perceived as one of greater-than-usual crisis on the continent.[4]

The combination of specific issues relating to a particular geographically located practice or sector and those concerning the corrupt practices of outside institutions, particularly multinational corporations, is typical of the international or 'global' social problem film as defined by Tait and deWaard (another contemporaneous example set in an African country is *The Constant Gardener* [2005], an Indiewood release from Focus Features in which the location is Kenya and the source of malfeasance the drugs industry). In *Blood Diamond*, such issues form the backdrop, characteristically, for a series of dramatic conflicts between the principals: fisherman Soloman Vandy (Djimon Hounsou), who finds and hides a huge diamond after being imprisoned by a rebel faction; Zimbabwean smuggler and former mercenary Danny Archer (Leonardo DiCaprio), who offers to help reunite Vandy with his family in return for a share in the proceeds of the diamond; and journalist Maddy Bowen (Jennifer Connelly), who agrees to use her contacts to assist Vandy in return for information from Archer that will enable her to expose those involved in the illegal trade. How exactly the two dimensions are combined, and with what effect in the overall positioning of the film, is the central issue addressed in this chapter. A number of overlapping oppositions can be established within which to locate the strategies employed by the film as an example of studio quality production. As was the case with *Inception*, examined in Chapter 2, *Blood Diamond* might be viewed as an example in which claims to quality are liable to be contested rather than more straightforward or entirely accepted. This remains a matter of degrees, however, as is the case with all the case studies analysed in this book and with the broader conception of quality Hollywood in general.

A key axis implicit in the social problem film is the relative weighting of what can be boiled down to the rival imperatives of serious *education* and popular *entertainment*. In their most socially concerned dimensions, films of this kind seek to educate the viewer to some extent, to provide enlightenment on what is usually presented as a pressing social issue. Didacticism is the distinguishing feature of the social problem film, Roffman and Purdy suggest, social themes being highlighted on the surface of the dramatic action rather than only emerging implicitly from beneath.[5] This is the primary claim of such films to quality status, as products designed, ultimately, to perform a 'worthwhile' role (whether or not specifically defined as 'political' in its implications), beyond or in addition to that of 'mere' entertainment or profitability. The opposition between education and entertainment is not an absolute one, though; the makers of such films would doubtless argue that the provision of a social message in entertaining form is likely to make it more effective *as* a message, by enabling it to reach a larger audience. How far this might involve compromise at the level of the message is a frequent source of critical attention in relation to films of this kind and is one of the issues considered in more detail below. Even if the two might work together in some respects, two distinct sets of dynamics can usually be identified.

Nested within the education/entertainment opposition are a number of others, including an opposition between claims that are made to the status of realism and what might be termed 'Hollywood confection' or fantasy: key poles in wider distinctions between that which is accorded or denied quality status. Realism, here, implies a serious and sustained engagement with something close to the on-the-ground or deeper background realities of whatever issues are being explored. Hollywood confection is a term I suggest to encompass a range of contrivances, conveniences and heightening devices typically employed in studio features of all kinds. Each of these modalities also has formal dimensions that make their own claims to one kind of status or the other, although these can closely overlap in some instances, as is suggested below. Another related opposition, of particular relevance to the territory occupied by *Blood Diamond*, concerns the extent to which such films trade in or seek to transcend familiar stereotypical treatments of the material, in this case the employment or questioning of prevailing – and usually racist – stereotypes of 'Africa', its peoples, or essentialist notions of 'African-ness'.

Social issues, 'education', and the limitations of Hollywood engagement

Much of the material that positions itself overtly as educative is situated close to the start of *Blood Diamond*, establishing a context that remains prominent on occasion but largely in the background for the majority of the running time. Opening titles locate the setting as 'Sierra Leone, 1999', successive lines of text informing us that 'Civil war rages for control of the diamond fields', 'Thousands have died and millions have become refugees', 'None of whom has ever seen a diamond'. A claim is made from the start for a location of real-world crisis and import rather than of purely fictional confection. A quiet, early morning scene features Vandy awakening his young son Dia (Kagiso Kuypers) and readying him for school, following which comes a sequence of intensely dramatised action in which troops from the rebel Revolutionary United Front (RUF) career into the village and eventually kidnap Vandy. Subsequent material includes a dramatisation (although relatively brief) of one of the activities for which the RUF became most notorious, the severing of the hands of some of their captives, a fate from which Vandy wins a last second reprieve.

Having established a sense of urgency and atrocity in relation to the situation on the ground in the West African state, the film then shifts to its most sustained 'education' sequence, one that serves to make a connection between these events – in a distanced, 'exotic' locale – and a world closer to that of the primary target audience of such productions at home and in the 'developed' world. The viewer is provided with a series of exchanges between delegates to a G8 conference on diamonds in Belgium (see Figure 5.1). These have the effective status of a mini-lecture, the full text of which – accompanied by footage that intercuts between the speakers and scenes from the mining area to which Vandy is taken – is worth reproducing in detail:

> *First speaker:* Throughout the history of Africa, whenever a substance of value is found the locals die in great number and in misery. Now, this was true of ivory, rubber, gold and oil. It is now true of diamonds. According to a devastating report by Global Witness, these stones are being used to purchase arms and finance civil war. We must act to prohibit the direct or indirect import of all rough diamonds from conflict zones.

> *Second speaker:* May I remind you that the US is responsible for two-thirds of all diamond purchases worldwide and I don't anticipate that demand diminishing.

Figure 5.1. Lecturing to the audience: part of the G8 sequence in *Blood Diamond* © Lonely Film Productions

> *Third speaker.* We must remember that these stones comprise only a small percentage of the legitimate diamond industry whose trade is crucial to the economies of many emerging nations.
> *Second speaker.* It's true. Current estimates are that conflict stones account for only 15 per cent of the market. But in a multi-billion dollar a year industry, that means hundreds of millions of dollars are available for weapons in the conflict zones.

The conference scenes conclude with applause for two representatives of the diamond industry said 'wholeheartedly' to endorse the proposal to ban the import of conflict stones; suited figures whose smug smiles suggest otherwise, as will prove to be the case. Relatively few further references to the underlying issue of the trade in blood diamonds are made during the main body of the film. Maddy at one point asks Archer whether he cares how many people die as a result of the deals he makes. His response includes a claim that she also, effectively, helps to sell blood diamonds, via seductive advertisements that appear in the magazine for which she writes. Soon afterwards, keeping his part of their deal, he explains to her how the diamond corporation featured in the film, Van De Kaap, maintains its ability to profit from conflict stones by handling them through an indirectly owned subsidiary. We are subsequently informed that a key strategy of the corporation is to keep diamonds off the market, to limit supply and so maintain high prices. Having taken control of the diamond fields of Sierra Leone, the

RUF threatens to flood the market; hence the benefit gained by Van De Kaap from prolonging the war (a South African private mercenary army with which the corporation is in league has sold arms to the rebels while also being employed against them by the government). At the end of the film, Maddy's article is shown to have unmasked Van De Kaap, partly through the documentation of the deal arranged with Vandy, through which he is paid £2 million for his stone and the return of the remainder of his family is arranged. Closing titles inform the viewer about the signing of the Kimberley Process in 2003, a certification scheme designed to curb the illicit trade. But, we are told, 'illegal diamonds are still finding their way to market. It is up to the consumer to insist that a diamond is conflict-free'.

What, then, should we make of this treatment of the issue of conflict diamonds? A number of relevant factual contexts are established, but only, it seems, to a limited extent. Much is left out of the picture. I should make it clear that my purpose in comparing what the film presents with some aspects of the broader reality of these issues is not primarily to make qualitative judgement of the film, as often appears to be the case in work that measures Hollywood treatment of real-world issues against an understanding of their reality. A frequent tendency in writing about Hollywood versions of historical events, for example, is to do little more than criticise such films for what are seen as their inaccuracies and failings. My aim is to offer an understanding of the particular ways studio films tend to handle such material; to *explain* rather than simply to criticise what can often be viewed as a typical Hollywood approach.

A notable feature of the stance taken by *Blood Diamond* is that final title, one that seeks to put the onus on the consumer. Implicitly, that means viewers of the film, should they be purchasers of diamonds at any point (that the latter is often likely to be the case is established briefly in a nod to the immense success achieved by the diamond industry in convincing populations that its products are the only acceptable norm for the contents of engagement and/ or wedding rings). This makes little rational sense. It appears to be widely accepted opinion that the Kimberly Process could never have been other than ineffective, given the ease with which diamonds are smuggled across national borders and the financial incentives available to various parties to forge certification paperwork.[6] How, then, could the consumer be expected to be responsible for knowledge of the provenance of diamonds? The only sense this really makes is as a rhetorical and deeply ideological exhortation: a way of seeking to make a direct link between the responsibilities of individual consumers/viewers and the events of the film. This can be understood in the context of a broader individualist ideology and its Hollywood dimension, in the processes of melodramatic-emotional allegiance such films seek to create – as a core component of studio film modality – between viewer and on-screen activity. Very little is offered in the way of any more analytical insight into the underlying issues, a quality that generally lies beyond the orbit of prevailing Hollywood norms.

Much more could have been said. A point made by Janine Roberts, in her exposé of the diamond trade – and particularly the activities of the dominant player, De Beers, for which Van De Kaap is an obvious stand-in – is that the part of the business that is the focus of this debate is only one of many highly dubious aspects of the industry.[7] Others include the very poor working and living conditions forced upon many miners in other countries, in which basic heath and safety precautions are often ignored. From the very beginning, Roberts argues, De Beers traded in conflict diamonds, via their use by its founder, Cecil Rhodes, to fund the extension of the British Empire in the late nineteenth century.[8] A case could be made, therefore, for the dubious provenance of diamonds on a scale much larger than that restricted to particular war zones, not to mention an array of other questionable anti-competitive practices pursued by De Beers.

The opening G8 statement about the historical costs of the discovery of valuables in Africa could also be accused of casting such a process in conveniently neutral language, with no reference to the colonial powers that were typically involved or to the legacy of imperialism that resulted (there is one later pointed reference to the colonial context, although only in passing, in a comment from a schoolteacher that the Belgians were the first to chop off hands in Africa). The particular situation of a 'failed state' such as Sierra Leone in this period can also be understood at least in part to be a product of the colonial heritage.[9]

To accuse the film of failing to supply such a wider context in any of these dimensions would be somewhat to miss the point, however, as it would be unrealistic to expect to find material of this kind – other than, perhaps, occasionally, in passing reference – in a studio production. To understand this is to acknowledge some of the structural limitations of the usual Hollywood mode of cinema, including productions such as this that make a show of including some degree of investment in social problems/issues of this nature. To go radically further would generally require a different modality and less individual-centred focus, most likely to be found in a documentary production of independent status that creates space for a more analytical or investigative approach to such material, or a very different kind of narrative orientation. It should come as no surprise, therefore, that the blood diamond issue is positioned largely in the background of the film or that the most prominent inclusion of such background, in the G8 sequence, should follow rather than precede a major action sequence and be intercut with some of its aftermath, including the larger-than-life presence of the RUF leader Captain Poison (David Harewood), a figure whose appearance and comments stand in vivid contrast to those of the bland suits at the G8. The dramatic events of the main narrative of the film are presented in a manner that is far more immediately compelling than any of the background, as would be expected of a studio production of this kind and in keeping with the tradition of the social problem film as examined by Roffman and Purdy.

A more detailed understanding of how a film such as *Blood Diamond* engages with social problems can be gained from an examination of its treatment of some broader issues relating to what is presented as a general 'African' context, rather than that only specific to the issue of blood diamonds in Sierra Leone. Part of its status as a social problem film is established in this terrain, in a general background of atrocity and human suffering. The use of such material has led to *Blood Diamond* being grouped by some commentators within a category described as 'the human rights film', along with a number of contemporary non-studio productions considered below such as *Shooting Dogs* (2005) and *Hotel Rwanda*.[10] This includes representation of RUF practices such as the severing of limbs and particularly the abuse of child soldiers that forms a significant, although minor, strand of the

Figure 5.2. Focusing on individuals: Vandy (Djimon Hounsou) almost reunited with his family at the refugee camp in *Blood Diamond* © Lonely Film Productions

plot via the experiences of Dia (forced to kill and to inject drugs, generally presented as being brainwashed and brutalised). Such material is typical of the kind of social problem that is perhaps most likely to receive Hollywood attention, in its vividly heightened capacity to generate an outraged response on the part of the viewer – with the added sentimental potential of a topic such as the abuse of children – but also to provide striking imagery and scenarios.

The blood diamond trade itself shares in some of this quality: as a social problem it is one that has more than usual capacity for a potent mixture of glamour and brutality, for heightened contrast between products of the highest luxury and a production context that involves elements of seemingly the lowest depravity. For all its dark and disturbing qualities, that is, this is material that lends itself to the stuff of stirring melodrama, in which Hollywood frequently trades, particularly when explored through a characteristic focus on the travails of a small group of pained individual protagonists. Less immediately dramatic and action-oriented evidence of a general impression of 'African suffering' is also provided through footage of the dispossessed and the background activities of agencies such as the World Food Programme, most notably in a sequence set at a vast refugee camp in neighbouring Guinea, where Vandy finds but is unable at this stage to be reunited with his wife and two daughters (see Figure 5.2). The broader backcloth of mass suffering implied by shots of the camp is once more outweighed – again, in a typically Hollywood manner – by closer focus on the melodramatic exchanges between Vandy and his family.

What the film offers in the way of explanatory accounts of the situation in Sierra Leone – either specifically, or as part of a broader African context – is a long way short of any real analysis, as might be expected for the same reasons as its limitations in relation to the context of conflict diamonds. There are no clearly marked 'educative' speeches about any of this, or any real evidence of an attempt to explain at all in the manner that might be found in more analytical sources.[11] What we are offered here are some of the opinions of Archer, and one or two other figures, counterposed with the position of Maddy, although the latter, notably, does not present any meaningful diagnosis of her own. Archer's views are broadly reactionary and simplistic in nature. His fallback line – also employed by two other characters – is the acronym 'TIA', which translates as the supposed truism 'This is Africa'. This is an essentialising construct, one that implies that things are just 'like this', always and inevitably, in Africa and that nothing can be done about it (and thus, implicitly, that a self-serving figure such as Archer is largely absolved of any guilt for pursuing his own ends). Archer's speech leading up to the first deployment of the acronym goes as follows:

> Peace Corps types only stay around long enough to realise they're not helping anyone. Government only wants to stay in power until they've stolen enough to go into exile somewhere else. And the rebels, they're not sure they want to take over; otherwise they'd have to govern this mess.

A shorter version of such sentiment is provided by the driver of a vehicle in which Archer, Vandy and Maddy ride as part of a convoy of journalists: 'Government bad, rebels worse. No one gives a toss any more.' How should we understand comments such as these, within the broader context of what the film appears to be saying? The answer is less than entirely clear, in a manner that seems functional to the positioning of a production of this kind. Such statements are marked as being cynical and world-weary, but as a cynicism that might seem

to be a product of experience. Maddy is positioned, largely in contrast, as something of a 'do-gooder', whose attitude might be considered – in these terms – to be naive. The attitude we are expected to
take towards Archer is far from clear-cut, however. Another significant marker of the quality status of *Blood Diamond*, in Hollywood
terms, is the characterisation of Archer as a far from entirely sympathetic figure. In this respect, despite many other differences, the
film has something centrally in common with *The Social Network* and
The Assassination of Jesse James. Archer seems in some core dimensions
to be an embodiment of an unreconstructed white-settler heritage,
given to expressions of apparently overt racism, along with the pursuit of self-centred activities that display no regard for their victims.
Not only does he smuggle conflict diamonds out of Sierra Leone, but
he also trades arms to the rebels in return and has a background as a
mercenary with what appears to be an entirely amoral private army.

The nature of Archer's character is such that the viewer might be
encouraged to dismiss his opinions about the broader situation. But
space is also left available for them to be accepted; or, perhaps more
likely, for the viewer not really to be required to come to a firm opinion on these matters, given the extent to which they remain in the
background. They do not have to be followed through as part of the
logic of the resolution of the main events of the narrative, a typically
evasive feature of the studio social problem format. No rival explanation is offered. In response to Maddy's question about whether or
not he cares how many die as a result of his activities, Archer's reply is
that 'people here kill themselves as a way of life. It's always been like
that', another essentialising comment that seems designed to absolve
himself from any responsibility. He then challenges Maddy in turn,
asking if she thinks she is going to change the outcome, to which her
response is typically Hollywood in its avoidance of any social level
of engagement. Not all Africans kill each other as a way of life, she
comments, reasonably enough, adding that: 'it's a shit, *shit* world, but
you know what? Good things are done every day, just apparently not
by you.' An appeal is made to a vague notion of 'good things being
done', rather than to anything involving structural causes, however
complex those might be, or broader prescriptions for improvement,
however difficult those might also remain.[12] This is the terrain on

which Hollywood is most comfortable, as a core aspect of the established classical/canonical narrative style: that of 'good things' done by individual agents rather than interventions at any more complex social, political or collective level. Archer, will, of course, turn out to do his own good thing, collaborating with Maddy in the exposure of the activities of Van De Kaap and eventually sacrificing himself in securing the escape of Vandy and Dia.

The precise manner in which Archer's character is articulated merits further attention, as a crucial axis around which the film revolves in its relative positionings towards the quality or more standard Hollywood ends of the spectrum, in relation to both his opinions and broader aspects of characterisation. This is an area in which the film makes a substantial commitment to a sustained degree of realism. Little effort is made in the majority of the film to soften the harsh edges of the character, although some background context-cum-justification is provided. Archer is not, generally, a likeable figure, although he is shown to be extremely capable, an issue to which we return below. DiCaprio's performance (picking up on the quality dimension of his star image, as outlined in Chapter 2) is a key component of the dynamic, complete with what sounds reasonably like an authentically harsh-edged white southern African accent and a tendency towards an unfriendly sneering demeanour. At times, Archer acts in an overtly racist manner. The film performs some typically Hollywood manoeuvres in this dimension, but it goes further than usual in establishing a number of unsympathetic characteristics that create an impression of distinction from the studio norm. These dynamics are most clearly in play during a series of exchanges between Archer and Vandy as the pair make their way from an army camp to the village where the diamond is hidden and where the latter hopes to find Dia.

Archer's general approach here is cold and domineering. He orders Vandy about, prompting the latter sarcastically to call him 'boss'. After Vandy puts them at risk during the night, Archer makes a number of distinctly unpleasant comments, referring to having tracked 'black terrorists' in Angola by the smell of their shit, a comment with blatantly racist connotations following earlier remarks about hunting baboons in the same manner. If Vandy puts his life at risk again, Archer threatens nastily, he will peel his face from his head.

In a later argument Archer calls Vandy 'my boy' and '*kaffir*', clearly exposing his racist background, after which the two scuffle when Vandy wants to go into a village to look for Dia. After a 'heartfelt' plea, Archer relents and accompanies Vandy that night (without any success), following which they talk in less hostile terms. Eventually, the two work together to triumph over the forces of both the RUF and the mercenary army in the recovery of the diamond and Dia.

This is, in the end, a classic instance of Hollywood reconciliation of apparent oppositions, and might be expected. In a sense, the distance established between the two exists primarily in order to be over-come, and to heighten the emotional impact of triumphant reconcili-ation when it occurs: a very standard Hollywood dynamic. But *Blood Diamond* goes significantly further than usual in the articulation of the first stage of the process. The hostility between the two seems uncom-fortably real and sustained, and grounded in Archer's background. It goes beyond the modality of the kind of hostile-but-not-really banter more typical of Hollywood treatments of such relationships (for example, that between the characters played by Bruce Willis and Samuel L. Jackson in *Die Hard with a Vengeance* [1995], another example in which the two eventually work together, as a team, to overcome both their antagonists and their own differences).

The manner in which this is articulated is related to the broader question of whether or not Archer will eventually 'do the right/good thing', which involves keeping his side of a bargain made with Vandy for them to share the proceeds from the diamond, a point on which we are encouraged to remain to some extent uncertain (the sustained maintenance of this uncertainty has something in common with the length of time the viewer is encouraged to remain in doubt about the potential guilt of Dave in *Mystic River*). The film treads a careful line here between conventional expectation and allowance for some doubt as to whether or not this will be fulfilled. Hollywood convention would lead us to expect that Archer must come good, but the writing and performance of the character make this appear significantly more in question than would usually be the case. When it comes to the crunch, when Vandy is held by the mercenaries and told to dig up the diamond for them, Archer appears to be taking the side of his former colleagues. Having proposed a split of the value of the diamond with

Figure 5.3. Ambiguous relationship: an exchange of looks between Archer
(Leonardo DiCaprio) and Vandy (Djimon Hounsou) in *Blood Diamond*
© Lonely Film Productions

his past commander, Colonel Coetzee (Arnold Vosloo), he instructs
Vandy to tell them where it is buried. He also whispers in Vandy's
ear, however, that 'they're going to shoot us both in the head', which
suggests that he is not really going along with Coetzee. Archer then
shouts aggressively at Vandy, in what might appear to be a theatrical
display for the benefit of Coetzee, and Vandy continues to refuse. At
this point Archer agrees a 70/30 split with Coetzee and commits
what appears to be a heinous act of betrayal, grabbing Dia from a
group in the background and revealing his status to Coetzee, thus
providing leverage to be used against Vandy.

What exactly Archer is doing here remains somewhat ambiguous,
however. On the one hand, he appears to have given up on Vandy and
to have betrayed him in the most cynical manner, by revealing the presence of Dia. But, on the other, the film provides further hints that this
is not the case. A number of looks are exchanged between Archer and
Vandy, and from Archer more generally (see Figure 5.3). These are not
heavily freighted with obvious meaning, as might have been the case, but
contain just sufficient to seem to confirm the impression that Archer
is 'up to something'; enough to make us suspect that he will eventually act for the good, even where aspects of his current behaviour suggest otherwise, as we would more generally be encouraged to expect
given his status as star-portrayed central protagonist. This impression is
increased, through further looks on the part of Archer, once the party

arrives at the point where the diamond is buried, eventually seeming to be confirmed when, amid the distraction of a pretence to unearth the rock, Archer grabs one soldier and Vandy hits another, after which the pair prevail.

Whether or not Archer might still be intent on betrayal at this point is left open, at the level of immediate events, whatever our more Hollywood-conventional expectations might be. As the trio make their way towards a hilltop rendezvous point, where they are to be picked up by a plane, Archer insists that Vandy hands over the diamond, a move that seems to signify dubious intent. He then radios the pilot of the aircraft, who instructs him to 'lose' Vandy and the child. But the counter-impression, that the two are working now as a team, is increased in subsequent scenes. Archer turns out to have been wounded in the exchanges with the mercenaries and is carried by Vandy – now, the stronger of the two, accompanied by 'heroically' building strains on the soundtrack – as they climb higher into the hills. Realising that he is not going to make it and in too much pain to continue, Archer gives Vandy the diamond, a gun and instructions and tells him to go, providing covering fire that helps to ensure the latter's escape with his son.

The death of Archer appears to be a device necessary to the film at this point, providing a way out of what might otherwise be an impossible bind resulting from the twin imperatives of Hollywood norm and relative marker of distinction. It saves the film, ultimately, from having to follow through the logic of his character. The question of whether or not he would, otherwise, have kept his side of the bargain is side-stepped. If he survived, very strong Hollywood convention would surely make the 'noble' act unavoidable: the lead character, played by a major star, could hardly be seen to act in any other way when it comes down to it. But for that to have happened, the film would risk being seen overtly to fall back on hoary cliché, a move that in this case would have clashed noticeably with the greater-than-usual degree of commitment to harsh realism manifested by the manner in which the character has primarily been drawn. A sacrificial death is itself cliché enough, of course, but one that obviates any need to resolve the question of what might have happened otherwise and that leaves the previous characterisation substantially intact. Archer's death also provides a convenient way to avoid having to follow through on the nature of the relationship that develops between the smuggler and Maddy, one that appears to be moving implicitly, but in an under-stated manner, in the direction of romance. For the two eventually to have come fully together, implicitly entailing some reconciliation of the very different values for which they stand, would have been the stuff of more obvious cliché than *Blood Diamond* appears to want to mobilise in these areas. The film is able to offer sufficient 'happy ending', in the form of the reuniting of Vandy and his family and the exposure of Van De Kaap's operation, to balance the more downbeat but necessary and heroic demise of Archer.

If Archer is allowed to remain a more plausibly realistic character in some respects than is the norm in Hollywood – his 'difficult' qualities more grounded and less easily shuffled off en route to his elevation to martyrdom – the film also performs the more conventional man-oeuvre of providing some elements of explanation/justification for his attitudes. He is, himself, to some extent, accorded the exculpatory status of a victim, telling Maddy of the rape and murder of his mother and decapitation of his father when he was nine years old, the context of which is not explained. He is also at pains to explain that he fought in Angola alongside black troops, although this does not seem to be enough to displace evidence of ingrained racism.

This is Hollywood: confection, coincidence and the persistence of stereotype

Other aspects of the characterisation of Archer contribute to the more conventional dynamics of the film, as do a number of contriv-ances beyond the convenience of his death. Dislikeable though he might be in some respects, Archer is presented as an extremely cap-able figure, in his traversal of the dangerous urban and rural landscapes of war-torn Sierra Leone. To some extent, his capability here seems implicitly to give added weight to the dubious opinions he has about the situation in this and other such countries. The impression is given that his views are based on sustained experience and engagement on the ground, unlike that of Maddy, who is presented as a dedicated journalist but one who is essentially a short-term visitor to theatres of this kind. His ability to master the landscape is also a key ingredient in the action-adventure dimension of the film, on which more below.

Contrivance is, in many respects, one of the bases of Hollywood narrative. At a very basic level, *Blood Diamond* depends on a number of coincidences, primarily those which ensure that Archer and Vandy both end up in the same Freetown jail and that the former overhears the words of the RUF officer who witnessed Vandy's possession of the diamond. Further coincidence involves the meeting of Archer and Maddy and the three-way dependent relationship that develops among the trio. Coincidences of this kind are more or less taken as read, as essential points of departure for Hollywood plots of any kind. *Blood Diamond* also provides numerous more overt moments of plot contrivance, however, elements that play a major part in its situation as a still largely mainstream-conventional production. These often take the form of outbreaks of heightened dramatic action – particularly involving plenty of fighting, gunfire and explosions – that occur at key moments in the development of the plot and of the interpersonal dynamics between the principals. An early example is found imme-diately after the key plot point constituted by Vandy's discovery of his large diamond. He is apprehended by a guard as he is about to hide the gem, but at precisely this moment army troops launch an attack on the RUF base, injuring the guard and so ensuring the survival of Vandy.

A similar action-dramatic contrivance occurs at another key moment, when Archer makes his proposal to Vandy, having secur-ing the latter's release from jail, offering to help him find his family in return for splitting the proceeds from the diamond. The sequence in which this is located begins with news reports of an incursion into Freetown by the RUF, but it is at exactly this moment that they are manifested on the screen. Several truckloads of rebel troops appear, heading directly towards the pair, prompting Archer's urgent demand: 'What's it going to be, yes or no? Yes or no?' Vandy's reply is an uncertain 'Where do we go?' that seems to be an implied assent, but one into which he appears forced by the pressure of the imme-diate source of danger. The dramatic stakes of the decision are, as a result, greatly heightened by a staging that, outside the world of

Hollywood, would be considered an unlikely coincidence of crisis at the local-personal and broader-canvas levels.

The force of events also seems to be such as to bypass the need for Vandy to have made any more considered decision (afterwards, when the two join a line of refugees leaving the city together, Vandy says he has agreed to nothing, to which Archer's response is that 'you have no choice'). Another such coincidence occurs in the later stages of the film, when Vandy is captured after trying to rescue Dia. He is ordered to dig up the diamond, a machete being held at the neck of his son. It is again at precisely this critical juncture that an attack ensues – this time, that of the mercenary forces – and permits Vandy to make off with Dia, the start of an action sequence in which Archer ends up protecting Dia amid the general mayhem that results. A similar effect occurs in the final parting between Vandy and Archer. If the former seems reluctant to leave the latter behind, an outbreak of gunfire from the pursuing mercenaries – who seem to have caught up at just the right moment to interrupt and displace this moment of quietly intense character interaction – again has the effect of putting the issue beyond the need for individual decision.

Outbreaks of action of these kinds often seem to short-circuit any other process in *Blood Diamond*, creating what appears to be a sheer force of circumstances in the diegetic universe, against which everything else falls away. They are also major components of the film in their own right, of course, both in themselves – offering particular kinds of cinematic experiences – and in the opportunities they create for character action, particularly on the part of Archer. At each level, as might be expected, this is a dimension in which the film is at its most mainstream-Hollywood in orientation and more so than any of the case studies included in this book other than *Inception*. If offering a seemingly authentic texture of performance in some respects, the figuration of Archer is one that also partakes of rather more implausible activity: super-accomplished white masculine behaviour of a kind that seems rooted in the separate universe of fiction-fantastical action heroics.

Two examples of this are the sequences in which Archer leads Vandy to safety in the heat of the RUF incursion into Freetown and that in which he takes command of a vehicle during an attack on the convoy

Figure 5.4. Heroic white male agency amid the mayhem: Archer (Leonardo DiCaprio) leads Vandy (Djimon Hounsou) through the war-torn streets of Freetown in *Blood Diamond* © Lonely Film Productions

of journalists. In each case he assumes charge in an indomitable manner, securing the safety of his charges (in the first case, Vandy, in the second, Vandy and Maddy) amid surroundings of chaos and slaughter. When Vandy, in the first of these sequences, asks 'Where do we go?', Archer's answer is: 'Follow me', which is exactly what he is required to do, it is implied, in order to survive. Archer leads him through a sustained series of immediate threats on the streets of the city: threading a way through stationary cars towards the start, from the surfaces of which machine-gun bullets ping in close proximity; finding cover behind various obstacles as they go, hitting the ground and crawling, when necessary; standing up and running at the opportune moment (see Figure 5.4). Around them are scenes of what appear to be directionless panic and death. In marked contrast, Archer offers direction and guidance, a constant series of instructions on what exactly to do and when: 'stay low', 'come on', 'this way', and the like. When they go to ground to avoid the impact of one explosion, for example, Archer keeps his arm on Vandy, telling him to 'wait' before getting up and adding 'now' to indicate the right time to move – as others, apparently lacking so perspicacious a guide, are gunned down in the road ahead.

A similar dynamic structures Archer's response to the attack on the convoy. When the driver of the vehicle in which he is travelling with Vandy and Maddy is shot, he shoves the body out of the door and slides behind the wheel to take charge once again. Under heavy machine-gun fire, those on the ground outside are being killed. A bus in which the trio had earlier been seated is strafed, its windows heavily bloodied. Where you would want to be in this situation, it is implied, is not amid the helpless collectivity of those on the bus, but in the capable hands of a source of hyper-capable individual white/male agency such as Archer, able to take direct action, as he does in the heightened sequence of skilful driving under fire that follows, again accompanied by verbal guidance to those who cower in the back seats (a type of Hollywood-conventional effective agency the absence of which from the two films examined in the previous chapter is among their clearest markers of distinction from the studio norm).

A number of dynamics are in play here that are of direct relevance to the positioning of *Blood Diamond* towards the more mainstream end of the Hollywood/quality spectrum. These relate both to the type of filmmaking that is embodied in such antics, further to be considered at the level of the visual qualities through which such action is manifested, and to the general politics of representation that is involved, particularly in relation to figurations of Africa and the reliance of the film on some familiar racial and gender stereotypes.

As far as the visual qualities of the film are concerned, these and other action sequences employ a number of core features of the intensified continuity approach cited in earlier chapters, and usually associated with mainstream as opposed to quality Hollywood style. The general impression is one of an urgent intensity, an effect created through devices such as the use of wavering, unstable camerawork and quick cutting, a style that is at its most heightened when the camera is situated in close proximity to the action. Longer shots that establish general orientation and larger views of the deployment of forces are outweighed by footage in which the camera is up close, giving the viewer the impression of being taken intimately into the heart of the action. Some shots offer something akin to a subjective position, that of a camera that seems itself to be responding, unstably, to the surrounding chaos – a wavering glimpse of a death here, someone else fleeing there – while others take a position akin to that of an additional protagonist situated closely alongside the principals.

This style, deployed in all the major action sequences of *Blood Diamond*, has potential to provide mixed resonances as far as the more general positioning of the film is concerned. At one level, they might seem to give an added sense of realism to the events, through the use of visual repertoires more traditionally associated with certain kinds of *vérité*-style documentary footage. Unstable camerawork of this variety seeks to confect an impression of realism by replicating the kinds of shortcomings in the images that might result from a case of actual reportage of unfolding events. Characteristic markers of this style include wavering motions from side to side and/or up and down, the occasional abrupt zoom and relatively fast cutting, including cutting into mobile camerawork that increases the overall impression of chaotic proximity to the action. The camera appears to be struggling to keep up and to be responding, at the limits of its capacity, to action for which it has been unprepared. On some occasions a slight strobing quality is given to the image, particularly visible in shots of fissiparous material such as exploding debris or a sudden spray of water or blood from a body, an effect created by manipulation of camera shutter angle (one of the best-known and most overt uses of this technique is found in the highly intensified battle sequences of *Saving Private Ryan* [1998]).

If a rhetorical claim to the status of realism is made through the employment of this style, it might serve to ground the rather more implausible aspects of the display of Archer's super-competence involved in numerous sequences of this kind. It could, therefore, be located among the film's markers of relative quality. At the same time, however, this approach had in this period become a familiar part of the Hollywood action film (associated particularly, but far from exclusively, with the *Bourne* franchise, from 2002), sufficiently so for it to signify not so much a claim to realism in itself but part of a conventional generic repertoire: a heightened (and thus clearly fabricated) pitch for a certain variety of realism – but one that is located within a format generally accorded lower cultural status, and thus generally an example of the more mainstream leanings of the film. It could cut either way, which is another dimension of the film that seems functional – if not deliberately designed for this purpose – to the overall positioning of a work of this kind that has feet in both the quality and more mainstream-conventional camps (an example of a division between these two positions within the work of a single director, Paul Greengrass, might be found in a comparison between the documentary-quality claims of the sober and fact-based ensemble drama *United 93* [2006] and the more conventional associations of such camerawork in his two entries in the *Bourne* series).

In general, the film is more classical in approach, like *Inception*, in reserving this kind of intensified style for its heightened action sequences. Some visuals also seek to create the kind of 'classy' impression found in the examples examined in the previous two chapters, but these are limited primarily to the opening passages and serve to establish an equilibrium that is disrupted by the incursion of the RUF. The film begins with Vandy striking a match and lighting a lantern that motivates a moderate form of pre-dawn chiaroscuro lighting of the kind found in *The Social Network* (not the more exaggerated variety employed at times in *The Assassination of Jesse James*). Classical *découpage*, mostly in mid and close shot interiors, is used to establish the waking of Dia and preparation for the trek to school. A number of more striking shots follow, including silhouettes and pink, orange and blue toned evocations of early morning sunlight in sky or reflected on water. The effect is to create a somewhat dreamy, idealised and aestheticised impression of the everyday lives of the Vandy family, before the idyll is shattered by the arrival of the rebels. Occasional 'scenic' images are deployed elsewhere in the film, particularly in the evocation of landscape. Most of the film is shot in a less marked manner, however. 'Magic hour' lighting is used in some instances, shooting just before sunset or after sunrise, when a low sun creates a soft, diffused and beautifying image quality. But this is employed in a standard directionally lit Hollywood manner rather than in pursuit of a more pronounced or overt beauty of image. Heightened forms are kept, in classical manner, for the evocation of heightened states, principally those of intensified action, rather than being used more liberally – another factor that contributes, although less overtly, to the overall balance of the production as a whole.

If the film makes formal claims to a grounding in reality in action sequences such as those examined above, its racial politics is rooted in far more dubious ideological territory. This is another dimension in which any of the progressive status traditionally associated with the social problem picture seems distinctly limited, the film drawing on a number of tropes familiar from what V.Y. Mudimbe terms the 'colonial library', a repository of discursive formations through which Africa has been understood in imperialist European terms.[13] Vandy is, in general, a positively coded figure, and so can be distinguished in this respect from a long tradition of more exclusively negative portrayals of black Africans in earlier Hollywood history.[14] At the same time, however, he also fits quite closely into a familiar stereotype, that of the 'Good African', drawn in a passive manner and as a figure largely unthreatening to prevailing racial inequalities. That Vandy is the one who follows and Archer is the leader embodies a core dimension of this very loaded figuration. It is also in this context that we should understand the manner in which Vandy seems repeatedly to be forced into decisions by circumstances, as detailed above, rather than as a result of his own active agency. In some scenes in the film, he seems to be accorded a reasonably strong individual presence and to be humanised in a standard Hollywood manner (the emotive outburst about his son, for example, that persuades Archer to go with him to look for Dia in the village at night). But in the key moments detailed above he seems to be stripped of any real ability to determine his own actions. That a plot/character rationale is provided for this difference between Archer and Vandy – the one, as mercenary-turned-smuggler, familiar with the world of action-thrills-danger; the other, as a fisherman, presumably not – merely seems to confirm some of the racially stereotypical constraints within which the film is structured.

These dynamics are complicated to a degree by the white-African status of Archer, but this only slightly militates against the stereotypical schema according to which he fits the equally familiar role of 'white helper' required by the sympathetic representative of the black African, a role shared in this case by Archer and Maddy (the less appealing dimensions of the 'helper' figure can, in this way, be projected onto Archer; Maddy is constructed as more unambiguously positive in intention and acting in some ways as his good conscience, although not capable of the gendered action exploits ultimately required to win the day). The 'good' black African is presented as a proud and reliable figure but as not being in control of his destiny, dependent on the help of such outsiders in order to be reunited with his family and/or to secure the proceeds of the diamond; just as, on a wider scale, black

Africa has often been seen as somehow in need of 'rescue' by what is usually cast as the wealthy, white 'West', rather than being accorded agency in its own right or its problems being understood at least partly to be rooted in the distinctly *un*helpful legacy of colonialism. In these respects, the film is implicated in a number of long-standing colonial discursive frameworks that share much in common with the Orientalist perspective examined by Edward Said, including the trope of Oriental (or, here, African) dependence on being rescued from its difficulties by representatives of the Occident.[15] As Margaret Higonnet suggests: 'Whatever their good intentions, Western films that raise issues of human rights often fall into a striking pattern that recapitulates the colonialist and paternalist representation of the white man who saves the people of color from themselves.'[16]

While *Blood Diamond* might express a cynical view of the effectiveness of any such rescue as attempted collectively by the United Nations (UN) or charitable agencies, largely through the opinions of Archer, it invests in them almost wholesale in the articulation of central character dynamics that form the most prominent dimension of the film. That Vandy ends up also helping Archer, briefly, when the latter is wounded and before he insists on being left behind, is only a brief and passing departure (it is, at least, a somewhat more substantial change from racist norms for it to be the white male hero who sacrifices himself to the escape of the black African, rather than the more familiar scenario in which a black sidekick or otherwise marginal character does the decent thing, or is otherwise disposed of, in favour of the securing of a white central couple). More generally, the film is also very familiar and conventional in its focus on an African locale only as a place of seemingly irresolvable crisis and suffering, or as a source of the exotic (in this case, in the extreme actions of the RUF), rather than as any more 'normal' or tractable background for dramatic action.

The characterisation of Archer as man-of-action and Vandy largely as passive recipient of his aid also resonates with a particular range of discursive constraints often applied to representations of black (African American) male figures in Hollywood, a phenomenon particularly noticeable in the realm of action cinema in recent decades. The dominant tradition here is for black characters not to be given the most assertive, all-out action roles, a tendency that, as Donald Bogle suggests, dates back to the deployment of the stereotype of the active and threatening 'brutal black brute' as a justification for racism in the early twentieth century (most notably in *The Birth of a Nation* [1915]).[17] The 'loose canon' figures of action films, those capable of exceptional heroic action but also often portrayed as in some ways potentially unstable, are usually white. Paired with such characters in a number of prominent instances – most notably the *Die Hard* and *Lethal Weapon* series – are black figures characterised as more nurturing, supportive and family-oriented, sharing some of the features of the traditional black 'mammy' stereotype. The latter is a more contained and constrained figure, as Ed Guerrero has suggested, one that seems to constitute less of a potential threat or problem to what can only be assumed to be a broadly racist social context (if it were not for the existence of such a context, it is hard to explain why such articulations would remain so persistent, despite the presence of some exceptions).[18] *Blood Diamond* seems to buy heavily into exactly this discursive regime in its opposition between Vandy (domesticated family man, and as such also to some extent feminised in this schema) and Archer (unattached and, as a result, it seems, rather than just coincidentally, capable of prodigious male-coded action exploits).

As a 'Good African', with no evident character flaws beyond an inability to perform some of the actions necessary to the situation in which he finds himself, Vandy is also positioned very schematically in the film as the opposite of the 'Bad/Evil/Nasty African' constituted principally by the RUF leader, Captain Poison. Vandy is positioned, in colonialist or neo-colonialist terms, as the 'civilised' African, as highlighted particularly by the commitment established on his part in the opening scene to the education of Dia (and the repeated refrain that Dia is going to become a doctor, a classic embodiment of rational/western 'civilisation'). He is structurally located as the type of African who has accepted something akin to the missionary project (the religious-symbolic status of the role of fisherman is resonant here): to educate and, supposedly, civilise, to gain Dia a better future than his own; ultimately, it seems, as articulated in this context, to buy into something akin to a westernising/modernising project.[19] Captain Poison, in contrast, can be understood as the latest in a long line of

Figure 5.5. Figures of the 'good' and 'bad' African: Vandy and Captain Poison (David Harewood) face-to-face in *Blood Diamond* © Lonely Film Productions

representations of the imaginary Africa of 'darkness' and 'savagery', a figure of nightmarish proportions in his organisation of activities such as the severing of hands, the recruitment of child soldiers and his general demeanour and appearance (see Figure 5.5).[20]

A demonic resonance is given to Poison, in particular, and the RUF in general, their activities being presented as more or less entirely beyond the pale and frequently associated with the flickering of flames (in night-time sequences in their camp and after the burning of a Freetown beach bar, where RUF figures dancing crazily amid the flames are made to be emblematic of the broader fall into chaos of the city). Like Archer, Poison is given lines that seek to provide some passing context for his actions, and a recognition of how they are being perceived, but in this case it is extremely attenuated and again without any specific context, just the comment that: 'You think I am a devil, but only because I have lived in hell.' That he also wants the diamond in order to escape provides a degree of parallel with Archer, and a modicum of greater resonance, but only in passing. Background reference is given in a faux BBC news report on the incursion into Freetown to the effect that 'atrocities' have been reported on both sides – which appears to have been true of the various parties involved in the civil war in Sierra Leone more generally[21] – but it is only those of one side that are given dramatic space.

Few other opportunities are provided for any more than passing representations of black Africans, beyond the background figures who perform familiar roles as either survivors, refugees or combatants. The teacher who makes the comment about Belgian colonialism is positioned in much the same manner as Vandy, in a smaller role, as a 'civilised' and 'civilising' presence, seeking to rehabilitate former child soldiers through education (he also reinforces the film's real ideological message about the supposed overriding importance of individual action, suggesting fatuously to Archer that even a bad man's life can be transformed by 'one moment of love'). A Freetown barman who figures in two scenes is also presented positively, as a friendly, knowing presence, and one who makes the point to Archer that the locals cannot simply flee the country as those from outside are able easily to do; but his is another minor role. Members of a black militia group into whose hands the principals fall briefly after the chase into the jungle are presented as a source of passing exotica more than anything else, turning out to be more naive and gullible than threatening when their leader falls for a quick-thinking (gendered) 'charm' routine from Maddy.

  Blood Diamond is far from alone in drawing on numerous tropes from the colonial library in its treatment of this kind of African terrain. A broadly similar focus on white 'helper' figures is also found in a number of non-Hollywood dramatisations of related issues, which suggests that the differences between work produced in and beyond the studios is one of relative degrees rather than being clear-cut. *Shooting Dogs*, a British production set during the genocide in Rwanda in the 1990s, is focused around the help provided by a white preacher, Christopher (John Hurt), and a young white teacher, Joe (Hugh Dancy), whose college becomes a (temporary) safe haven for Tutsis threatened with slaughter by Hutu militia. A notable exception is the performance of the central helping role by a black figure in the international co-production *Hotel Rwanda* (distributed by the American independent Lions Gate), based on the true story of the Hutu hotel manager Paul Rusesabagina (Don Cheadle). It is ultimately the white/western-characterised UN that rescues the group given sanctuary by Paul in his hotel, however, while additional assistance is provided from afar by the Belgian head of the company that owns the establishment. Paul is also figured very clearly as a white/European-oriented and mediating figure in his role as provider of western luxuries to his guests, even if he soon realises that any sense of being a part of that world is subject to withdrawal once the chips are down. Both films offer a critique of the extremely limited mandate given to the UN in Rwanda, each dramatising an almost identical situation in which UN troops are unable to intervene in the slaughter that surrounds them.

Some more pointed background context is provided in *Hotel Rwanda* as far as the post-colonial context is concerned, the point being made that the Hutu/Tutsi divide was a fabrication of the Belgian colonial power. This is an important point, absent from *Shooting Dogs*, suggesting that conflict of the kind experienced in the 1990s was not a product of some inevitable African 'savagery' but of a particular outside historical intervention which created the basis for subsequent events even if not their most immediate trigger.[22] Whether or not the existence of this extra dimension might be attributed to the non-Hollywood nature of the film seems open to question, however, particularly given that, like all the background supplied in these films, it is only given passing mention. *Shooting Dogs* and *Hotel Rwanda* both also risk falling into overly simplistic tropes of the kind used in *Blood Diamond* in their depiction of the Hutu militia in the demonic shape of sinister, chanting, arm-waving rag-tag mobs (even if this were an accurate representation of their appearance, the deployment of such images – and little else to add any human substance – brings into play a history of invidious associations). *Shooting Dogs* and *Hotel Rwanda* also share with *Blood Diamond* the confection of elements of personal-individual 'happy ending' that balance, to varying extents, their more downbeat emphasis on the broader massacre of innocents.

In both cases, an acknowledgement of large-scale killing – and effective criticism of the west, including specifically the United States – is combined with more upbeat personal-sentimental dynamics that might be accused of to some extent undermining or sugaring the broader message. A more political element of critique exists in these films than is found in *Blood Diamond*. Both include, for example, the same tendentious State Department attempt to hedge around the use of the term 'genocide' in relation to the mass killings. This seems to be in keeping with their non-Hollywood origins and relatively less mainstream industrial location, which generally permits more scope for the inclusion of such material. But any such difference seems qualified by the use of some of the more conventional strategies outlined above. The most obvious difference between these examples and *Blood Diamond* is the absence of any overt action heroics in the non-Hollywood instances, in which the heroism is a quiet matter of resolution and refusing to bow down to threats, rather than active exploits of the kind associated with Archer. This is a feature of another international social problem film set in Africa, *The Constant Gardener*, a conspiracy narrative, the focus of which is on the activities of a dishonest drug company acting with the complicity of senior British officials. The focus here, again, is almost entirely on white foreground characters against which Africa presents little more than 'exotic' background and figures of suffering/exploitation.

The degree of action heroics also distinguishes *Blood Diamond* from the main tradition of the social problem film, or from other political dramas of various periods that would be prime candidates for problem-related quality status. For Roffman and Purdy, the approach of classical-era problem films resulted from a combination of a particular set of social circumstances (including the Depression, Roosevelt's 'New Deal', the war against fascism and postwar idealism) and core conventions of classical Hollywood narrative as shaped by the consistent ideological frameworks inscribed in the production code. Changes at both levels undermined the particular formula of the time, they suggest, but a number of similarities can be identified in problem films of subsequent decades. Overt action sequences tend not to figure centrally in the format, the dominant tendency of which is to lean towards psychological forms of dramatic conflict (see, for example, the approach taken to HIV/AIDS in *Philadelphia* [1993] or to the evils of the tobacco industry in *The Insider* [1999]). This might be somewhat less the case in instances in which the 'problem' is located within a conflict situation, where a number of distinctions can be made between different approaches. Action often tends to happen *around*, or to be followed by, the main protagonists, rather than being enacted by them, in examples such as some of the treatments of Reagan-era issues in central America (more likely to be found in films produced in the independent sector, such as *Under Fire* [1983] and *Salvador* [1986]). Films that take on issues relating to the American-led wars on Iraq in 1991 and 2003 vary considerably in these terms, from examples that question (at least to some degree) to those which seem to reinstate capacity for heroic action in such spheres.[23]

Combining education and entertainment?

The focus on individual heroic action in an example such as *Blood Diamond*, and its use to ensure the achievement of individual/personal goals, is one of many issues that raise questions about the potential effectiveness of Hollywood or other commercially oriented films as sources of education about the kinds of problems they address. Does the primary focus at this level displace or undermine serious engagement in the issues, or reduce any scope such films might have to bring about change? A displacement of this kind certainly appears to take place at the textual level, as is suggested by a number of scholars who have addressed *Blood Diamond* and the other Africa-set examples cited above from this perspective. An 'aesthetic of closure', Margaret Higonnet suggests, 'inhibits the call to action by the audience that leaves the theatre'.[24] Elizabeth Goldberg identifies a mechanism common to a number of these and related examples in which the achievement of closure by the central protagonist(s) is followed by a movement in which 'the narrative field opens to foreground the historic referent' – typically, via closing titles of the kind found in *Blood Diamond, Hotel Rwanda* and many others.[25] We might add, though, that the former is dramatised and personalised, in a manner designed to give the viewer a vicarious experience from the inside, while the latter remains much more distant and abstract, and thus likely perhaps to have less impact on the viewer.

The result seems akin to that identified by Roffman and Purdy in the social problem films of the classical era, in which they suggest issues are raised only to be 'exorcised' onto 'safe targets contained within a dramatic rather than a social context. The effect is cathartic, purging us for the time being of anxieties and guilts over the state of the world'.[26] This does not mean we should assume that *no* educational impact can result, however, or that any such act of displacement at the textual level need entirely condition the experience of the viewer. This returns us to the somewhat dismissive verdict of Robert Ray on the problem films of the postwar decades, cited in the Introduction. Ray suggests that any concern with social issues is merely – and, he implies, ineffectively – 'grafted on' to the principal dramatic appeal of the narrative. Exactly how such different dimensions might interact in the experience of the viewer is likely to be more complex and difficult to determine with any certainty.

The diamond industry certainly took *Blood Diamond* seriously enough, its trade group, the World Diamond Council, spending a reported $15 million on a public relations campaign designed to combat any negative impact on the business.[27] The film prompted wider news coverage of the conflict diamonds issue, giving it a currency during the week of release despite the fact that the events it depicted were from the previous decade. The PR response of the industry also figured prominently in such coverage, however.[28] The studio itself seemed to encourage viewers to explore the issues further, the film's website providing links to the campaigning groups Amnesty International and Global Witness. The film opened in the US on 10 December, during the Christmas shopping period, the peak selling season for diamonds. What its impact might have been on actual sales remains unclear. A survey conducted by the Jewelry Consumer Opinion Council was reported to have found that, among consumers who saw *Blood Diamond*, two-thirds said it would not affect their willingness to purchase diamond jewellery; whether that implied that one-third *would* be affected was left unaddressed.[29]

At the domestic box office, the film performed disappointingly, suggesting a relatively limited direct reach, even if surrounding coverage might have brought the issues to a larger constituency. Given a solidly mainstream but not blockbuster-scale release on 1,910 screens, *Blood Diamond* grossed $57 million on a budget estimated at $100 million, although it took twice as much in the overseas market, perhaps partly on the basis of its international setting, achieving a final theatrical gross of $171 million.[30] In its advance round-up of offerings for the holiday season, *Variety* suggested that Warner had 'a challenge on its hands' with the film, on the basis of its 'politically aware' characteristics, although this seems likely to have been mitigated from the studio point of view by the presence of DiCaprio as one of the biggest star names of the time.[31] It was only when DiCaprio was signed on that the project had secured the go-ahead on large-budget scale, according to the director, Edward Zwick, in keeping with the kinds of constraints typically experienced by features with some aspirations towards the quality end of the spectrum, as seen in previous chapters. This is another case in which the deal involved a funding partner, Virtual Studios, as cited in the previous chapter, as a mitigator of any perceived risk. An earlier script circulating in Hollywood at the end of the 1990s had involved the hunt for a diamond but was said by Zwick to have been 'in the vein of an Indiana Jones movie', implying a project with fewer quality aspirations.[32] The director says he decided to pursue the wider ramifications of the scenario, bringing in consultants including Alex Yearsley from the human rights group Global Witness, whose work had played a key role in bringing public attention to the issue of conflict diamonds, which added to the more serious/educative credentials of the production.

As far as its key marketing materials are concerned, the film was positioned as solidly mainstream (as also suggested by the size of its opening), posters and trailers emphasising a combination of the presence of DiCaprio and the individual action-oriented dimensions, as would be expected for an entirely standard studio release. The main poster is dominated by DiCaprio's face, with Hounsou behind him, and both set in front of a flaming battleground, the red and yellow tones of which are reflected in their images as typical signifiers of 'explosive' action-adventure. The tag-line is 'From the director of *Glory* and *The Last Samurai*', seeking to create associations with titles rather than the name of Zwick himself and with no mention of the social problem dimension of the film. The centrality of diamonds is made clear in the trailer but not in any even vaguely political context, the emphasis being entirely on a mainstream-oriented combination of action and close interpersonal relations.

Zwick himself offers a typically Hollywood take on the question of the relative positioning of the film, commenting: 'I believe that ideas and entertainment can co-exist' and not seeming at all interested, in interview, in exploring any of the real tensions that might result in this or any other case.[33] Although his name was unlikely to be familiar to a wider public – hence its absence from the poster – Zwick's reputation within Hollywood at the time was for exactly the kind of mixture of quality and more mainstream-conventional resonances offered by *Blood Diamond*, as manifested in other examples such as *Glory* (1989), notable for featuring an all-black Civil War regiment, the Gulf war drama *Courage Under Fire* (1996), *The Siege* (1998), a prescient pre-9/11 dramatisation of the impact of Islamic militant attacks on Manhattan, and would-be 'epic' historical dramas such as *Legends of the Fall* (1994) and *The Last Samurai* (2003). This is exactly the kind of territory often associated, negatively, with the term 'middlebrow', as suggested in the Introduction, and liable to be viewed within prevailing hierarchies as either somewhat pretentious, in mainstream terms, or as lacking any real substance of engagement in serious issues. From a more positive Hollywood-oriented perspective, however, Zwick is a figure whose name is often associated in biographical sketches with terms such as 'thoughtful', 'intelligent' and 'cerebral' (such quality credentials being strengthened by his role as a non-directing producer of Indiewood titles such as *Shakespeare in Love* [1998] and *Traffic* [2000] and his involvement with critically approved television series including *Thirtysomething* [1987–91] and *My So-Called Life* [1994–95]).[34]

Press coverage suggested that each of the three main performers, as well as the director, had investments of some kind in the serious dimensions of the film: Hounsou as a West African with connections to the part of the world in which it was set, Connelly as a figure who had become an Amnesty International ambassador for human rights education in 2005 and DiCaprio as a star said to be strongly concerned about issues related to the exploitation of global resources.[35] This is another dimension in which Hollywood figures have often tried to present themselves as using their influence in pursuit of worthy causes rather than just for commercial gain, and in a process of transfer – one way or the other – between the on-screen and external worlds.

It is notable that the 'extras' provided on the DVD/Blu-ray release also tend to put the emphasis on the more serious/realistic dimensions of the film, framing it in a manner that skews more towards the quality end of the spectrum for those sufficiently interested to consume such para-textual material, in a manner similar in some respects to that noted in relation to *Inception* in Chapter 2. These include a 60-minute investigation of the contemporary state of the diamond trade by the Sierra Leone journalist Sorious Samora, which demonstrates the ease with which diamonds could still be smuggled out of the country and the ready market for undocumented stones in New York. Zwick's commentary on *Blood Diamond* tends to stress its serious dimensions and the sense of responsibility he felt when representing material with such real-world resonance. Much is also made here of the 'authentic' nature of DiCaprio's accent and performance, resulting in part from spending time with real mercenaries, the subject of a short extra of its own. Another focuses on the staging of the Freetown invasion/chase sequence, again putting the emphasis on the claims it makes to realism – including the role of Samora as a consultant – and entirely ignoring the more fantastical dimension of the action-heroics themselves. The general tenor of these paratexts, taken as a whole, is to add to the more serious/quality weightiness of the production, but to do so in a manner that seems ideally suited to the studio context; that is, to do so precisely as optional 'extras', without intruding directly on the main fabric of the film itself.

Judgements about the educative potential of the film such as those made by writers from the human rights perspective are closely related to these broader questions of relative degrees of quality: whether such films tackle social issues in a serious and substantial manner (quality), or whether these serve as little more than 'exotic' backdrop for more commercially oriented forms of entertainment; whether such films might succeed in getting across a 'message', or whether any such material is little more than a point of departure for less challenging forms of action-adventure. This is also a major point of orientation for prominent journalistic critics, as might be expected, from which the film received mixed responses, a number of which suggest that the combination of the two dimensions is problematic.

For Manohla Dargis in *The New York Times*, the film is 'a textbook example of how easily commercialism can trump do-goodism, particularly in Hollywood'.[36] The film 'means well', Dargis suggests, 'but it also means box-office business' and 'there's an insolvable disconnect between this serious story and the frivolous way it has been told'. Kenneth Turan in the *Los Angeles Times* acknowledges similar grounds for criticism but prefers to accentuate the positive, suggesting that 'it should be recognised that movies like this have become as rare and potentially valuable as the stone that sets its plot in motion'.[37]

A weakness for 'the Hollywood emotional moment and convenient plot resolutions' are, for this critic, 'overshadowed by the film's willingness to risk disturbing an audience's sense of the world and how it is run'. Stephanie Zacharek, on the Salon website, identifies a similarly 'uneasy hybrid' of 'preachy entertainment that wants to offer thrills, too'.[38] On the one hand, she suggests, 'no one with a conscience should buy a diamond unless he or she knows where it came from. On the other, should Zwick really be using a glorified action movie to scold us?' Such doubts appeared to be quite widespread, the film earning a distinctly modest 62 per cent approval rating on the aggregation site Rotten Tomatoes.[39] A notable split is visible here, however, between the findings of critics and the wider arena of online viewer responses. *Blood Diamond* scores an impressive 90 per cent audience rating on Rotten Tomatoes and a similarly high average rating of four-and-a-half out of five stars in customer reviews on Amazon, which suggests that such concerns figure less prominently for viewers other than professional critics.

The number of Amazon reviewers who give disapproving scores to the film is strikingly low. Nine out of a total of 390 are listed as offering the lowest ranking of one star, but of these only four are actually based on their opinion of the film itself, the rest being the result of various forms of complaint about the quality of formats on which it was bought from the retailer.[40] Of these four, only one expresses a complaint based on the 'message' being undermined by other, more mainstream qualities. Another suggests, somewhat surprisingly, that the film cares *only* about its message rather than providing ingredients such as emotional involvement and compelling action sequences. The other two negative reviews are brief and without comment on the issues dimension of the film. Of 13 two-star reviews, five offer broad criticism of Hollywood-style treatment in one way or another, while two complain that the film is 'too preachy', the rest offering more general reservations. The most positive Amazon responses, meanwhile, suggest that the film offered many viewers what they found to be a successful mixture of 'message' and more familiar Hollywood ingredients such as action, emotional turmoil and enjoyable star performances, despite the conclusions of some critics. A total of 213 out of 390 give *Blood Diamond* the maximum five-star rating (with another 118 at four-star). Of these, according to my reading of the comments, at least 108 give strong praise of some kind to the simultaneous presence of both dimensions of the film, whether briefly or in more developed argument (some 38 refer positively to the social issues dimension alone while 28 praise other qualities without reference to these; comments from the remainder do not fit clearly into any of these categories, as is often the case with such responses).

Of those who express opinions on such issues with any clarity, it seems that the combination of qualities offered by the film was appreciated by Amazon viewers to a greater extent than it was by professional critics. This, in itself, might be related to hierarchical processes of boundary-marking of the kind that are central to the focus of this book, as seen in some of the responses to *Inception* examined in Chapter 2. Critics in general (or, perhaps, critics of particular kinds) appear more likely than most viewers to be invested in the maintenance of quality/non-quality distinctions, the identification of which can be seen as part of their stock-in-trade. It is not surprising, therefore, that some critics (although far from all of those writing for 'quality' outlets) might seem more queasy than the majority of viewers in their response to the manner in which a film such as *Blood Diamond* mixes elements of significant/important social context with very Hollywood-conventional fabrication.

Notes

1   Peter Roffman and Jim Purdy, *The Hollywood Social Problem Film: Madness, Despair, and Politics from the Depression to the Fifties*, Bloomington: Indiana University Press, 1981, p. viii

2   Kay Sloan, *The Loud Silents: Origins of the Social Problem Film*, Chicago: University of Illinois Press, 1988

3   R. Colin Tait and Andrew de Waard, *The Cinema of Steven Soderbergh*, London: Wallflower, 2013, p. 150

4   Paul D. Williams, *War and Conflict in Africa*, Cambridge: Polity, 2011, p. 1

5   Roffman and Peurdy, *The Hollywood Social Problem Film*, p. viii

6   Janine Roberts, *Glitter and Greed: The Secret World of the Diamond Cartel*, New York: Disinformation, 2007, who cites the conclusion of a US General Accounting Office report from 2006 that any such guarantees 'are little more than worthless illusions', p. xi

7   Roberts, *Glitter and Greed*
8   Ibid., p. 84
9   See William Reno, *Corruption and State Politics in Sierra Leone*, Cambridge: Cambridge University Press, 1995. Not all of the blame can be put on the colonial past, as Williams argues, which does not explain the specific triggers of particular contemporary contexts, but it remains 'an important underlying factor'; Williams, *War and Conflict in Africa*, p. 7
10   See, for example, Joyce Ashuntantang, 'Hollywood's representations of human rights: The case of Terry George's *Hotel Rwanda*' in MaryEllen Higgins, ed., *Hollywood's Africa after 1994*, Athens: Ohio University Press, 2012
11   Sources such as Williams, *War and Conflict in Africa*
12   See Williams, *War and Conflict in Africa*, Part III
13   V.Y. Mudimbe, *The Invention of Africa: Gnosis, Philosphy and the Order of Knowledge*, Bloomington: Indiana University Press, 1988
14   For more on this history, see Kenneth Cameron, *Africa on Film: Beyond Black and White*, New York: Continuum, 1994
15   Edward Said, *Orientalism: Western Conceptions of the Orient*, London: Routledge, 1978
16   Margaret Higonnet, with Ethel R. Higonnet, 'The troubled terrain of human rights films' in Higgins, ed., *Hollywood's Africa after 1994*, 2012
17   Donald Bogle, *Toms, Coons, Mutattoes, Mammies, and Bucks: An Interpretive History of Blacks in American Films*, New York: Continuum, 1989
18   Ed Guerrero, *Framing Blackness: The African-American Image in Film*, Philadelphia: Temple University Press, 1993
19   For more on the model of 'conversion' implied in the emphasis on religion, education and modernisation, see Mudimbe, *The Invention of Africa*
20   Cameron suggests that by the 1960s African figures in film were similarly divided between the 'dangerous' and the good; *Africa on Film*, p. 127
21   Greg Campbell, *Blood Diamonds: Tracing the Deadly Path of the World's Most Precious Stones*, New York: Basic Books, 2012, p. 143
22   See Williams, *War and Conflict in Africa*, pp. 121–7
23   See Geoff King, 'Reassertions of Hollywood heroic agency in the Iraq War film' in Claire Molloy and Yannis Tzioumakis eds, *Routledge Companion to Film and Politics*, London: Routledge, 2016
24   Margaret Higonnet, 'The troubled terrain of human rights films', p. 51
25   Elizabeth Golding, *Beyond Terror: Gender, Narrative, Human Rights*, New Brunswick: Rutgers University Press, 2007, pp. 37–8

26   Roffman and Purdy, *The Hollywood Social Problem Film*, p. 305
27   T.L. Stanley, 'Gem sellers launch blitz against *Blood Diamond*', *Advertising Age*, 11 December 2006, p. 12
28   Rekha Sharma, 'News on the rocks: Exploring the agenda-setting effects of *Blood Diamond* in print and broadcast news', *Media, War & Conflict*, vol. 5, no. 3, 2012
29   Susan Thea Posnock, 'Blood Diamond splatter on sales looks light', *National Jeweler*, vol. 101, no. 1, January 2007
30   Figures from boxofficemojo.com
31   Ian Mohr, 'Studios seek year-end surge', *Variety*, 11–17 December 2006
32   Marc Santora, 'Hollywood's multifaceted cause du jour', *The New York Times*, 3 December 2006, via nytimes.com
33   See, for example, interview in Kim Williamson, 'Cover story: Director's chair: Blood Diamond', *Boxoffice*, vol. 142, no. 11, November 2006, pp. 30–1
34   See, for example, biography provided by the Internet Movie DataBase, via imdb.com, and 'All Movie Guide' biog provided on the website of *The New York Times*, http://movies.nytimes.com/person/118079/Edward-Zwick/biography, and Yahoo biography, http://uk.movies.yahoo.com/person/edward-zwick/biography.html;_ylt=Anr1hZSDfaN2g_cuwYWtSxixl8sF;_ylu=X3oDMTI2ajBnaD-lrBG1pdANQZXJzb24gRW50aXR5IEFib3V0BHBvcwMxBHNlY-wNNZWRpYUVudGl0eUFib3V0TGlua3NQYWNrYWdlQXNz-ZW1ibHk-;_ylg=X3oDMTE2ZW9pOWNpBGludGwDZ2IEbGFu ZwNlbi1nYgRwc3RhaWQBHBzdGNhdAMEcHQD;_ylv=3
35   Williamson, 'Cover story'
36   Manohla Dargis, 'Diamonds and the devil, amid the anguish of Africa', 8 December 2006, via nytimes.com
37   Kenneth Turan, 'Blood Diamond', 8 December 2006, via latimes.com
38   Stephanie Zacharek, 'Blood Diamond', 8 December 2006, via salon.com
39   http://www.rottentomatoes.com/m/blood_diamond/
40   Reviews accessed 25 March 2013, starting at http://www.amazon.com/Blood-Diamond/product-reviews/B000OLRH10/ref=cm_cr_pr_fltrmsg?ie=UTF8&showViewpoints=0

6

Artificiality or intelligence?

Spielberg, Kubrick and rival versions of quality

The focus of this book so far has been on the existence of elements of quality in Hollywood in the hierarchical sense emphasised in the Introduction, in the ascription of what is conventionally taken to be a (relatively) higher status to certain cultural forms, or those which borrow from or claim resonances with these. That is, quality in the sense of 'doing certain kinds of things' that are accorded a particular position in prevailing cultural schemas, rather than specifically in terms of an evaluative judgement of 'how well' a particular thing is done in its own terms (whatever slippage might often exist between the two). The latter is a type of judgement that can be made across the whole of the cultural spectrum, rather than being restricted to particular sectors discursively situated higher on the conventionally established scale. Examples can be identified of works of the most popular/commercial orientation that are judged to have been mounted particularly well, with a degree of skill of execution and achievement that lifts them above the norm, without necessarily entailing any claims to higher cultural status of the kind elaborated above. These two kinds of

judgement can also overlap, however, and be related to similar underlying discursive frameworks.

The career of Steven Spielberg provides a useful site within
which to consider further the nature and implications of these different notions of quality, including as it does notable examples of
each: highly popular, mainstream 'crowd-pleasing' and often also critically acclaimed films such as *Jaws* (1975), *Close Encounters of the Third
Kind* (1977), *Raiders of the Lost Ark* (1981), *E.T. The Extraterrestrial*
(1982) and *Jurassic Park* (1993); and those that pitch for more elevated
and 'serious' or 'worthy' status, or that seem to wear such an appeal
on their sleeve, such as *The Color Purple* (1985), *Schindler's List* (1993),
Amistad (1997), *Munich* (2005) and *Lincoln* (2012) (plus a number that
might be located somewhere in between the two). At the same time,
Spielberg's work has regularly been criticised for its dependence on
certain characteristics, particularly the sentimental and the emotionally manipulative, that are often associated with positions of lower
quality in both senses, an accusation that has been made of examples
of his work at the most popular and more 'lofty' ends of the scale.

These issues are addressed here primarily through the framework
provided by another of Spielberg's films, *A.I. Artificial Intelligence*
(2001), a production that opens up an interesting route into various dimensions of quality through its dual patrimony as a film made
by Spielberg but from a project originally developed over a lengthy
period by Stanley Kubrick – a figure of very different repute. This
chapter begins with a sketch of the qualities with which the two filmmakers are primarily associated: Spielberg as what might be termed
a highly successful popular sentimentalist, making some excursions
into avowedly 'serious' quality territory; Kubrick as a figure associated
with a more rigorously 'artistic' approach and with the production of
a number of features that significantly push the boundaries of this variety of quality within the studio environment, most notably in films
such as *Dr Strangelove or: How I Learned to Stop Worrying and Love the
Bomb* (1964), *2001: A Space Odyssey* (1968) and *A Clockwork Orange*
(1971). This is followed by an analysis of the extent to which either
such qualities can be identified in *A.I.* and how distinctions between
the two – and concomitant notions of quality – are articulated in critical discourses surrounding the film.

If the work of Spielberg is identified most closely with quality at the level of the particularly skilled deployment of approaches designed for popular appeal, of making mainstream Hollywood films particularly well (rather than claims to quality of a hierarchical nature), this chapter also explores the basis on which judgements of this kind are made. I draw here particularly on Warren Buckland's reading of Spielberg, one that offers a positive evaluation of the filmmaker based on the attribution to his work of qualities such as coherence and organic unity, concepts drawn from a critical tradition that returns us to some of the key strands of the broader quality debate explored throughout this book.

Contrasting quality reputations

The reputation of Kubrick lies at the upper end of the Hollywood quality spectrum, probably as close to its summit as that of any film-maker of the post-classical studio era and considerably more so than any considered so far in this book. While much of the Hollywood quality tradition – historical and more recent – has been located in a cultural region often labelled disparagingly as 'middlebrow', Kubrick's *oeuvre* has been accorded higher status (although not entirely uncontested), including association with venerated established 'high art' traditions of modernism (a position also sometimes given in part to some of the films of the Hollywood 'Renaissance' of the late 1960s and 1970s). A particular basis for this judgement is the denial in most of his work of a strong sense of emotional proximity to central characters, an absence of any clear or unambiguous sense of allegiance of the kind that is one of the core features of most Hollywood production. Apart from *Spartacus* (1960), a film over which he did not have control and subsequently disowned, James Naremore suggests that *Paths of Glory* (1957) is 'the only one of his pictures that centres on an admirable character with whom the audience can feel comfortable identification.'[1] In most, if not all, of Kubrick's subsequent work, the relationship with characters offered to the viewer is either distant (particularly *2001: A Space Odyssey*), distinctly uncomfortable (notably *A Clockwork Orange* and *The Shining* [1980]), or somewhere between the two. This is a strong marker of distinction from the Hollywood norm, in some cases considerably more pronounced than the degree of distance from character found in several of the case studies examined above.

Kubrick's films have often been characterised as exhibiting a cold and distanced aesthetic, although Naremore usefully suggests that this exists in relationship with potentially more emotive subject matter: 'A dialectic or tension between the rational and irrational can be seen everywhere in his work, so that he usually leaves the impression of a fastidious, highly controlled or "cool" technician dealing with absurd, violent or sexually "hot" material.'[2] Whatever exact conclusion we might reach, the terms in which this is put are ones that invoke weighty artistic traditions. For Naremore, Kubrick belongs to 'the twilight of international modernism', in the company of august figures such as the writers Franz Kafka, James Joyce, Bertolt Brecht and Harold Pinter. His work demonstrates

> a preoccupation with several of the leading ideological or aesthetic tendencies of high modernism: a concern for media-specific form, a resistance to censorship, a preference for satire and irony over sentiment, a dislike of conventional narrative realism, a reluctance to allow the audience to identify with leading characters and an interest in the relationship between instrumental rationality and its ever-present shadow, the irrational unconscious.[3]

A similar (and similarly approved) cultural location is evoked by Robert Kolker, who notes that the sources for the director's work are primarily literary rather than cinematic and suggests that his films 'have an intellectual complexity associated more with the literature of words than that of film'.[4]

The films of Spielberg are customarily located very differently, diametrically opposite those of Kubrick in some key respects – and hence lower in established cultural status – particularly in their association with large outpourings of sentimental emotion, an acute version of which is offered, for example, at the climax of E.T. Spielberg films tend to offer a very mainstream-conventionally comfortable and affirmative form of allegiance with character, even when they deal with darker material. One indication of the difference between the two filmmakers is their use of music. Spielberg characteristically works to the accompaniment of swelling scores by John Williams – highly conventional in their underpinning of what can be seen as a strongly manipulative form of emotional engagement – while Kubrick often uses music to reinforce or establish the tonal disjunction that Naremore identifies as a central component of his output, including the use of 'Singin' in the Rain' during a rape sequence in *A Clockwork Orange*. The films through which Spielberg's reputation was established as a major Hollywood presence (*Jaws, Close Encounters of the Third Kind, Raiders of the Lost Ark* and *E.T.*) are very mainstream and affirmative popular entertainments that might be viewed as distinctly accomplished in their own ways but not the kind of material usually associated with the higher quality end of the spectrum. His subsequent inclusion of a strand of avowedly more serious work – alongside further action-adventures such as *Jurassic Park* and its first sequel (1997), and sequels to *Raiders of the Lost Ark* (1984, 1989, 2008) – was treated with some suspicion by many critics, for various reasons particular to his own case.[5] These also include the more general difficulty faced by figures who seek to change their repute, particularly in the move from popular commercial success to more elevated status, as is demonstrated in Robert Kapsis' study of the contested reputation of Alfred Hitchcock and the thriller genre with which he is strongly associated.[6]

With their focus on 'important' social issues and their generally sombre approach, examples such as *Schindler's List, Amistad, Munich* and *Lincoln* fit solidly into the broader Hollywood quality tradition, as classic examples of status-seeking 'Oscar bait', as does *The Color Purple* with its basis in a work of literary fiction. They maintain some of the qualities through which Spielberg's work contrasts with that of Kubrick, however, particularly in their retention of a central strain of the sentimental, even if sometimes in more muted form. A very Hollywood-conventional position is offered to the viewer amid the traumas depicted in *Schindler's List* and *Amistad*, for example, while any harshness that exists in Spielberg's version of Alice Walker's *The Color Purple* seems to exist primarily, if not solely, in order eventually to be subjected to large-scale emotional transcendence. While Kubrick's work might be politically ambiguous, and far from necessarily progressive, Spielberg's has often been viewed as politically reactionary in its ideological implications.[7] This and his sheer commercial success, and the resultant power he has wielded as a major Hollywood player, has contributed to a quite widespread tendency for his work to be viewed with suspicion or to be denigrated, particularly (but not exclusively) by left-leaning critics. When Spielberg has made films with quality credentials this has often been interpreted as a straining for respectability – and/or as involving a 'dumbing down' or making palatable of more serious material – rather than something truly meritorious in its own right. Similar evaluative judgement might be made of many examples of the studio quality tradition more generally, as suggested in the Introduction. My main purpose here is not to enter into the merits or otherwise of such perspectives, but to establish them as components of the prevailing reputation of the filmmaker. They sit alongside the enormous audience popularity of most of Spielberg's output, of course, although that in itself is part of the grounds on which hierarchically based claims to quality status are more likely to be challenged than affirmed.

Negative judgements about Spielberg have not gone uncontested. Claims have been made to the status of quality on the basis of the level of accomplishment with which popular-conventional material is articulated in his work, as considered further below, particularly in relation to the reading offered by Buckland. Some similar arguments are made by Nigel Morris, although these also include attempts to claim for the filmmaker some of the higher 'artistic' status gained by Kubrick and are thus worthy of some attention at this point.[8] Contrary to the suggestion by Kolker and other commentators that his films effectively force viewers into particular subject positions, Morris argues that Spielberg's work is capable of embodying contradictions that result in the kind of ambiguity often associated with art cinema, in examples including the political dimensions of films such as *Jaws* and *Munich*. The most sustained argument employed by Morris, in relation to higher-level claims that might be made on the part of Spielberg, relates to elements of self-reflexivity and allusion that he identifies throughout the director's body of work. Repeated images such as shafts of bright light, silhouetted figures viewed against screen-like backdrops and projector-like circular elements are read by Morris as reflexive references to the cinematic apparatus, while many examples are provided of allusions to images or scenes from a wide range of other films, including works associated with quality or art-cinema traditions.

In the view of Morris, such references are overt and evident to viewers, although this seems to be greatly over-stated. *Saving Private Ryan* (1998), for Morris, is 'an essay in metatextuality [...] testing the limits of representation'.[9] Further, seeking to move on to the terrain associated with Kubrick, he reads it as 'a modernist throwback, multifaceted, cubist, despite surface conventionality'.[10] This seems hugely exaggerated, at best, bearing little resemblance to anything lying within a 'normal' range of experiences of viewing the film. Kolker acknowledges the existence of elements of self-referentiality in Spielberg's films but concludes, more convincingly, that these do not have a distancing effect or function to undermine the fundamental process of audience engagement in narrative events.[11] Morris might be right to suggest that Spielberg's films are open, potentially, to a greater variety of readings than has been assumed by some of his critics, but it is difficult to read his interpretation here as anything more than over-compensation for the degree to which he believes Spielberg to have been sold short by others, another typical feature of critical dispute over the cultural standing of particular filmmakers, genres or other cultural forms. As such, it is of interest primarily as evidence of the manner in which reputations for quality of one kind or another can be subject to contest, among academics as well as in the wider public-critical sphere.

The freedom Spielberg has had to pursue less obviously commercial quality productions such as *Schindler's List* and *Amistad* is not difficult to explain. The industrial clout gained by his blockbuster successes from *Jaws* onwards (notwithstanding the box office flop of *1941* [1979]) was such as to put him in a close-to-unique position of being able to obtain studio support for almost anything he might suggest, an extreme instance of the importance for quality productions of the presence at their heart of figures with greater than usual power. This was partly a matter of the desire of studios to maintain or obtain his services, and partly of anticipations of likely success with any such material – if potentially lesser than with more obviously commercial projects – on the basis of his track record. If anyone was going to be allowed to make a three-hour monochrome feature set during the Nazi Holocaust, it was going to be Spielberg; likewise, if anyone was likely to be viewed as capable of doing this in a manner that might not be off-putting to a large audience, that would also be Spielberg. We can add to this the substantial stake Spielberg has gained in the industry, initially through the creation of his own company, Amblin Entertainment, in 1984, and subsequently in his role as one of the joint founders of the new studio, DreamWorks, a decade later. As it turned out, *Schindler's List* proved to be another big hit in its own right, achieving a worldwide gross of $321 million on a budget of $22 million. As noted above, Spielberg's subsequent serious projects have been interwoven with more obviously commercial – and hier-archically much lower-status – films, including a number of sequels to highly successful mainstream originals. This can thus be seen as a version of the 'one for me, one for them' approach (maybe often more than one for 'them') that has governed the ability of other filmmakers to create space for more personal, less commercial-seeming projects within the studio environment (see, for example, aspects of the career of Martin Scorsese).

The space gained by Kubrick to pursue a series of distinctly less conventional features without any such exchange appears in greater need of explanation. After early independent productions includ-ing *Fear and Desire* (1953), *Killer's Kiss* (1955) and *The Killing* (1956), Kubrick worked consistently with major studios but with a degree of autonomy rare even for the most established of directors. This was, again and as usual, conditional largely on initial financial suc-cess. Despite their unconventional qualities, a number of the films through which the director's reputation was established were signifi-cant box office hits, associated in part with the wider currents of the Hollywood Renaissance of the period. As Naremore records, *Dr Strangelove*, co-produced by Columbia and Kubrick's own company, Hawk Films, was one of the biggest successes of 1964; *2001*, famously sold to a late-1960s youth audience as 'the ultimate trip', became one of the biggest earners in the history of MGM; and *A Clockwork Orange*, because of, probably more than in spite of, the controversy with which it was surrounded, became one of Warner's biggest hits of the decade.[12]

In 1970 Kubrick signed a three-picture deal with Warner that constituted 'one of the most attractive contracts any director has ever received', under which the studio would fund the purchase, development and production of properties for him to direct, giving him a guarantee of final cut and with 40 per cent of any profits going to Hawk.[13] He stayed with the studio for the remainder of his career, continuing to receive support from senior executives despite diminishing commercial returns. His appeal to the studio appears to have been based on a combination of the prestige he brought to its output and the economy with which he operated, suggesting both the importance that can in some cases be attributed to the former but also some of the pragmatic limitations by which it is usually accompanied. As Naremore puts it, Terry Semel, deputy chief executive officer of Warner, 'believed that Kubrick strengthened the studio's image on Wall Street, and appreciated the fact that his late [generally less successful] films were shot with relatively small, efficient crews'.[14] An important additional source of the autonomy he achieved was the fact that from the independently produced *Lolita* (1962) onwards, all his films were shot in England, at considerable physical distance from Hollywood, where Kubrick gained the reputation of a maverick recluse, further adding to his associations with filmmaking beyond the studio norm.

Placing *A.I.*: between Kubrick and Spielberg

Given the strongly contrasting associations brought by the two film-makers, it is unsurprising that few accounts of *A.I.* have been able to resist the temptation of seeking to credit particular aspects of the film to either Kubrick or Spielberg, or to engage in evaluative judgements about the relative merits of the potential contributions of each. A common assumption – either as the basis of argument or a premise against which to suggest the contrary – has been that Kubrick's more cool and distanced approach to such material was subjected to a process of 'Spielbergification' that would typically be seen as a negative process, given the relative positions of the two in the prevailing cultural hierarchy (although scope exists for these relative valuations to be reversed from a more populist position). The principal accusation in such accounts is that Spielberg is responsible for the injection of substantial doses of sentimental heartstring-pulling into the film, to which the narrative lends itself quite readily, in its tale of the search for love undertaken by a state-of-the-art 'mecha' robot boy, David (Haley Joel Osment), after his rejection by his adoptive mother, Monica (Frances O'Connor). The film contains a number of sequences that involve heightened sentiment of the kind frequently associated with Spielberg, particularly the scenes in which David is abandoned by Monica and the closing sequence in which he is briefly reunited with a simulacrum of her figure created in the distant future. *A.I.* also includes other elements that have the appearance of typical Spielberg material, most notably a central parallel with the story of *Pinocchio*, a source of potentially somewhat child-like (rather than darker) fairytale resonance and well established as a favourite of the director. A sequence in which the story is read aloud to David and to Monica's real son, Martin (Jake Thomas), is strongly reminiscent of an equivalent involving the emotive reading of *Peter Pan* in *E.T.*

The pointed attribution of such elements to one filmmaker or the other – pointed in the sense often of entailing value-judgements – can be a tricky business, however. It might easily be assumed that the *Pinocchio* dimension was added by Spielberg, so much does it seem to be in tune with his established sensibility, but it proves to have already been in place in the script material developed under Kubrick during his years of preparation for the film.[15] Debate has also focused on the ending, or more specifically an earlier potential end-point that precedes the sequences set in the distant future. Searching for the Blue Fairy from *Pinocchio*, a character he thinks will be able to turn him into a real boy, David is led to a statue of the figure in the remains of a fairytale theme park that lies in the depths of a drowned future Manhattan. As he sits repeating his prayer to the Blue Fairy, the camera pulls away, leaving him in suspended animation, seemingly waiting endlessly in vain (see Figure 6.1). As what could be taken to be a poignant but devastating undermining of the myth, this was viewed by some (myself included) as a powerful and satisfying ending for the film. Instead, we are taken 2,000 years into a more distant future, after

Figure 6.1. Preferred ending? David's (Haley Joel Osment) submersible waiting in vain for the answer to his prayers to the Blue Fairy in *A.I. Artificial Intelligence* © Warner Bros. and DreamWorks LLC

the extinction of humanity, in which the memories of David provide a heavily evolved mecha species with their only direct access to knowledge of their human creators, and the brief reincarnation of a simulacrum of Monica, who can be brought back for just a single day. The closing scenes are intensely emotional, in a slow-burning manner, ending on a note that mixes sadness with a sense of considerable achievement on the part of David, after Monica declares her love for him and we are told he is able to sleep for the first time. It is easy to project the actual and earlier potential endings onto the reputations of Spielberg and Kubrick, respectively, but the position again appears to be much less clear-cut, the last act of the film also featuring in the material developed under Kubrick's earlier direction.[16]

The finished article remains a work that includes many points of similarity with Kubrick's *oeuvre*, including a central underlying thematic concern with the opposition between the emotional and the rational, the human and the technological. It offers in many ways a typically bleak, non-Hollywood portrait of humanity, located like most of the films examined in this book within the variety of quality that emphasises the darker or more complex dimension of reality while also providing some scope (variable from one example to another) for the creation of more ameliorative impressions of moral uplift. The world of the start of the film is one in which global warming has led to flooded coastal cities and the population is diminished. Sequences at the 'Flesh Fair' depict human cruelty and vindictiveness, in the destruction of a mish-mash of obsolete mecha before baying crowds, the artificial beings seeming here to embody characteristics more 'human' than those of their destroyers. Such material might well be found in a more conventional Hollywood treatment, but it would be expected to be counterposed by the presence of more positive representatives of the species, whose values would be seen eventually to prevail or at least to be maintained as a source of strong viewer allegiance. David himself seems in some respects the most human character, akin to the status of the computer HAL in *2001*. By the end of the film, humanity, as such, is no more, its demise not even dramatised or mourned but occurring entirely off-screen in the gap between the two final acts. The underpinnings of the film also include many of the key philosophical and theoretical issues that occupied Kubrick's thoughts and fed into his films – and their distinctiveness within Hollywood – throughout his career.[17]

The setting up of oppositions between the human/emotional and technological/rational is a frequent mainstay of science fiction cinema, but the studio norm is for this to be subjected to a typically Hollywood variety of 'magical' reconciliation. The usual scenario is for a notion of the human to be subjected to threat by the realm of the coldly scientific/technical/rational – either within humanity or an external source of threat – but for this to be overcome. The human prevails, although this usually entails some manipulation of the technical/rational against itself, the implicit message being that the two can be reconciled as long as the latter is subordinated to the primacy of the former (see, for example, the *Terminator* and *Matrix* series, among many other examples). It is a considerable break with the norm for the human to be shown to have become extinct, and not even for any fight to be dramatised but for this to be presented as a long-achieved fait accompli. The ending, then, can be taken as a bleak one, but it is also ambiguous – another familiar Kubrick tendency in itself – and mixed with positive resonances of a variety more likely to be associated with the work of Spielberg. If this is a future in which humanity has not survived, it can be seen to have evolved in the transition to a higher level of mecha, another way of reconciling the opposition, even if one that does not seem particularly heartening as far as the fate of humans themselves are concerned.

When David is eventually reunited with his creator, Professor Hobby (William Hurt), the latter reveals that David's progress since being abandoned by Monica has been monitored to test his response to the situation. Where would his reasoning take him: 'To the logical conclusion – the Blue Fairy is part of the great human flaw to wish for things that don't exist. Or to the greatest singular human gift, the ability to chase down our dreams', the latter being something no machine had ever done before. What is implied here, although not stated outright, is that David has *already* transcended the limits of mecha, akin to his desire; the very pursuit of the dream, based on a fairytale, is itself evidence that he has gained certain characteristics of the human/real. At the point of the potential alternative ending, that is, the pursuit of the dream has been established as a positive, human characteristic, not a hapless myth. If the film were to have ended here, however, the resonances overall would have been considerably more bleak in character.

The closing scenes with the simulacrum of Monica are very sadly toned and bittersweet emotionally, but the final lines from the voice-over narrator indicate that David is now able to find rest, having received Monica's declaration of love. He goes to sleep and we are told that 'for the first time in his life, he went to that place where dreams are born' (see Figure 6.2). Earlier, the capacity to dream is equated by Hobby with something close to the human, with 'an inner world of metaphor, of intuition, of self-motivated reasoning, of dreams'. What *A.I.* seems to dramatise, then, is the beginnings of the transcendence of the human into other forms that might be more benign than the portrait of humanity provided by much of the film. This is another respect in which it seems to have something in common with *2001*, the final protagonist of which – the astronaut David Bowman (Keir Dullea) – also experiences what appears to be a simulated environment before seeming to be transcended in the birth of the 'Star Child' figure that appears at the end. There are also some major points of

Figure 6.2 To sleep, perchance to dream? David (Haley Joel Osment) at peace at the end of *A.I. Artificial Intelligence* © Warner Bros. and DreamWorks LLC

difference between the two, however, and between *A.I.* and the qualities with which Kubrick is generally associated.

A.I. seems to buy into the fairytale/dream dimension, as a straightforwardly positive marker of humanity, in a manner that does not seem typical of Kubrick's films. While Kubrick had a career-long fascination with fairytales, as Naremore and others have suggested, this appears to have been part of a darker and more pessimistic vision; the irrational to be counterposed to the rational-logical in Kubrick is generally viewed as that of a dark and threatening unconscious, not that of wish-fulfilment dreams of idealised love. The latter seem to be embodied textually in the more emotional level of engagement offered by *A.I.*, that which seems closer to the approach associated with the more mainstream-conventional sensibility of Spielberg. The notion that humanity is characterised positively by the chasing down of dreams – rather than a more negative/logical conclusion or the subversion of wish-fulfilment by the more darkly irrational – seems typically much more Spielberg than Kubrick. The chasing down of dreams is also, of course, more likely to be associated with mainstream fantasy (in the broadest sense of the term) than with some of the characteristics associated with either the quality tradition in general or the particular version found in the work of Kubrick. This and the closing tone certainly make the film less distinctive, in Hollywood terms, than would otherwise be the case.

The resonances of the closing sequences are still distinctly mixed, however, and not clear-cut. A careful balance seems to be created between relatively more positive and negative components, and moment-by-moment shifts between one and the other (at one point, for example, it seems that there is no chance of bringing back Monica; then we are led to expect that this will be possible and is about to happen; but it turns out that she can only be resurrected, bitter-sweetly, for a single day). Such tonal modulation might situate the film somewhere in between what would usually be expected of the two filmmakers, but the effect is more outwardly emotional in its language – offering scope for the production of a combination of tears of sadness and of joy – than would be characteristic of Kubrick.

It is worth returning here briefly to the question of the different usages of music often associated with the two filmmakers. A musical score by Spielberg's regular collaborator, John Williams, plays an important part in the heartstring-tugging emotive sequences, but in a manner that is quiet and generally more muted than in Spielberg at his most heavily melodramatic. The score also includes some distinctly bleak, cool and distant tones, in some cases reminiscent of similar material employed during the second half of *2001*. This, then, is another dimension in which the film can be seen to be drawing to varying degrees on the kinds of qualities associated with each, although it is notable that the music that plays over the closing credits – and thus leaving the final impression – centres on a highly emotional female vocal of a devotional kind that seems much more conventional than the closing disjunctions sometimes offered by Kubrick.

Visually, too, the film mixes very typically Spielberg imagery such as flooding white backlighting, in some key sequences – and ameliorative golden-edged, halo-creating rim-lighting, in others – with effects that create a more dislocating impression. The latter include various images of David in the earlier sequences at home, in which his appearance is distorted, creating an impression of alienation that emphasises his non-human form. In a heavily unfocused first

Figure 6.3. Dislocating impression: David (Haley Joel Osment) as viewed through an overhead light fitting in *A.I. Artificial Intelligence* © Warner Bros. and DreamWorks LLC

sighting, his figure is elongated in a manner that seems to antici- pate the shape of the super-mecha of the final act. He is also viewed through the misshaping vertically ridged glass of interior doors and in some cases oddly framed (including a high angle above the dining table in which his head is positioned within the circular shape of a light fitting) (see Figure 6.3). The repeated use of circular shapes in the production design is another link with *2001*, in each case capable of being read as symbolic of a cyclical process of evolution. In the often intentionally flat, non-blinking performance of Osment, David is given a persona that shifts between the extremely cute (accessible to mainstream-conventional sentimental viewer attachment) and the potentially sinister (distinctly less so).

If the offering of explicitly emotional material tilts the film in the direction of the more familiar mainstream, *A.I.* also provides a number of points of reflexive consideration of this and other central under- lying themes, a dimension more likely to be associated with quality production (even if this remains mostly implicit rather than overt). The film lends itself to analysis in terms of its reliance on an appeal to the emotions but it is also clearly largely *about* the nature of emotional experience and its importance to notions of the human. A number of

Figure 6.4. Imaginary reconciliation of oppositions: Flat Fact, to be combined with Fairy Tale, in the Dr Know oracle terminal in *A.I. Artificial Intelligence* © Warner Bros. and DreamWorks LLC

parallel oppositions are established, including those between mecha and 'orga' and between logical conclusion and the chasing down of dreams. When David and his accomplice in the middle part of the film, Gigolo Joe (Jude Law), visit a computer oracle terminal in search of information about the location of the Blue Fairy, the categories within which questions can be posed include 'Flat Fact' and 'Fairy Tale' (see Figure 6.4). But it is only when a simultaneous combination of the two is used that they make any progress; another apparent reconciliation of the opposition.

It is tempting also to relate the orga/mecha opposition back to the distinction between notions of the organic and mechanical that were shown in the Introduction and Chapter 1 to play an important historical role in the underpinning of hierarchical conceptions of quality. In its long period of painstaking evolution, primarily under the tutelage of Kubrick, *A.I.* itself would seem to be located more closely to the domain of the 'organic' work of art/culture than that of 'mechanical' assembly. As what remains a Hollywood production, however, brought to fruition by a figure at the heart of the industry, it might be said to have feet in both camps and thus in some ways to straddle the opposition (as do the more advanced mechas of the diegesis). The

position occupied by Spielberg in this schema – particularly in relation to notions of the organic whole – is considered further below.

Exactly how far any such dimensions can be separated out in detail
between what was brought to the film by Kubrick and Spielberg
remains open to question and speculative interpretation, however, as
tends usually to be the case in collaborative enterprises. The issue is
further complicated if the roles of other participants are taken into
account. Brian Aldiss, author of the short story 'Supertoys Last All
Summer Long', which provided the starting point for the film, was
involved in the early stages of development but left after disagreeing
with Kubrick about the resonances of the *Pinocchio* dimension with
his material – an indication of the filmmaker's commitment to this
component. A subsequent treatment was developed by the science
fiction writer Ian Watson, who is credited for 'screen story'. Another
collaborator was the novelist Sara Maitland, who was asked 'to bring
more emotional and fairy-tale magic' to the narrative.[18] Had debate
about the film not been so over-determined by the Kubrick/Spielberg
axis – and if it were not the norm for such writers of treatments to
receive little credit for the final work, the screenplay being attributed
to Spielberg – it is possible that similar discussion might have been
framed at least partly in terms of Watson versus Maitland. The closer
we look at such issues, the more complex the ascription of relative
degrees of authorship tends to become. The manner in which such
issues are expressed remains of significance in its own right, however,
as one facet of discourses relating to the attribution of quality, whatever reservations might exist as far as the reality is concerned.

A number of different positions are taken on the dominant Kubrick/
Spielberg issue by commentators of various kinds. These range from
the suggestion that the contributions of Kubrick and Spielberg are
inseparable, so closely is the film a production of their collaboration,
to claims that they clash rather than producing a unified outcome.
According to the version of events provided in the production notes
distributed on the release of *A.I.*, and as a result widely reported,
Kubrick suggested that he produce the film for Spielberg to direct,
the latter quoting the former as saying: 'I think this movie is closer to
your sensibility than mine.'[19] Jan Harlan, executive producer of the film
and of a number of other Kubrick titles – and therefore someone who

could be considered a strong inside authority – suggests that Kubrick would have been proud of Spielberg's film (implicitly countering any criticism that suggested otherwise), also indicating at one point a distinct difference between the approaches of the two that accords with more general accounts of the kind offered above: 'Stanley's version was too black and cynical for an expensive film that had to appeal to a broad family audience. Steven had the ability to lighten the tone without changing the substance.'[20] In another contribution to the same book, however, a volume that emphasises its roots in the long-term intellectual preoccupations of Kubrick, he suggests somewhat differently that it is 'almost impossible to separate out what was Stanley's and what was Steven's in the finished film, so seamlessly did the collaboration work and so profoundly did Steven understand what Stanley was trying to achieve'.[21] Spielberg's long-time producing partner Kathleen Kennedy, meanwhile, asserts in the production notes: 'There is no question that this is a movie that has Steven Spielberg's sensibilities all over it. But the subtext is all Kubrick.'[22]

'Official' accounts of this kind vary somewhat in their emphasis, then, but are all entirely positive about the nature of the collaboration and its result, as would be expected from their position as supportive paratexts. The clear tendency is to emphasise the basis of the project in the ideas of Kubrick but to see Spielberg as a worthy inheritor of his mantle, if giving a somewhat more commercial slant to the material. The opinion of critics tended to be more judgemental, in a manner that helps to underline the nature of the basis on which prevailing notions of quality are often established within public discourse.

The contrasting reputations of the two filmmakers are strongly to the fore in reviews from prominent critics, as might be expected, and generally marshalled – implicitly if not always explicitly – in terms of the quality distinctions suggested above. A widespread verdict is that *A.I.* is a 'mish-mash' or 'schizoid' in nature, failing to unify qualities associated with Kubrick and Spielberg. A relatively mild version of this is offered by Kenneth Turan in the *Los Angeles Times*. Turan situates the film within the quality arena in general, concluding that it 'was not created to fill a market need, but in service of a shared personal vision', while suggesting the difficulty of resolving the different positions of its co-creators: 'Kubrick's frigid aloofness and analytical distance couldn't be more different from Spielberg's hard-to-shake passion for cozy sentiment and audience acceptance, and joining the two sensibilities has proved problematical.'[23] In another mixed review, which separates the two filmmakers in terms that share similarly hierarchical/evaluative premises, A.O. Scott in *The New York Times* suggests: 'Spielberg seems to be attempting the improbable feat of melding Kubrick's chilly, analytical style with his own warmer, needier sensibility.'[24] The final scenes, Scott suggests, 'are likely to provoke argument, confusion and a good deal of resistance' – as they do from other critics – although Scott reads the conclusion positively, as a fusion of 'the cathartic comfort of infantile wish fulfillment' with acknowledgement of the 'unspoken moral of all our fairy tales' that to be human is to be mortal and to die. For this critic, Spielberg (specifically credited for this dimension and contrary to his wider reputation) is 'Refusing to cuddle us or lull us into easy sleep'.

A number of others are more critical of the ending. For Roger Ebert, in the *Chicago Sun-Times*, the film is both 'wonderful and maddening', with 'a couple of possible earlier endings that would have resulted in a tougher movie' (that is, it is implied, higher quality), while the actual conclusion is 'too facile and sentimental, given what has gone before'.[25] For J. Hoberman, in the *Village Voice*, the film suggests that 'Spielberg the historian is in remission; Steven the regressive has returned with a vengeance' with a 'fascinatingly schizoid, frequently ridiculous, and never less than heartfelt mishmash'. At the point where David is left praying underwater to the Blue Fairy, he suggests, 'For an unforgettable moment, I thought that Spielberg would really leave us with a bizarre, albeit truly despairing, image of eternity: Pinocchio frozen forever in a world where Jiminy Cricket is mute and Disney dead'. But, he suggests, upping the rhetoric: 'Not to worry. The shamelessly milked miracle arrives 2000 (and one?) years later, replete with thunderous wonder, appropriate white light, and a symbiotic reunion so obliterating in its solipsism it could split your skull.'[26] Peter Rainer, in *New York* magazine, takes a similar line, suggesting that Spielberg bathes David 'in a nimbus that would make Pinocchio warp with envy. David's love for his mother, as it's played out, is another example of brackish material making its way through Spielberg's cosmic car wash'.[27] Although '*A.I.* bears strong evidence of the darker, kinkier, and more unforgiving Kubrick movie it might have been [...] at almost every opportunity Spielberg, who also wrote the script, softens Kubrick's misanthropy'. For Charles Taylor, on Salon, the final act is one in which 'Spielberg's worst heartwarming instincts take over', while Mick LaSalle, of the San Francisco Chronicle, suggests that 'the most vicious parodist of Spielberg could not devise anything more precious, more shallow or more patently ridiculous'.[28] The pairing of Kubrick and Spielberg is 'a coupling from hell', offering the worst traits of each: 'So we end up with the structureless, meandering, slow-motion endlessness of Kubrick combined with the fuzzy, cuddly mindlessness of Spielberg.'

Kubrick is accorded qualities similar to those elaborated earlier in this chapter (chilly, aloof, analytical, misanthropic, as well as slow-moving), which might not be taken positively in all cases but underline a location closer to that of art cinema than mainstream Hollywood. Spielberg, unsurprisingly, is generally associated with 'softer' characteristics, the language of which is often critical if not derogatory: cosy sentiment and cuddly mindlessness; warmth but in the context of neediness and striving for audience acceptance; regression and solipsism; shameless milking; bathing in brackish waters (neither fresh nor salty) and the warm suds of a car wash. It is not difficult to tease out the judgements of cultural value implied in the use of such terminology, including a broad distinction-marking elitism expressed in terms that draw on conventionally gendered tropes of a kind familiar from the history of negative judgements of popular culture.

There were also some unambiguously positive reviews, although these were in a minority, including a gushing response in the trade paper, Variety, which suggests that the film is colder and more analytical than previous Spielberg films, and so accepts the same underlying framework of quality distinction: 'Brakes have been put on what might have been sentimentalised or emotionally milked situations.'[29] Although 'buffs and tradesters' would argue about the relative contributions of the two filmmakers, the general audience would be confronted by 'an unusually ambitious science fiction film' that this industry-oriented reviewer locates clearly within quality terrain, employing a familiar rhetorical opposition of the kind often found in viewer responses to such films posted online:

> Viewers predisposed against highfalutin films that take themselves seriously no doubt will turn off and ask what happened to the old Spielberg. But those gagging on the glut of cinematic junk food should welcome this brilliantly made visionary work that's bursting with provocative ideas.

A.I. gained an overall rating of 73 per cent on the review aggregation site Rotten Tomatoes, on the basis of 190 reviews, with viewer responses significantly lower, at 58 per cent, suggesting that the film generally appealed relatively more to critics than to other members of the audience. Viewer reactions as measured by reviews posted on amazon.com also suggest sharp divergences of opinion, although notably those strongly favouring the film number almost twice as many as those strongly against. The results here are quite polarised. Of a total of 779, 'star' rankings are as follows: five-star, 303; four-star, 149; three-star, 83; two-star, 91; one-star, 153.[30] I have chosen here, along similar lines to the previous chapter, to analyse the responses of those in the five- and one-star categories, in an attempt to gain a sense of some of the terms in which the film is most strongly embraced or rejected.[31] Among five-star reviewers, according to my interpretation, 128 (42 per cent of the total in this category) provide comments that suggest an appreciation of the film in quality terms such as its 'thought-provoking' dimensions or related points of distinction from the Hollywood norm, expressed either briefly or in more developed terms. Many of these also indicate approval of the overtly emotional qualities of the film, however, suggesting that these two bases of appeal need not be mutually exclusive. It is quite common, among these respondents, for the film to be seen as simultaneously 'thought-provoking' and 'heart-wrenching'. A total of 82 (27 per cent of this category) include the emotional as at least one ground for admiring *A.I.* The same quite substantial number gives specific credit, in more or less elaborated terms, to the combinations of qualities brought by the partnership of Kubrick and Spielberg, although some of those who highlight the emotional dimension – many admitting the shedding of tears – do so more exclusively in relation to Spielberg. A substantial proportion, however, make positive comments that combine the marking of points of distinction in the film with the appreciation of its (more conventional) emotionally heartstring-tugging elements *and* give credit overall to the blend of sensibilities brought by the two filmmakers, whether or not they identify the latter specifically as the source of the different dimensions of the work. Just four (1.3 per cent of the five-star ratings) give sole credit to Kubrick, while a more substantial 56 (18 per cent) attribute the positive qualities they find in the film to Spielberg alone, which is unsurprising given the much greater general audience familiarity of his previous work and his name.

Very few of those who give five-star reviews (just two) consider the combination of the two filmmakers to have jarred, a conclusion reached by a slightly larger number (nine, or 5.8 per cent) of the total of 153 who condemn *A.I.* to the lowest category one-star bracket. The number of these who blame Spielberg specifically for what they see as the shortcomings of the film is also quite small (nine), while 12 (7.8 per cent) complain about an excess of the sentimental and 15 (9.8 per cent) object to the ending, either generally or again on the grounds of sentimentality. None of the one-star reviews blames Kubrick by name, although the terms in which the film is rejected include a number of qualities that might more generally be associated with his work or certain versions of quality more generally. Nine, for example, find the film too cold, lacking a source of identification or a hero figure. Another seven find the film too dark, dreary or downbeat. By far the most common ground of rejection – as often found in viewer-response dislike of less mainstream titles – is that the film is boring, too long and/or too slow, a factor cited by 52 reviewers (34 per cent of those in this category), another dimension that might resonate with the Kubrick *oeuvre*, although there is no evidence to suggest that this is familiar to most of the one-star reviewers (the contributions of which are generally – although not exclusively – shorter and less developed than some of the more positive responses).

Overall, such responses seems fairly typical of those found to Hollywood quality films of the kind examined in this book. Those who celebrate the film as simultaneously 'thought-provoking' and 'heart-wrenching' are perhaps the ideal audience for such productions, their responses marking out what is both more and less distinctive – in studio terms – in the dimensions offered to the viewer. It is clear, however, that this is not a mix that appeals to everyone, as indicated in both the terms in which the film is rejected by a significant minority and the vociferous nature of some of these responses, including a number of rhetorical declarations that the film is the worst the viewer has ever seen – and by its disappointing box office performance.

A co-production between Kubrick's studio home, Warner, and Spielberg's DreamWorks, with a budget put at between $90 million and $100 million, *A.I.* was given a release of blockbuster scale, in 3,242 theatres, similar to that of the two biggest earners of the year, *Lord of the Rings: The Fellowship of the Ring* and *Harry Potter and the Philosopher's Stone* (opened in 3,359 and 3,672 theatres respectively). This signified distinctly mainstream-commercial ambition rather than aspirations to the status of specifically artistic quality.[32] It took only $78.6 million (compared with $314 million and $317 million domestic grosses for *Lord of the Rings* and *Harry Potter*), although this was supplemented by greater success overseas, where the film earned twice as much. The total of $235.9 million would not have represented any great success in the theatrical market, when marketing and distribution costs were deducted, but would not be likely to be considered a disaster once DVD and other revenue streams were taken into account.

The Kubrick/Spielberg factor also featured in trade press reporting of the release of *A.I.*, the initial performance of which in its opening Independence Day week was considered to be 'respectable' at $29.4 million.[33] A key measure of likely success in the large-opening blockbuster-scale arena is the extent of the revenue drop experienced in the immediately following weeks, the point at which *A.I.* demonstrated its limitations, falling 52 per cent in week two and a further 63 per cent in its third week.[34] Just over a week before release, *Variety* reported unidentified Warner executives suggesting that the name of Kubrick was 'dominating the pre-release chatter', which would be unlikely to be considered an ideal situation, but with hopes that 'Spielberg's trademark blend of sci-fi and child wonderment' would prevail.[35] Up to this point, marketing for the film had been 'enigmatic', leaving 'industryites wondering what the film has going for it aside from Steven Spielberg'. A high level of secrecy having surrounded the production, a gesture in which Spielberg sought to maintain a Kubrick tradition, 'Insiders' were reported to have described the film as 'one part Kubrick and three parts "E.T."'.[36]

After the second and third week disappointments, however, this did not appear to be how the film seemed in the marketplace, despite the presence of the director's name above the title in posters and at the climax of the main trailer. The trailer itself leans towards the quality-distinctive in its associations, beginning with full-screen text providing a 'warning' about the employment of the series of codewords required to activate what is subsequently described as 'a robot child'. The spelling out of more concrete elements of plot is then intermingled with the voicing and appearance on screen of the sequence of abstract terms that constitute the code, the impression created by which is distinctly oblique, 'arty' and coolly toned, by studio standards. Warner president of distribution Dan Fellman suggested that 'moviegoers have viewed it as a more challenging film of the Kubrick variety than as a commercial, Spielberg type of pic', which seems in keeping with the resonances provided by the trailer.[37] On this basis, expectations seemed to be adjusted, or at least face could be saved, by noting that the film had already exceeded the domestic gross of $55.7 million achieved by Kubrick's final film, *Eyes Wide Shut*, which opened at the same time of year in 1999. *A.I.* also performed disappointingly in the prestige stakes, earning Oscar nominations only in secondary categories (visual effects and score) and no wins.

Valuing Spielberg: orga vs. mecha?

If some, notably Morris, have sought to elevate Spielberg's films to the status of higher-cultural products, my main focus here is on valorisations of the filmmaker on the basis of their quality as *popular* entertainments perceived to be of a particularly high standard. A useful starting point is the intervention offered by Tom Shone in *Blockbuster: How the Jaws and Jedi Generation Turned Hollywood into a Boom-town*, a work that seeks to situate itself in a populist position, as opposed to academic analysis, similar to that in which it situates Spielberg's films in relation to established versions of quality. Taking *Jaws* as a key exemplar, Shone marks out a number of distinctions. First, the film is distinguished from contemporary blockbusters such as *The Poseidon Adventure* (1972) that are largely dismissed for their claims to self-importance of a kind associated with earlier traditions of the star-heavy prestige film. *Jaws*, in contrast, has a lighter and more witty touch, absent of any such pretentions. A key marker of this for Shone is the inclusion within the film of particular kinds of character detail that add an extra dimension of nuance to the work, seen as elevating its quality but as doing so in a subtle manner and without any heavy-handedness. One such example is a touching moment in which the young son of Chief Brody (Roy Scheider) mimics his father's finger-steepling gesture as the two are seated together at the dinner table.[38]

I would agree that this is precisely the kind of detail that contributes to the quality of the film, in evaluative terms, giving it an extra degree of resonance beyond that which might usually be expected of work in this popular generic locale, without undermining any of the more conventional appeal overall. Shone wraps this into a heavily over-stated conclusion, however. Usually, to find such touches, he suggests, it was necessary at the time to watch 'something far more boring – some chamber piece about marital disintegration by John Cassavetes, say – and yet here were such things popping up in a movie starring a scary rubber shark'.[39] This, he suggests, 'was nothing short of revolutionary: you could have finger-steepling and scary rubber sharks *in the same movie*'.[40] He continues, in the same rhetorical manner: 'Spielberg had completely upended the pyramid of American film, ridding the blockbuster of its rather desperate bids for "prestige" while also visiting on it the sort of filigree dramatic technique normally associated with films much higher up the brow.'[41] This marked, apparently, the end of 'the old system of cinematic apartheid that had existed before, dictating that popular movies must be dumb and highbrow films boring'.

Little of this rhetorical framework stands up to close examination, depending as it does on the assumption that works of independent or art-cinema status such as those of John Cassavetes are inherently 'boring' (which is far from the case and the kind of judgement that assumes a particular viewing position) or that there was ever any system within which 'popular movies must be dumb' (a similarly unsustainable generalisation in relation to any period of Hollywood history). It only makes sense as part of Shone's attempt to set himself up, in the selling of his own general-audience-oriented book, as a populist debunker of pretension (something done more overtly in later passages in which he mocks academic analysis of examples such as *Alien* [1979] and *Blade Runner* [1982]). A similar over-simplification follows when Shone distinguishes Spielberg's films from the cinema associated with the Hollywood Renaissance of the late 1960s and 1970s. Here, Shone offers an inversion of the more widely prevailing value-judgement, according to which the Renaissance is accorded a quality status seen to have been undermined by the success of blockbusters from the likes of Spielberg and George Lucas. If Spielberg 'turns out to have been the most talented filmmaker of his generation', without any of the angst involved, say, in the work of Martin Scorsese, then 'What was the point of all those hours passed in the dark confines of the art house [are these screens somehow darker than those of the multiplex?], boning up on Ukrainian cinema, watching the unwatchable'.[42]

It is easy to dismiss such tendentious rhetoric, but the oppositions, and the assumptions behind them, are not untypical of the kinds of interventions found in this discursive territory (including some of the forms of expression found in viewer responses from Amazon cited in earlier chapters). It is not necessary to caricature and dismiss art cinema, outside a world of rather cheap 'witty' point-scoring, to argue for the existence of some qualities often associated with that domain within works of more overtly popular appeal. At the other end of the scale, Shone also draws on familiar discursive tropes in distinguishing *Jaws* (in particular, among some other examples) from later varieties of the blockbuster of the kind cited as negative markers of quality in Chapter 1 of this book. A sound recording of an early audience screening of *Jaws* identified one aural highlight in the collective scream that greeted one moment of horror, Shone reports. Another such moment was then added to the film, creating two screams but each less potent than the original single moment. This, for Shone, 'contains a telling diagnosis of the problems to which the blockbuster would be heir – all its inflationary drives, gratuitous escalations, Pyrrhic redundancies'.[43]

My point here is not necessarily to question the preferences expressed in accounts such as these, but to identify the nature of the value–judgements on which they are based and the discursive frameworks within which these are articulated. And even here, when valorising work of popular appeal, the process remains close to what is involved in broader, hierarchically based articulations of quality. Much of what Shone praises falls into categories such as the subtle, the nuanced and the restrained that have featured in notions of quality examined elsewhere in this book (Spielberg's light touch, his highly economic delineation of some aspects of character in *Jaws*, as opposed to the 'everything but the kitchen sink' approach often associated with subsequent blockbuster franchises such as the *Transformers* series). Even within the most popular of productions, therefore, a similar process of distinction-marking can occur, and on some very similar grounds. Missing from these might be markers such as complexity or darkness of conclusion, and general world-view; the latter are found in some examples included by Shone, particularly *Alien* and *Blade Runner*, but this is precisely why they have generally been more attractive to certain kinds of academic analysis and have sometimes been accorded a higher cultural status, and also why they were less successful as feel-good crowd-pleasers on release than the likes of *Jaws*, *Star Wars* and *E. T.*

Qualities with a similar cultural location are established as the basis of what makes Spielberg's films superior to other blockbusters in the more substantial academic engagement offered by Warren Buckland, a close study of the formal characteristics of the work. Buckland starts from a position similar to that of Shone, seeking to identify what he also sees as 'slight differences in filmmaking, small details constituting the elusive quality that elevate[s] Spielberg's blockbusters over other blockbusters'.[44] His focus is exclusively on the more popular of the filmmaker's works, not those accused of straining for other kinds of prestige. The basis of such quality in this account lies in the achievement of an 'organic unity' in the work, a notion with a long history in the study of aesthetics, defined here as 'a whole that is more than the sum of its parts, in that the whole possesses an *added value* not contained in any of its parts, for the parts have reached their highest degree or best possible level of integration'.[45] Key terms deployed by Buckland are 'balance' and 'coherence', drawn from a tradition of film criticism rooted particularly in the work of V.F. Perkins and, Buckland suggests, from the implicit assumptions expressed in a number of how-to guides on filmmaking.

For Perkins, writing in the early 1970s, when film had achieved considerable recognition as an art in its own right through the process detailed via the account of Shyon Baumann in the Introduction of this book, the 'battle for prestige' had been won.[46] Film was thus freed from the need to try to define itself in terms drawn from other arts, or from a general, capitalised notion of Art (however much these might seem to have remained in play for some notions of the quality film, as seen in the preceding chapters). Instead, the medium could be defined according to what Perkins identifies as its two principal underlying tendencies: the power to capture the appearance of the real world and, alternatively, the capacity to provide an ideal image, ordered by the will of the filmmaker.[47] The fiction film offers the possibility of a synthesis between these two imperatives. While some might seek a notion of 'pure' cinema rooted in either one or the other (film as 'essentially' realist or 'essentially' expressive), what Perkins valorises is 'an ideal compromise' between the two.[48] The aim of the filmmaker, he suggests, should be to achieve a balance between 'the twin criteria of order and credibility' by seeking 'to organize the world to the point where it becomes most meaningful but to resist ordering it out of all resemblance to the real world which it attempts to evoke'.[49] The ideal achievement, according to these criteria, is for an image simultaneously to be both a recording of what happens within the diegesis and an expressive device that heightens its significance, without the expressive dimension seeming in any way imposed upon the material.

This is very much within the parameters of notions of classical filmmaking, in which style is meant to be subordinated to the demands of narrative and not to obtrude in its own right, as is suggested by Adrian Martin, another of the sources on which Buckland draws.[50] We return here to the debate about notions of the classical and the post-classical or the mannerist – and the underlying values implied in the use of such categories – encountered in Chapter 4. A privileging of organic unity also provides a frequent reference point, as Buckland suggests, in the writings of Noel Carroll. It is against such a notion that Carroll is critical of what he terms the 'demonstrative expressiveness' of some of the Hollywood Renaissance films of the 1960s and 1970s.[51] Similar qualities are valorised by Stefan Sharff, also cited by Buckland, whose concept of 'significant form' likewise suggests an added value that results at the level of the whole from the combination of its parts, another position the value-judgements of which are founded on notions such as unity and organic integration.[52] Buckland also identifies related sources of quality in the narrative strategies employed by films, a 'successful' example being one that paces the disclosure of narrative information in a particular manner, 'so that information is withheld from spectators until the most appropriate time (the narration must be uncommunicative at certain times in order to keep the audience involved)'.[53]

Buckland then proceeds to analyse a selection of Spielberg's works, including some of his early TV productions, evaluating them according to the extent to which they achieve organic unity, either overall or in what are considered to be particularly successful sequences. Some of the early work is found distinctly lacking, although with occasional signs of what was to come. A Spielberg-directed episode of the Universal TV series *Night Gallery* ('Eyes', 1969), for example, is generally judged negatively. It is deemed to have slipped often into mannerism (and this is seen, precisely, as a descent, in hierarchical terms) in its tendency to reach for what are seen as excessively stylised touches. These are viewed as a means through which the director could mark his distinctive presence, but are criticised for not being organically integrated into the material. The first of Spielberg's films judged to have manifested organic unity in a large number of scenes is *Jaws*, on which I focus here as the main example of this approach (Buckland's book includes only very brief consideration of *A.I.*).

Two of the opening scenes, including the bridge between them, employ graphic matches (a regular Spielberg trait). In the first case, the match is between two ocean horizon shots: first, the night sea after the shark death that begins the film; second, a similar shot from the perspective of Chief Brody the following morning. The second, less exact match involves two shots through doorways of the Brody home. In each case, Buckland suggests, the match might appear to be 'a distracting mannerist stylistic trick'; that is, a bad thing, to be

Figure 6.5. 'Manifesting organic unity': tension between foreground and background in *Jaws* © Universal Studios

disparaged.[54] But each is then judged to have greater resonance. The first links the two scenes at the thematic level, according to Buckland, through the subsequent impact on Brody of the chain of events started with the death of the initial victim. The transition 'goes beyond pedestrian rendition and pushes the film towards significant form and organic unity', Buckland argues, although it is a moot point, perhaps, how far any such thematic issues are really in play in a passing and early moment such as this.[55] The second is said to emphasise family unity, another source of thematic relevance that provides motivation and thus counters any accusation of arbitrary mannerism, although this is a very fleeting moment and it seems, again, to be asked to carry a good deal of baggage in this reading.

Buckland expresses further admiration for the manner in which Spielberg handles a following sequence during which Brody takes the telephone call that proves to be alerting him to the fact that a girl has gone missing – the victim from the opening scene. This is staged in depth, with Brody to one side of the screen in the foreground while in the background his wife cleans a wound on the hand of their son, Michael, and agrees that he can go swimming afterwards (see Figure 6.5). As Buckland suggests, the controlling of narrative information at this point is such that viewers are able to put together the two pieces of knowledge, 'and realize that it is not a good idea for Michael to go swimming in the shark-infested waters with a bloody wound on his hand', but that this is not apparent to the parents. Tension exists, he suggests, between not just foreground and background but between the image and the viewer: 'This is an extremely effective shot, using the framing, foreground-background, shot duration, and omniscient narrative to engage the audience. Even at this early stage, *Jaws* is manifesting organic unity.'[56]

If the latter is another brief and passing moment, Buckland finds similar qualities in a more celebrated high-point of the film, the sequence that culminates in the second shark attack, after Brody has been prevailed upon to keep the beaches open ahead of the 4 July weekend. A sustained tension is created between events occurring in the foreground, middle ground and background, through various partly obscured views, as Brody watches nervously on the shore and he and the film viewer experience a number of false alarms. These culminate in Spielberg's deployment of a zoom/dolly – a simultaneous zooming out and tracking in of the camera that maintains the framing of Brody's figure while creating a yawning effect in the background, as a result of the change in depth of field. This is a showy effect that seems entirely motivated as an expression of character subjectivity and that climaxes what is undoubtedly an impressively choreographed sequence. A number of other sequences that are deemed to achieve organic unity are subsequently examined from a selection of films including *Close Encounters of the Third Kind*, *Raiders of the Lost Ark* and *Jurassic Park*.

Other writers have taken a similar approach (collectively, sometimes labelled *mise-en-scène* criticism), recent proponents including John Gibbs and Steven Peacock, each also putting their emphasis on the appreciation of qualities such as subtlety and coherence.[57] As Gibbs suggests, the valorisation of coherence as an aesthetic standard can be dated back as far as the writing of Plato and Aristotle, sources the citation of which bring their own imprimateur of quality/prestige and associations with the classical in more literal-historical terms.[58] It was also a major tenet of the literary New Criticism of the mid twentieth century, another source of intellectual standing of particular relevance during the development of academic film studies from the early 1960s.[59] The imitation of an action in drama should be that of 'a single, unified action and one that is a whole', Aristotle suggests in his *Poetics*, the most familiar source of the concept.[60] The structure should be such that the transposition or removal of any one section should change the whole: 'If the presence or absence of something has no discernible effect, it is not part of the whole', as would be said of an effect of style that is considered to be arbitrarily imposed.[61]

The same source is cited by the art historian E.H. Gombrich, although Gombrich suggests that unity in itself is no guarantor of quality but should be accompanied by some sense of complexity, within which organic unity counts for more.[62] Steven Peacock puts his focus primarily on small-scale aspects of form (implicitly suggesting the subtle, although without using this term as such) and the role of expressive criticism in seeking to evoke these.[63] Such material can be understood, here more explicitly than in some accounts, as providing an ideal resource for the mobilisation by critics of their own cultural capital, as demonstrated by their ability not just to identify but to evoke such qualities in prose. This helps to explain the wider favouring of qualities such as subtlety and organic unity: they lend themselves to a particular form of analysis that provides a particular (superior) kind of position to the analyst, whether at an academic or more journalistic level.

Against qualities such as organic unity and subtlety, as sources of negative value-judgement, are set familiar suspects of the kind seen above in the rhetoric of Shone, in the reservations of Buckland about the devices employed in some cases by Spielberg, and in earlier parts of this book. In films in which form is seen overtly to have been imposed on content, Perkins suggests: 'Asserted meanings, crude juxtapositions, tend to be both blatant and unclear, like over-amplified noises bellowing from a faulty loudspeaker.'[64] It is notable that when Buckland criticises some of what he sees as 'forced, artless' visuals, imposed by Spielberg on his episode of *Night Gallery*, he goes on to describe this approach as 'mechanical', reinforcing the sense of continuity between this discourse and the historical opposition between notions of the organic and the mechanical considered in the Introduction and Chapter 1.[65] The mechanical here is viewed as the fake, the artificially confected; that which is imposed from outside rather than seeming to emerge seamlessly from the material itself. This is another opposition that seems rhetorical, however. The difference, really, is one of *seeming*, of appearances rather than substance. It is not

that the effects valorised by Buckland, for example, or others employing this approach, actually emerge 'naturally' from somewhere. They
are just as much imposed as those which are criticised. The difference
is that some such effects are more carefully disguised than others.

A similar point might be made in relation to the process of fictional
confection and coincidence identified in *Blood Diamond* in the previous chapter. The fact that events at the micro/personal and macro/
social level are often closely conjoined might also be seen as a source
of organic unity, of tightly integrated textual organisation in which
the general speed and effective mobilisation of such material tends to
distract attention from quite how contrived it really is. Organic unity,
that is, might be viewed itself as a form of smoothly accomplished
fakery! The point is not necessarily to judge it as such, in negative
evaluative terms, but to suggest that it need not be seen as in any way
inherently superior.

That some might prefer the creation of an impression of organic
unity might seem reasonable enough, as a situated value-judgement,
but they do so from a particular position that needs to be acknowledged. A notable absence from writing in the tradition cited above is
any attempt to explore the underlying basis of the value-judgements
that are being made. Notions such as organic unity and subtlety tend
to be taken here at face value, as markers of superior quality, the
broader socio-cultural or historical basis of which is not subjected to
analysis. This is the case even in some work located within what initially presents itself as a more critical context, as in two contributions
in which such values feature prominently in a collection titled *Valuing
Films*, the introduction of which by Laura Hubner promises to inves-
tigate the 'political and discursive frameworks that prioritize certain
forms of value over others'.[66]

Each of these adopts to some extent a perspective of the kind associated with Perkins, in which organic unity is deployed as a measure
of value, but neither subjects the basis of this measure to any sustained critical interrogation. Instead, it is largely accepted, unquestioned, as a measuring rod. This is certainly the case in the first, in
which James Walters argues for the use of this kind of coherence as a
basis of evaluative judgement of the 'twist' film. Tom Brown offers a
somewhat more complex account, in an examination of the critical

tendency for spectacle to be under-valued in Hollywood films. This includes, among others, the suggestion that spectacle can form part of the organic unity of a film and so can, in effect, be rescued for critical respectability on this basis. That spectacle can be read this way – as contributing to thematic or other narrative dimensions – is an argument I have made myself elsewhere. But to *value* certain forms of spectacle more highly on this basis is to mobilise a particular set of discursive assumptions the nature of which requires further analysis.

What, then, of the underlying bases of these terms of reference? Qualities such as organic unity or subtlety should not be seen as offering a neutral basis for evaluation, however widespread their adoption. They are socially and historically situated, as are all value-judgements, and need to be understood as such, as part of particular cultural-taste formations. As Jane Feuer puts it, using the language of reception theory in the context of quality television, 'there can never be a judgement of quality in the absolute sense' but in relation to 'one's interpretive community or reading formation'.[67] To appreciate the organic unity of a text as such, including the various subtleties through which this is achieved, requires certain resources of cultural capital. At the same time, as suggested above, to express this in writing, in reviews or book-length studies, is to deploy such capital, to gain a return of some kind on the investment entailed in its accumulation. In both cases, what is also involved is the implicit marking of distinctions from those *not* equipped with such resources. The resonance the terms of the approach sketched above has with the earlier historical period considered in the Introduction – one in which a newly evolving 'mass' audience was seen as a threat to existing cultural and social hierarchies – further suggests some of what might be seen to be at stake here, particularly given a prevailing context in which certain types of Hollywood film are identified as a source of cultural lowering or diminishment.

The valorisation of organic unity and the subtle can be understood as part of a wider discursive process in which such markers of distinction are used to help to maintain existing cultural boundaries, regardless of whether or not this might be the avowed intent of those who use such an approach. A policing function is implied here: the defence of that which requires more cultural capital in order fully to be appreciated against that which needs less. This is the case whether this involves the appreciation of qualities associated with 'higher' cultural forms in their own right – the 'literary' or the 'artistic' – or the nuances approved in a broadly similar manner under the label of organic unity within work of an otherwise more popular/commercial orientation. This is one way perhaps to explain the valorisation of types of filmmaking – or other cultural production – in which the expressive employment of form is not too readily apparent but considered ideally to disappear into the content. The contribution made by form in such cases remains apparent to those with the requisite resources but is not likely to be noticeable to most of those in the broader target audience. A more 'heavy-handed' approach, of the kind denigrated by critics in this tradition, might be more likely to come to the attention of – and thus be able explicitly to be appreciated by – viewers who lack the particular kind of cultural upbringing and education that encourages the valorisation of the subtle.

At issue here might partly be the particular dimension of the noticing and appreciation of form in its own right. It might be argued, contrary to what I have suggested above, that the kinds of organic unity achieved by a figure such as Spielberg make some highly mainstream-oriented films more pleasurable for a large audience, regardless of its ability to understand why or to be able to identify the particular devices that are responsible for the effectiveness of the work as one of popular entertainment (this is effectively what Buckland suggests). It is not the norm for consumers of popular culture to require explicit knowledge of the formal qualities that make such works enjoyable in particular ways; their operations are, usually, at a level that is not consciously noticed. But the appreciation of formal qualities is widely taken to be a marker of a 'superior' level of engagement, in relation to films or other cultural products situated at any level in the broader cultural hierarchy (including, for example, a 'sophisticated' understanding of the traditions of a 'low' genre such as horror). The 'sin' of the heavy-handed, then, might be to threaten the relative exclusivity of the terrain of those who can appreciate the subtle deployment of form. A figure such as Quentin Tarantino might be evoked here, one whose expressive uses of form tend to lie at the overt end of the scale, and thus tend to be more widely accessible as such – more noticeable to more viewers, less disguised – and therefore liable to be questioned by some from the kind of perspective outlined above (the heavy-handed and 'obvious' versus the kind of nuance celebrated, for example, by David Bordwell in the examples of art filmmaking cited in Chapter 1).

A more frequent target of critics who draw on these discourses, however, may be a particular understanding of the contemporary blockbuster, noted much less for the use of overtly expressive formal devices than for a general sense of noise, clamorous spectacle and lack of subtlety. Here, the operative distinction appears more clearly to be located in what comes down to matters of the kinds of social class locations (combined with some others, including age and gender) with which such productions are associated. If earlier periods such as those examined by Raymond Williams and Leo Lowenthal were ones in which cultural boundaries were defended in the context of the perceived threat to some sectors from a rising popular or 'mass' culture, a similar dynamic seems to underlie the fears expressed in recent decades about the supposed undermining of qualities such as classical restraint by what are seen as the heightened commercial imperatives underlying the contemporary blockbuster franchise. Opposed to classical notions of organic unity and subtlety are, in this account, the demands of what Richard Maltby term a 'commercial aesthetic', one in which different elements might be included in a film not so much in order to achieve balance and unity but as a result of a more cynical courting of particular audience constituencies; 'one that is essentially opportunistic in its economic motivation'.[68] To associate the latter with the Hollywood of the last several decades, as distinct from an earlier 'classical' period is to be guilty of further over-simplification, however. Maltby's use of the concept is in relation to Hollywood history as a whole, not just to a particular era, and the point has often been made that much of the cinema of what is known as the classical era is far from an embodiment of the kinds of (idealised) qualities sometimes associated with the term.

If the distrust of what is viewed as mechanical imposition of expressive effects can be seen as part of a historical response to perceived threats to particular groups resulting from the spread of various forms of mass/popular culture, this discourse can also be situated within a broader tradition of suspicion of the image, examined by Rosalind Galt, one that brings together a number of strands considered in this book.[69] Galt identifies a long-standing denigration of the image within film theory of various kinds. This is traced back to a wider cultural tradition rooted in the separation between idea and image established by Plato, and the favouring of the former, a phenomenon described by Galt as part of 'the foundational language of Western aesthetics'.[70] The longer-term historical context is the same here as that evoked in Chapter 1 in relation to discourses that establish value-laden distinctions between narrative and spectacle. Some more recent elaborations within film theory and elsewhere have inherited this suspicion of the image itself, Galt suggests, and have also 'replicated the hierarchy within the image'.[71] If particular kinds of images are subjected to the most heightened suspicion – those seen, for example, as 'too colourful' or 'too cosmetic', overly decorative, labelled by Galt as the 'pretty' – the emphasis on organic unity in the work of critics such as Perkins and his adherents might be seen as offering a way effectively of containing any such distrust. That which might be considered 'a distracting stylistic mannerist trick', to cite Buckland, language that is akin to the suspicion of the image explored by Galt, can more safely be accommodated when provided with a rationale that exists in the realm of ideas, such as a thematic significance. That which might otherwise be viewed as 'superficial', a key term in the widespread tendency examined by Galt, gains a sense of 'deeper' meaning.

The kind of language employed in relation to the object of distrust by writers otherwise as different in level of engagement as Buckland and Shone suggests the existence of a broader cultural complex within which these discourses can be located. Language of this type seems to betray a certain anxiety about the existence of such qualities and suggests another link to the explanation offered by Galt, for whom the suspicion of the supposedly 'seductive' qualities of the visually pleasing image is rooted in a deeply embedded conjunction of patriarchal and Orientalist discourses.[72] We can return here to the valorisation of classical qualities in the history of art, a topic addressed in Chapter 4. The favouring of what were seen as neoclassical works

in the eighteenth century involved a rejection of more overtly decorative forms such as the baroque and the rococo, Galt suggests, the
qualities of the latter tending to be associated, negatively, with both
the feminine and the foreign, particularly the Asian.[73] Neoclassical
notions such as these 'continue to structure film criticism', with all the
baggage that this entails, Galt argues (although there might be exceptions to this tradition), despite what she suggests is their inability to
comprehend the more elaborate styles of some filmmakers.[74]

The valorisation of organic unity and coherence might also have
ideological implications in left/right terms, as is implied in the suggestion by Galt that the pretty can have a radical potential it is not
usually accorded (for feminist, queer or left-leaning perspectives).
To emphasise unity and coherence within deeply divided societies
such as those of the capitalist 'west' might be to risk glossing over
the many disjunctures upon which such societies are founded. Todd
Berliner makes a good rival argument to those of Perkins, Carroll,
Sharff and Buckland for the potential aesthetic merit of 'the illogic,
imbalance, and disproportion one finds in many great artworks', this
in the context of the analysis of such qualities as manifested by celebrated films from the Hollywood Renaissance in the 1970s.[75] As
Richard Shusterman argues, even if the pragmatic value of organic
unity is recognised (as, for example, in its capacity to satisfy a 'need
[or desire] to perceive and experience satisfying unities in the dis-
ordered flux of experience'), it should not be fetishised or seen as
the only valued approach. Merit can also be found, he suggests, in
rival qualities such as fragmentation and incoherence.[76] It is possible
to make sweeping and reductive claims in either direction, the key
point here being that this is something open to contest and debate,
without any point of neutral value-judgement. If the pretty has radical potential for Galt, she notes that this is not *necessarily* so, any
more than it should necessarily be treated as an object of suspicion.
Likewise, it is not necessary to make any argument in favour of the
kinds of qualities criticised by Buckland in some of the early work of
Spielberg in order to argue the need for a critical interrogation of the
usually unstated values that underpin the privileging of criteria such
as organic unity or subtlety. That such qualities can have pragmatic
value is a point central to Buckland's approach. It might be these

dimensions that make Spielberg's films work particularly effectively for particular audiences, in a particular socio-economic conjuncture (one that would be likely to include sedimented assumptions based on the kinds of histories of aesthetic judgement traced by Galt), which would be sufficient to justify this as a basis of measurement at that level.

The same might be said of the longer tradition of valuing organic unity as a major thread in the history of 'classical' western art and literature. It appears to have proved to be an effective approach in a great many cases over time. Plenty of other forms have also proved effective without being founded on this principle, however, particularly with popular audiences (including many films that are far from entirely classical or unified in their texture). This suggests that organic unity is only one specific basis for positive valuation and one that implies a certain cultural location, in this case benefiting in its hegemonic prevalence from the massive weight of accumulated cultural authority that accompanies notions such as these as a result of their centuries-long association with classical form.[77] Value-judgements of this nature are rarely put in such proximate terms, however, but are usually presented – explicitly or implicitly – as if neutral, objective and/or universal.

We can be led here into broader debates about the nature of aesthetic judgement and a fundamental split between those who argue for universals of one kind or another – art as an evolutionary universal, for example, or the judgement of beauty as one that should involve a Kantian exercise of disinterested rationality[78] – or for the socially constructed nature of all such judgements.[79] Whatever origins some might argue for in the distant past – as in the evolutionary argument – it seems clear to me that these are essentially historical and socio-cultural matters as we experience them, our preferences being shaped by various conjunctions of inherited assumptions and within the frameworks of prevailing discursive horizons of the kinds encountered on various occasions in this book. It is not possible to step outside these, into some entirely neutral space that escapes the process of distinction-marking. I would certainly position myself within such frameworks, inhabiting some of the key quality assumptions explored above in my own preferences. This does not mean that it is not possible to interrogate the bases on which these are founded, just that this is always done from a particularly situated position. I often appreciate the subtle and the organically unified myself and tend to favour the kinds of quality films examined here, along with products of Indiewood and the unattached indie sector, above the more conventional studio blockbuster. I might also find myself making distinctions in my own preferences between some of the products of quality Hollywood, or the Indiewood sector, and those of the often more highly valued independent or art-film sectors (although not in all cases). I do so as the product of a particular (white, male, middle-class, academic) background. That we can feel such preferences strongly, at what is experienced as an individual 'gut' level, reinforced by the views of like-minded critical institutions, should not be taken as evidence for any larger claims that might be made for the value of such qualities in their own right, however, but as a demonstration of the power of the socio-cultural grounds we inevitably occupy and on which the processes of distinction-marking are made.

Notes

1   James Naremore, *On Kubrick*, London: BFI, 2007, p. 82
2   Ibid., p. 246
3   Ibid., pp. 3–4
4   Robert Kolker, *A Cinema of Loneliness: Penn, Stone, Kubrick, Scorsese, Spielberg, Altman*, 3rd edition, Oxford: Oxford University Press, 2000, p. 101
5   For examples, see Nigel Morris, *The Cinema of Steven Spielberg: Empire of Light*, London: Wallflower, 2007
6   Robert Kapsis, *Hitchcock: The Making of a Reputation*, Chicago: University of Chicago Press, 1992
7   See, for example, the reading of Spielberg in Michael Ryan and Douglas Kellner, *Camera Politica: The Politics and Ideology of Contemporary Hollywood Film*, Bloomington: Indiana University Press, 1988, Chapter 8; as well as Kolker, *A Cinema of Loneliness*
8   Morris, *The Cinema of Steven Spielberg*
9   Ibid., p. 285
10   Ibid., p. 287
11   Kolker, *A Cinema of Loneliness*, p. 290

12   Naremore, *On Kubrick*, pp. 19, 20, 22

13   Ibid., p. 21

14   Ibid., p. 23

15   On the genesis of the film, see Jane Struthers, 'The birth of *A.I.*' in Jan Harlan and Jane Struthers, eds, *A.I. Artificial Intelligence From Stanley Kubrick to Steven Spielberg: The Vision Behind the Film*, London: Thames & Hudson, 2009

16   Struthers, 'The birth of *A.I.*'

17   Ibid.

18   Ibid.

19   Kathleen Kennedy, 'A.I.: Artificial Intelligence: Production notes', http://cinema.com/articles/611/ai-artificial-intelligence-production-notes.phtml. Much the same point is repeated by Spielberg in a 'Creating *A.I.*' feature on the DVD/Blu-ray release

20   Jan Harlan, 'Afterword: The two masters' in Harlan and Struthers, *A.I. Artificial Intelligence*, p. 148

21   'Blown by a strong wind over the legal mountains' in Harlan and Struthers, *A.I. Artifical Intelligence*, p. 8

22   Kennedy, 'A.I.: Artificial Intelligence: Production notes'

23   Kenneth Turan, 'Movie review: Mechanically inclined', 29 June 2001, via latimes.com

24   A.O Scott, 'Film review; Do androids long for mom?', 29 June 2001, via nytimes.com

25   Roger Ebert, 'A.I. Artificial Intelligence', 29 June 2001, entry for the film at rottentomatoes.com

26   J. Hobernman, 'The mommy returns', 26 June 2001, entry at rottentomatoes.com

27   Peter Rainer, 'The ultimate boy toy', 29 October 2001, entry at rottentomatoes.com

28   Charles Taylor, 'Artificial maturity', salon.com, 29 June 2001; Mick LaSalle, *San Francisco Chronicle*, 29 June 2001; both via rottentomatoes.com

29   Todd McCarthy, 'Review: A.I. Artificial Intelligence', 18 June 2001, via rottentomatoes.com

30   Sample accessed 16 May 2013 at http://www.amazon.com/A-I-Artificial-Intelligence-Widescreen-Two-Disc/product-reviews/B00003CXXP/ref=cm_cr_dp_see_all_summary?ie=UTF8&showViewpoints=1

31   For further rationale for this approach, see Martin Barker, *A Toxic Genre: The Iraq War Films*, London: Pluto Press, 2011, p. 16

32   These and the following figures are from the film's entries on Internet Movie Database (imdb.com) and Box Office Mojo (boxofficemojo.com)

33   Carl DiOrio and Dade Hayes, 'Distrib's summer bummer', *Variety*, 16 July 2001, via variety.com

34   Carl DiOrio, 'Goldilocks rocks B.O.', *Variety*, 15 July 2001, via variety. com

35   Dade Hayes, 'Summer expectations soar', 22 May 2001, via variety.com

36   Ibid. The point about secrecy is from Rachel Amramowitz, 'Summer sneaks', *Los Angeles Times*, 6 May 2001, via latimes.com

37   DiOrio, 'Goldilocks rocks B.O.'

38   Tom Shone, *Blockbuster: How the Jaws and Jedi Generation Turned Hollywood into a Boom-town*, London: Simon & Schuster, 2004, p. 33

39   Ibid., p. 33

40   Ibid., p. 33, emphasis in original

41   Ibid., p. 33

42   Ibid., p. 80

43   Ibid., pp. 25–6

44   Warren Buckland, *Directed by Steven Spielberg: Poetics of the Contemporary Hollywood Blockbuster*, New York: Continuum, 2006, p. 1

45   Ibid., p. 4

46   V.F. Perkins, *Film as Film: Understanding and Judging Movies*, Harmondsworth: Penguin, 1972/1986, p. 10

47   Ibid., pp. 60–61

48   Ibid., p. 62

49   Ibid., pp. 69, 70

50   Adrian Martin, '*Mise-en-scène* is dead, or the expressive, the excessive and the stylish', Continuum, vol. 6, no. 2, 1993, p. 3

51   Noel Carroll, *Interpreting the Moving Image*, Cambridge: Cambridge University Press, 1998

52   Stefan Sharff, *The Elements of Cinema: Toward a Theory of Cinesthetic Impact*, New York: Columbia University Press, 1982

53   Buckland, *Directed by Steven Spielberg*, p. 51

54   Ibid., pp. 90, 92

55   Ibid., p. 91

56   Ibid., p. 92

57   For a history of this tendency, see Martin, '*Mise-en-scène* is dead'

58   John Gibbs, *Mise-en-Scène: Film Style and Interpretation*, London: Wallflower, 2002, p. 40

59   On its use in relation to film evaluation as early as the 1930s, see Janet Staiger, 'The revenge of the film education movement: Cult movies and fan interpretive behaviors', *Reception: Texts, Readers, Audiences, History*, vol. 1, fall 2008

60   Aristotle, *Poetics*, Harmondsworth: Penguin, 1996, p. 15

61   Ibid., p. 15

62   Ernst Gombrich, 'Norm and form' in *Gombrich on the Renaissance: Volume 1, Norm and Form*, London: Phaidon, 4th edition, 1985, p. 77

63   Steven Peacock, *Hollywood and Intimacy: Style, Moments, Magnificence*, Basingstoke: Palgrave Macmillan, 2012. For more on expressive criticism, see Martin, '*Mise-en-scène* is dead'

64   Perkins, *Film as Film*, p. 119, comments directed in this case at a rather different example, Eisenstein's *Battleship Potemkin* (1925)

65   Buckland, *Directed by Steven Spielberg*, p. 64

66   Laura Hubner, 'Introduction: Valuing film' in Laura Hubner, ed., *Valuing Films: Shifting Perceptions of Worth*, Basingstoke: Palgrave Macmillan, 2011. The two essays are James Walters, 'The value of coherence in the contemporary twist film', and Tom Brown, 'Spectacle and value in classical Hollywood cinema'

67   Jane Feuer, 'HBO and the concept of quality TV' in McCabe and Akass, eds, *Quality TV: Contemporary American Television and Beyond*, London: I.B.Tauris, 2007, p. 146. The concept of reception community is from Stanley Fish, that of reading formation from Tony Bennett. Organic unity has also been used as an unquestioned basis for the ascription of quality to certain forms of television, as in Sarah Caldwell, 'Is quality television any good', also in McCabe and Akass, *Quality TV*, p. 30

68   Richard Maltby, *Hollywood Cinema: An Introduction*, Oxford: Blackwell, 1995, p. 7

69   Rosalind Galt, 'Pretty: Film theory, aesthetics, and the history of the troublesome image', *Camera Obscura*, vol. 24, no. 2, 2009, p. 91

70   Ibid., p. 3

71   Ibid., p. 3

72   For a more extended version of this argument, see Rosalind Galt, *Pretty: Film and the Decorative Image*, New York: Columbia University Press, 2011

73   Ibid., pp. 242–4

74 Ibid., p. 248
75 Todd Berliner, *Hollywood Incoherent: Narration in Seventies Cinema*, Austin: University of Texas Press, 2010, p. 28
76 Richard Shusterman, *Pragmatist Aesthetics: Living Beauty, Rethinking Art*, Oxford: Rowan & Littlefield, 2000, p. 76. As Shusterman suggests, a strong critique of the privileging of organic unity has been made by theorists of deconstruction such as Jacques Derrida, who emphasise the extent to which that which is viewed as within any such whole is also fundamentally constituted by that which exists outside.
77 For more on this background, and some suggestions relating to the basis of its long-standing appeal, see N.J. Lowe, *The Classical Plot and the Invention of Western Narrative*, Cambridge: Cambridge University Press, 2000, pp. 260–1
78 For examples of each of these positions see, respectively, Denis Dutton, *The Art Instinct: Beauty, Pleasure, and Human Evolution*, Oxford: Oxford University Press, 2009; and Roger Scruton, *Beauty: A Very Short Introduction*, Oxford: Oxford University Press, 2011
79 For a discussion by one of the founders of what became known as the 'institutional theory of art', from an art-philosophical tradition, see George Dickie, *Art and Value*, Oxford: Blackwell, 2001

A brief conclusion

As for Hollywood, the space it retains for work that lies in the quality territory as defined in this book seems to remain intact, despite the extent to which this is often questioned, including the suggestion by Spielberg that *Lincoln* (2012) came close to achieving a release only on cable television; that even he might have struggled to bring such a work to theatres. This book has sought to outline some of the key parameters of such films and to explain some of the reasons for their existence – and the broader contexts in which they might be situated, at various levels – as a still significant if minor part of the studio land-scape. It is clear that the space for such work remains limited and is usually conditional on the involvement of personnel with particularly strong track records or industrial clout. The bounds of difference are also restricted, departures from prevailing studio norms often being limited in scope and balanced by the presence of more conventional features.

The most frequent markers of distinction in the case studies exam-ined in this book, which I take to represent at least some broader trends, are a relative complexity of narrative (variable) and a (par-tial) undermining of some of the qualities usually associated with the

Hollywood heroic protagonist. At the level of visual style, the most common feature is a somewhat traditionally classical approach, implicitly positioned as 'classy' and restrained, one in which an intensification of continuity is generally absent or restricted to heightened action sequences, and only an occasional use of approaches marked as more overtly 'artistic'. The studio quality film is rarely radical in the ideological implications of its stance, even when overtly addressing social issues and doing so more than might be the norm, while sharing with many indie and art-cinema features a basis of appeal to viewers that is at least partially elitist in its offering of markers of distinction from the qualities associated with the Hollywood mainstream. This is usually combined with broader sources of attraction, however, the 'ideal' target audience – as manifested by some of the critical and viewer responses considered in this book – seeming to be that which takes pleasure simultaneously from both levels of engagement.

The individual case study examples on which I have focused can be located among a broader range of films that make similar claims to quality status, although there are a number of points at which lines blur between what we might find within the output of the main studios and either their speciality divisions or other relatively substantial independent operations. Some films with quality credentials might seem distinctly more likely to come from one part of this terrain than another, as I have suggested at various points in this book, but there are also considerable overlaps. As a blockbuster or science fiction with certain quality dimensions, *Inception* can be located alongside other examples such as *The Matrix* (1999), as was suggested in Chapter 2, as well as Nolan's own *The Dark Knight* (2008) and his subsequent *Interstellar* (2014). It can also be viewed in the context of earlier examples of studio 'twist' films such as *The Sixth Sense* (1999), and contemporary 'altered reality state' films such as *The Adjustment Bureau* (2011, from Universal) and *Source Code* (2011, from the mainstream-oriented independent, Summit Entertainment). It is perhaps harder to find a close equivalent of *The Social Network*, in its particular mix of qualities, but the general location is similar to that of other examples from the same period such as *Moneyball* (2011, Columbia) and *The Wolf of Wall Street* (2013, Paramount), in broad positioning as generally 'smart' contemporary studio narratives, and another Sorkin-scripted dramatisation of the world of tech business, *Steve Jobs* (2015, Universal). *Steve Jobs*, based on a biography of the Apple co-founder, also offers an illustration of the difficulties that can beset such productions, however. Initially set up like *The Social Network* as a David Fincher film at Sony, it was dropped by the studio after a number of difficulties, including the departure of the director in what was reported to be a disagreement about the size of his fee and his level of control over all aspects of the production. Like all these examples, *The Social Network* can be considered under the heading of the biopic, a category that has had quality associations dating back at least to the 1930s, Academy Award prestige winning examples of which range – in more recent decades – from *Out of Africa* (1985, Universal) to *A Beautiful Mind* (2001, Universal and DreamWorks) and the music biographies *Ray* (2004, Universal) and *Walk the Line* (2005, Fox).

For other films of broadly the same period similar in approach and texture to *The Assassination of Jesse James*, we have to look more to the Indiewood divisions or to some unattached independents that have relatively substantial ambitions, as was suggested in Chapter 4 in the use of comparators such as *There Will Be Blood* (2007), *No Country for Old Men* (2007) and *Killing Them Softly* (2012). Quality films with dimensions similar to those of *Mystic River* can be found in other 'brooding' examples including Christopher Nolan's *Insomnia* (2002, Warner), *Gone Baby Gone* (2007, another Denis Lehane adaptation, from Miramax) and *Gone Girl* (2014, Fox). Why *Gone Baby Gone*, a film from the same fictional source with aspects of setting and mood similar to those of *Mystic River*, might have been situated within a speciality division, albeit one as large as Miramax, rather than the main arm of a studio, might come down to a slightly different balance of qualities, stars, or the relationships of those involved (Eastwood's long-standing connection with Warner versus Ben Affleck's with Miramax).

Which side of the studio line some such films fall might be a matter of such variables, or particular company strategies (including, of course, whether or not a studio has a speciality wing), or might sometimes appear a more arbitrary outcome of individual circumstances. Among other films that might be judged to be quality treatments of the crime (or related con-artist format) of different kinds from other periods – with some more generic components but other claims to quality status – we might include examples ranging from *Heat* (1995, Warner, with two big performance parts for Robert DeNiro and Al Pacino) and *LA Confidential* (1997, Warner) in the 1990s to *American Hustle* (Columbia, 2013). We might also cite others featuring major platforms for award-garnering acting, examples in one recent year from across the studio/speciality/independent lines including Spielberg's *Lincoln* (DreamWorks, Fox, for which Daniel Day-Lewis took the top Academy Award), *The Dallas Buyer's Club* (2013, Universal's Focus Features) and *August Osage County* (2013, The Weinstein Company); earlier studio main division examples include *Terms of Endearment* (1984, Paramount, best actress for Shirley MacLaine), *Rain Man* (1988, United Artists, best actor for Dustin Hoffman), *American Beauty* (1999, DreamWorks, best actor for Kevin Spacey), *The Insider* (1999, Disney/Touchstone, nomination for Russell Crowe and a meaty role also for Al Pacino) and *Ray* (best actor for Jamie Foxx).

A number of other comparable films are already considered alongside *Blood Diamond* in Chapter 5, although those that treat relatively similar issues in Africa are mostly from the independent or Indiewood sectors and the film is unusual for the social problem film in its employment of so much Hollywood-style heroic action. Additional internationally focused social problem films from the studios in the same era would include *Syriana* (2005, Warner), *Rendition* (2007, Warner's New Line), *Argo* (2012, Warner) and *Zero Dark Thirty* (2012, Columbia), while a sample focused on domestic politics could range from Oliver Stone's *JFK* (1991, Warner) to *Bulworth* and *The Siege* (both 1998, Fox), *Frost/Nixon* (2008, Universal) and *The Ides of March* (2011, distributed by Sony).

A.I., in Chapter 6, is used in a somewhat different fashion than the other case studies, less as an example of a particular type of quality film in itself – although it can stand as this as well – than as a way to open up the various issues explored in relation to the different reputations of Kubrick and Spielberg. Crossing over various of the above categories, including a number of genre entries, would be quality-claiming studio main division films the reputations of which are based to a significant extent on the status of others who have gained recognition as auteur directors. To suggest just a few, dating back into the early 1990s (this survey excludes the many less conventional studio features that could be identified in the earlier period of the Hollywood Renaissance, taken as a reference point for some forms of quality in subsequent decades): the Coen brothers (*Miller's Crossing* [1990], Fox; *Barton Fink* [1991], Fox as distributor but not producer; *The Hudsucker Proxy* [1994], Warner; *O' Brother Where Art Thou?* [2000], Disney's Touchstone and Universal; *True Grit* [2010], Paramount); Steven Soderbergh (*Out of Sight* [1998], Universal; *Erin Brockovich* [2000], Universal and Columbia; *The Good German* [2006], Warner; *The Informant* [2009], Warner); David Fincher (*Seven* [1995], New Line [Warner]; *Fight Club* [1999], Fox; *Zodiac* [2007], Paramount and Warner; *Gone Girl*); Martin Scorsese (*The Aviator* [2004], Warner and Miramax; *The Departed* [2006], Warner; *Shutter Island* [2010], Paramount; *Hugo* [2011], Paramount; *The Wolf of Wall Street*).

One format with strong and long-standing quality associations not included in the case studies in this book is the more literary-fictional adaptation. Its absence is partly a matter of space and partly related to the fact that this has been a realm particularly associated with the studio speciality divisions of recent decades. Studio examples persist as well, however. Titles cited in Chapter 1 such as *Extremely Loud and Incredibly Close* (2011, Warner and Paramount), *Life of Pi* (2012, Fox 2000) and *The Great Gatsby* (2013, Warner) join a tradition that dates back to the beginnings of Hollywood and that has continued across the decades, a fairly random sample from the 1980s onwards including *Empire of the Sun* (1987, Spielberg, Warner), *Dangerous Liaisons* (1988, Warner), *Wuthering Heights* (1992, Paramount), *The Remains of the Day* (1993, Columbia, co-produced with Merchant Ivory), *The Age of Innocence* (1993, Scorsese, Columbia), *Sense and Sensibility* (1995, Columbia), *Snow Falling on Cedars* (1999, Universal), *Revolutionary Road* (2008, DreamWorks), *The Book Thief* (2013, Fox 2000) and *Inherent Vice* (2014, Warner).

That such films continue to be produced by the majors, alongside the surviving speciality divisions, is notable and evidence that there remains more to contemporary Hollywood than the blockbuster franchise regime that constitutes its strategic core. This, I believe, is likely to remain the case on an ongoing basis. The main examples examined in this book cover a period from 2001 *(A.I.)* to 2010 *(Inception* and *The Social Network)*, with others in between from 2003 *(Mystic River)*, 2006 *(Blood Diamond)* and 2007 *(The Assassination of Jesse James)*. The quality film as defined here is not restricted to this particular period, however. It has plenty of predecessors, in both the recent and more distant past. Examples continue to appear up to the time of this writing and are likely to do so into the future. If nowhere else, each year's Oscar nominations can be relied upon to provide examples, along with their rivals or partners from the indie and Indiewood domains.

The studio quality film might often appear to be under threat, and its numbers might wax and wane, in particular changing circumstances either at the studios in general or in any particular case. But the argument of this book is that it is a persistent phenomenon, driven by the various factors examined above, that is never likely to be absent from the Hollywood roster. This is the case whether the films exist alongside or in the place of the productions of what remain of the speciality divisions. Even when their numbers are few and if some might seem to have the status of one-offs rather than representing concerted trends, their existence remains worthy of note and an examination of their textual qualities and production histories is revealing of the conditions within which any such space is available. The terms in which quality is ascribed, or debated, in this domain also provide an insight into how exactly the concept of 'the mainstream' is articulated, either explicitly or implicitly: the former (quality) implies some notion of the other (non-quality/mainstream) and usually involves a mixture of the two, the exact balance of which is variable across the kind of range encountered above. An exploration of this specific terrain, as offered in this book, can also shed light on broader processes of cultural distinction-marking and their roots in long-standing discursive complexes that remain operative today.

Select bibliography

Adorno, Theodor, and Max Horkheimer, 'The Culture Industries', in *Dialectic of Enlightenment*, London: Verso, 1997

Allen, Robert, and Douglas Gomery, *Film History: Theory and Practice*, New York: McGraw-Hill, 1985

Andrews, David, 'Towards an inclusive, exclusive approach to art cinema', in Rosalind Galt and Karl Schoonover, eds, *Global Art Cinema: New Theories and Histories*, Oxford: Oxford University Press, 2010

——*Theorizing Art Cinemas: Foreign, Cult, Avant-Garde, and Beyond*, Austin: University of Texas Press, 2013

Aristotle, *Poetics*, Harmondsworth: Penguin, 1996

Ashuntantang, Joyce, 'Hollywood's Representations of Human Rights: The Case of Terry George's Hotel Rwanda', in MaryEllen Higgins, ed, *Hollywood's Africa after 1994*, Athens: Ohio University Press, 2012

Bakhtin, Mikhail, *Rabelais and His World*, Bloomington: Indiana University Press, 1984

Balio, Tino, *Hollywood in the New Millennium*, Basingstoke: Palgrave Macmillan, 2013

Barker, Martin, *A Toxic Genre: The Iraq War Films*, London: Pluto Press, 2011

Barthes, Roland, *S/Z*, New York: Hill and Wang, 1974

Bauman, Shyon, *Hollywood Highbrow: From Entertainment to Art*, Princeton: Princeton University Press, 2007

Becker, Howard, *Art Worlds*, Berkeley: University of California Press, 1982

Berliner, Todd, *Hollywood Incoherent: Narration in Seventies Cinema*, Austin: University of Texas Press, 2010

Blank, Grant, *Critics, Ratings, and Society: The Sociology of Reviews*, Lanham, MD: Rowman and Littlefield, 2007

Bogle, Donald, *Toms, Coons, Mutattoes, Mammies, and Bucks: An Interpretive History of Blacks in American Films*, New York: Continuum, 1989

Bordwell, David, Janet Staiger and Kristen Thompson, *The Classical Hollywood: Film Style and Mode of Production to 1960*, London: Routledge, 1985

——*Narration in the Fiction Film*, London: Routledge 1986

——*Figures Traced in Light: On Cinematic Staging*, Berkeley: University of California Press, 2005

——*The Way Hollywood Tells It: Story and Style in Modern Movies*, Berkeley: University of California Press, 2006

Brooker, Will, *Hunting the Dark Knight: Twenty-First Century Batman*, London: I.B. Tauris, 2012

Bourdieu, Pierre, *The Field of Cultural Production*, London: Routledge, 1983

Bowser, Eileen, *The Transformation of Cinema 1907-1915*, Berkeley: University of California Press, 1990

Boyer, Michael Vincent, *The Hollywood Culture War: What You Don't Know CAN Hurt You!*, Xlibris Corporation, 2008

Brown, Tom, 'Spectacle and Value in Classical Hollywood Cinema', in Hubner, ed., *Valuing Films: Shifting Perceptions of Worth*, Basingstoke: Palgrave Macmillan, 2011

Buckland, Warren, *Directed by Steven Spielberg: Poetics of the Contemporary Hollywood Blockbuster*, New York: Continuum, 2006

——ed., *Puzzle Films: Complex Storytelling in Contemporary Cinema*, Oxford: Blackwell, 2009

Cagle, Chris, 'Two modes of prestige film', *Screen*, vol. 48, no. 3, Autumn 2007

Caldwell, John Thornton, *Production Culture: Industrial Reflexivity and Critical Practice in Film and Television*, Durham & London: Duke University Press, 2008

Caldwell, Sarah, 'Is Quality Television Any Good', in Janet McCabe and Kim Akass, eds, *Quality TV: Contemporary American Television and Beyond*, London: I.B. Tauris, 2007

Cameron, Kenneth, *Africa on Film: Beyond Black and White*, New York: Continuum, 1994

Carroll, Noel, *Interpreting the Moving Image*, Cambridge: Cambridge University Press, 1998

Collins, Jim, *Bring on the Books for Everybody: How Literary Culture Became Popular Culture*, Durham: Duke University Press, 2010

Dickie, George, *Art and Value*, Oxford: Blackwell, 2001

Doherty, Thomas, 'The Death of Film Criticism', *The Chronicle of Higher Education*, 28 February 2010, at http://chronicle.com/article/The-Death-of-Film-Criticism/64352/

Dutton, Denis, *The Art Instinct: Beauty, Pleasure, and Human Evolution*, Oxford: Oxford University Press, 2009

Ellis, John, 'The Quality Film Adventure: British Critics and the Cinema', in Andrew Higson, ed, *Dissolving Views: Key Writings on British Cinema*, London: Cassell, 1996

Elsaesser, Thomas, 'The Mind Game Film', in Buckland, ed., *Puzzle Films: Complex Storytelling in Contemporary Cinema*, Oxford: Blackwell, 2009

English, James, *The Economy of Prestige: Prizes, Awards, and the Circulation of Cultural Value*, Cambridge, Mass.: Harvard University Press, 2005

DiMaggio, Paul, and Paul Hirsch, 'Production Organizations in the Arts', *American Behavioral Scientist*, vol. 19, no. 6, July/August 1976

Epstein, Edward Jay, *The Big Picture: Money and Power in Hollywood*, New York: Random House, 2006

——*The Hollywood Economist: The Hidden Financial Reality Behind the Movies*, Brooklyn: Melville House, second edition, 2012

Feuer, Jane, Paul Kerr and Tise Vahimagi (eds), *MTM: Quality Television*, London: BFI, 1984

——'HBO and the Concept of Quality TV', in Janet McCabe and Kim Akass, eds, *Quality TV: Contemporary American Television and Beyond*, London: I.B. Tauris, 2007

Fish, Stanley, *Is there A Text in This Class: The Authority of Interpretive Communities*, Cambridge, Mass.: Harvard University Press, 1980

Frandsen, Sanne, 'Organizational image, Identification, and Cynical Distance: Prestigious Professionals in a Low-Prestige Organization', *Management Communication Quarterly*, vol. 26, no. 3, 2012

Gabler, Neal, *An Empire of Their Own: How the Jews Invented Hollywood*, New York: Anchor, 1988

Galt, Rosalind, 'Pretty: Film Theory, Aesthetics, and the History of the Troublesome Image', *Camera Obscura*, 91, vol. 24, no, 2, 2009

——*Pretty: Film and the Decorative Image*, New York: Columbia University Press, 2011

Gibbs, John, *Mise-en-Scène: Film Style and Interpretation*, London: Wallflower, 2002

Gray, Jonathan, *Show Sold Separately: Promos, Spoilers, and Other Media Paratexts*, New York: New York University Press, 2010

Goldberg, Elizabeth, *Beyond Terror: Gender, Narrative, Human Rights*, New Brunswick: Rutgers University Press, 2007

Goldman, William, *Adventures in the Screen Trade: A Personal View of Hollywood*, London: Abacus, 1983

Gombrich, E.H., 'Norm and Form', in *Gombrich on the Renaissance: Volume 1, Norm and Form*, London: Phaidon, fourth edition, 1985

Grainge, Paul, *Brand Hollywood: Selling Entertainment in a Global Media Age*, London, Routledge, 2008

Guerrero, Ed, *Framing Blackness: The African-American Image in Film*, Philadelphia: Temple University Press, 1993

Harlan, Jan, and Jane Struthers, eds, *A.I. Artificial Intelligence From Stanley Kubrick to Steven Spielberg: The Vision Behind the Film*, London: Thames & Hudson, 2009

Hesmondhalgh, David, *The Culture Industries*, London: Sage, 2007

Higonnet, Margaret, with Ethel R. Higonnet, 'The Troubled Terrain of Human Rights Films', in MaryEllen Higgins, ed, *Hollywood's Africa after 1994*, Athens: Ohio University Press, 2012

Higson, Andrew, *English Heritage, English Cinema: Costume Drama Since 1980*, Oxford: Oxford University Press, 2003

Holbrook, Morris, and Michela Addis, 'Art versus Commerce in the Movie Industry: A Two-Path Model of Motion-Picture Success', *Journal of Cultural Economics*, vol.32, no.2, 2008

Hubner, Laura, ed., *Valuing Films: Shifting Perceptions of Worth*, Basingstoke: Palgrave Macmillan, 2011

Kapsis, Robert, *Hitchcock: The Making of a Reputation*, Chicago: University of Chicago Press, 1992

Keating, Patrick, *Hollywood Lighting: From the Silent Era to Film Noir*, New York: Columbia University Press, 2010

——'The Art of Cinematography', *Trinity: The Magazine of Trinity University*, January 2010

King, Geoff, *Spectacular Narratives: Hollywood in the Age of the Blockbuster*, London: I.B. Tauris, 2000

——*American Independent Cinema*, London: I.B. Tauris, 2005

——*Indiewood, USA: Where Hollywood meets Independent Cinema*, London: I.B. Tauris, 2009

——*Indie 2.0: Change and Continuity in Contemporary American Indie Film*, London: I.B.Tauris, 2014

——'Reassertions of Hollywood heroic agency in the Iraq war film', in Claire Molloy andYannis Tzioumakis (eds), *Routledge Companion to Film and Politics*, London: Routledge, 2015

Klinger, Barbara, *Melodrama and Meaning: History, Culture and the Films of Douglas Sirk*, New York: Wiley, 2004

Kolker, Robert Philip, *A Cinema of Loneliness: Penn, Stone, Kubrick, Scorsese, Spielberg, Altman*, Third Edition, Oxford: Oxford University Press, 2000

Koszarski, Richard, *An Evening's Entertainment: The Age of the Silent Feature Picture, 1915-1928*, Berkeley: University of California Press, 1990

Kovács, András Bálint, *Screening Modernism: European Art Cinema, 1950-1980*, Chicago: University of Chicago Press, 2007

Leitch, Thomas, *Film Adaptation and Its Discontents: From* Gone with the Wind *to* The Passion of the Christ, Baltimore: Johns Hopkins University Press, 2007

Levine, Lawrence, *Highbrow/Lowbrow: The Emergence of Cultural Hierarchy in America*, Cambridge, MA: Harvard University Press, 1988

Lowe, N.J., *The Classical Plot and the Invention of Western Narrative*, Cambridge: Cambridge University Press, 2000

Lowenthal, Leo, *Literature and Mass Culture*, New Brunswick: Transaction Books, 1984

Macdonald, Dwight, 'Masscult and Midcult' in *Masscult and Midcult: Essays Against the American Grain*, New York: New York Review of Books, 2011, 35. Originally published 1962

MacDowell, James, *Happy Endings in Hollywood Cinema: Cliché, Convention and the Final Couple*, Edinburgh University Press, 2013

Maltby, Richard, 'The Production Code and the Hays Office', in Tino Balio, ed., *Grand Design: Hollywood as a Modern Business Enterprise, 1930-1939*, Berkeley: University of California Press, 1993

——*Hollywood Cinema: An Introduction*, Oxford: Blackwell, 1995

Martin, Adrian, 'Mise-en-scène is Dead, Or The Expressive, The Excessive and The Stylish', *Continuum*, vol. 6. no. 2, 1992

McCabe, Janet, and Kim Akass, eds, *Quality TV: Contemporary American Television and Beyond*, London: I.B.Tauris, 2007

Medved, Michael, *Hollywood vs. America*, New York: Harper, 1993, 3; first published 1992

Monk, Claire, *Heritage Film Audiences: Period Films and Contemporary Audiences in the UK*, Edinburgh: Edinburgh University Press, 2011

Morris, Nigel, *The Cinema of Steven Spielberg: Empire of Light*, London: Wallflower, 2007

Mudimbe, V.Y., *The Invention of Africa: Gnosis, Philosophy and the Order of Knowledge*, Bloomington: Indiana University Press, 1988

Naremore, James, *On Kubrick*, London: BFI, 2007

Neale, Steve, *Genre and Hollywood*, London: Routledge, 2000

Newman, Michael Z., 'New media, young audiences and discourses of attention: from Sesame Street to "snack culture"', *Media, Culture & Society*, 32, 4, 2010

—— and Elana Levine, *Legitimating Television: Media Convergence and Cultural Status*, New York and London: Routledge, 2012

Obst, Linda, *Sleepless in Hollywood: Tales from the New Abnormal in the Movie Business*, New York: Simon & Schuster, 2013

Peacock, Steven, *Hollywood and Intimacy: Style, Moments, Magnificence*, Basingstoke: Palgrave Macmillan, 2012

Pekurny, Robert, 'Coping with Television Production', in James Ettema and D. Charles Whitney, *Individuals in Mass Media Organizations: Creativity and Constraint*, London: Sage, 1982

Perkins, Claire, *American Smart Cinema*, Edinburgh: Edinburgh University Press, 2012

Perkins, V.F., *Film as Film: Understanding and Judging Movies*, Harmondsworth: Penguin, 1972/1986

Prince, Stephen, *A New Pot of Gold: Hollywood Under the Electronic Rainbow, 1980-1989*, New York: Charles Scribner's Sons, 2000

——*Digital Visual Effects in Cinema: The Seduction of Reality*, New Brunswick: Rutgers University Press, 2010

Purse, Lisa, *Digital Imaging in Popular Culture*, Edinburgh: Edinburgh University Press, 2013

Radway, Janice, *A Feeling for Books: The Book-of-the-Month Club, Literary Taste, and Middle-Class Desire*, Chapel Hill: University of North Carolina Press, 1999

Ray, Robert, *A Certain Tendency of the Hollywood Cinema, 1930-1980*, Princeton: Princeton University Press, 1985

Reno, William, *Corruption and State Politics in Sierra Leone*, Cambridge: Cambridge University Press, 1995

Roberts, Janine, *Glitter and Greed: The Secret World of the Diamond Cartel*, New York: Disinformation, 2007

Roffman, Peter, and Jim Purdy, *The Hollywood Social Problem Film: Madness, Despair, and Politics from the Depression to the Fifties*, Bloomington: Indiana University Press, 1981

Roger, Ariel, *Cinematic Appeals: The Experience of New Movie Technologies*, New York: Columbia University Press, 2013

Ryan, Michael, and Douglas Kellner, *Camera Politica: The Politics and Ideology of Contemporary Hollywood Film*, Bloomington: Indiana University Press, 1988

Said, Edward, *Orientalism: Western Conceptions of the Orient*, London: Routledge, 1978

Salt, Barry, *Film Style and Technology: History and Analysis*, London: Starword, 1992

Schatz, Thomas, *Hollywood Genres*, Austin: University of Texas Press, 1981

——*The Genius of the System*, New York: Metropolitan Books, 1988

——*Boom and Bust: American Cinema in the 1940s*, Berkeley, University of California Press, 1997

Sconce, Jeffrey, 'Irony, nihilism and the new American "smart" film', *Screen*, 43, no. 4, Winter 2002

Scruton, Roger, *Beauty: A Very Short Introduction*, Oxford: Oxford University Press, 2011

Sharff, Stefan, *The Elements of Cinema: Toward a Theory of Cinesthetic Impact*, New York: Columbia University Press, 1982

Sharma, Rekha, 'News on the rocks: Exploring the agenda-setting effects of Blood Diamond in print and broadcast news', *Media, War & Conflict*, vol. 5, no. 3, 2012

Shearman, John, *Mannerism*, Harmondsworth: Penguin, 1967/1990

Shiner, Larry, *The Invention of Art: A Cultural History*, Chicago: University of Chicago Press, 2001

Shone, Tom, *Blockbuster*, London: Simon & Schuster, 2004

Shusterman, Richard, *Pragmatic Aesthetics: Living Beauty, Rethinking Art*, Oxford: Rowman & Littlefield, 2000

Sloan, Kay, *The Loud Silents: Origins of the Social Problem Film*, Chicago: University of Illinois Press, 1988

Staiger, Janet, 'The Revenge of the Film Education Movement: Cult Movies and Fan Interpretive Behaviors', *Reception: Texts, Readers, Audiences, History*, vol. 1, Fall 2008

Stewart, Garrett, *Framed Time: Toward a Postfilmic Cinema*. Chicago: Chicago University Press, 2007

Tait, R. Colin, and Andrew deWaard, *The Cinema of Steven Soderbergh*, London: Wallflower, 2013

Thanouli, Eleftheria, *Post-Classical Cinema: An International Poetics of Film Narration*, London: Wallflower, 2009

Thomson, Irene Taviss, *Culture Wars and Enduring American Dilemmas*, Ann Arbor: University of Michigan Press, 2010

Thompson, Robert, *Television's Second Golden Age: From Hill Street Blues to ER*, Syracuse: Syracuse University Press, 1996

Truffaut, Francois, 'A Certain Tendency of the French Cinema', in Bill Nichols, ed., *Movies and Methods*, Volume 1, Berkeley: University of California Press, 1976

Tzioumakis, Yannis, '"Independent", "Indie" and "Indiewood": Towards a periodisation of contemporary (post-1980) American independent cinema', in Geoff King, Claire Molloy and Tzioumakis, eds, *American Independent Cinema: Indie, Indiewood and Beyond*, London: Routledge, 2013

Turow, Joseph, 'Unconventional Programs on Commercial Television', in James Ettema and D. Charles Whitney, *Individuals in Mass Media Organizations: Creativity and Constraint*, London: Sage, 1982

Uricchio, William, and Roberta Pearson, *Reframing Culture: The Case of the Vitagraph Quality Films*, Princeton: Princeton University Press, 1993

Vernallis, Carol, *Unruly Media: YouTube, Music Video, and the New Digital Cinema*, Oxford: Oxford University Press, 2013

Walters, James, 'The Value of Coherence in the Contemporary Twist Film' in Laura Hubner, ed., *Valuing Films: Shifting Perceptions of Worth*, Basingstoke: Palgrave Macmillan, 2011

Williams, Paul D., *War and Conflict in Africa*, Cambridge: Polity, 2011

Williams, Raymond, *Culture and Society 1780-1950*, Harmondsworth: Penguin, 1961

Wyatt, Justin, *High Concept: Movies and Marketing in Hollywood*, Austin: University of Texas Press, 1994

Index